MORRIS R. COHEN AND THE SCIENTIFIC IDEAL

Morris Raphael Cohen, 1880-1947
(Courtesy of the Archives of the City College of New York)

MORRIS R. COHEN AND THE SCIENTIFIC IDEAL

David A. Hollinger

The MIT Press
Cambridge, Massachusetts, and London, England

This book was set in IBM Composer Press Roman by Techdata Associates Inc., printed on R & E Book, and bound in MBL-4405 by The Colonial Press Inc. in the United States of America

Library of Congress Cataloging in Publication Data

Hollinger, David A
  Morris R. Cohen and the scientific ideal.

  Includes bibliographical references and index.
  1. Cohen, Morris Raphael, 1880-1947. I. Title
B945.C54H64   191   75-12850
ISBN 0-262-08084-2

To Joan

CONTENTS

Guide to Abbreviations Used in Notes

RN	*Reason and Nature* (1931)
LSO	*Law and the Social Order* (1933)
ILSM	*Introduction to Logic and Scientific Method* (1934)
PL	*Preface to Logic* (1944)
FL	*Faith of a Liberal* (1946)
MHH	*The Meaning of Human History* (1947; 2nd ed., 1961)
SBGS	*Source Book in Greek Science* (1948)
DJ	*A Dreamer's Journey* (1949)
SPS	*Studies in Philosophy and Science* (1949)
RWJ	*Reflections of a Wondering Jew* (1950)
RL	*Reason and Law* (1950)
KSD	*King Saul's Daughter* (1952)
AT	*American Thought* (1954)
Portrait	*Portrait of a Philosopher: Morris R. Cohen in Life and Letters* (1961), edited by Leonora Cohen Rosenfield
Tribute	*A Tribute to Morris Raphael Cohen, Teacher and Philosopher* (1928), edited by Max Grossman
Cohen MSS	Papers of Morris R. Cohen, in possession of Leonora Cohen Rosenfield, Washington, D. C.
NR	*New Republic*
JP	*Journal of Philosophy*
PR	*Philosophical Review*

To *Vanity Fair*, he was the professor's professor, the authority in the sphere of academic intellect, the man to ask about the meaning of the Einstein theory.[1] To *Commentary*, he was "the Paul Bunyan of the Jewish intellectuals," a folk hero with "gigantic mental prowess."[2] To the *New Masses*, he was the complete bourgeois liberal, the reliable register of the bankrupt middle-class mind.[3] To Harold J. Laski, he was "the subtlest mind in American philosophy"; to the *New York Times*, "an almost legendary figure in the liberal tradition."[4] To many of his learned colleagues in philosophy and cultural criticism, he was "the Socratic personality of our time," the independent, rational thinker who "fell victim to no fashionable solution, no modish formulas, no sentimental enthusiasms or hysterical despairs."[5] To the editor of the *Modern Monthly* in 1934, he was, along with John Dewey and Bertrand Russell, an ideal symposiast, a person whose views on contemporary moral and intellectual issues were bound to compel attention.[6]

An imposing and often commanding presence in American intellectual life less than forty years ago, Morris Raphael Cohen (1880-1947) made a remarkably quick transition from influence to obsolescence. Today it is impossible to see him as a great thinker, yet Cohen was undeniably "great" within the limited terms of his generation's needs and aspirations. He would not have attained eminence had he not been able to offer something then in demand. What functions did he perform for his contemporaries? What qualities in Cohen, and what circumstances in American intellectual discourse, served to make him a major figure in the 1920s and 1930s? Every thinker is, of course, "a man of his own times," but some thinkers retain a substantial constituency in subsequent epochs. Cohen did not. He turned out to be much more of a "period piece" than did some of his contemporaries who had comparable stature in the eyes of the academic and literary community of about 1930. Cohen's career promises, therefore, to help us understand the differences between his age and ours.

The inquiry would be less worthy of pursuit had Cohen been obviously and exclusively identified with ideological traditions and intellectual communities that have since withered. In that case his career could be expected to illuminate only "differences between his age and ours" that we have already recognized and charted. Cohen's historicity is, in fact, not so easily defined; nor do we so thoroughly comprehend the aspects of the recent past to which his career gives us access. Indeed, Cohen was intimately and extensively involved in the creation of the very sphere of modern intellectual discourse to which his works now seem persistently irrelevant.

As the first Russian-born Jew to come to prominence as a public moralist and as a professional philosopher, Cohen was a pivotal figure in the accommodation of East European Jewry to American culture. He was a crucial exemplar, to the sons of immigrants, of what it meant to be an "American intellectual." Moreover, he represented to numerous thinkers of native stock the hope that Jewish immigrants and their progeny would substantially enrich and liberalize American intellectual life. Cohen was a consolidating agent in the formation of the secular, ethnically diverse, left-of-center intelligentsia that was to become institutionalized, by the 1940s, in the liberal-arts departments of several major universities and in many journals of opinion.

Cohen's influence on the development of this community of discourse was exercised not only through his critical essays in the *New Republic* and in professional journals, but also through personal contact in and around New York City. At the City College of New York, where he taught until his retirement in 1938, he was mentor to many of the leading scholars and writers of the following several decades, including William Barrett, Lewis Feuer, Louis Finklestein, Paul Goodman, Sidney Hook, Joseph Lash, Richard Morris, Ernest Nagel, Benjamin Nelson, Herbert Schneider, Samuel Thorne, Paul Weiss, Morton White, Philip Wiener, and Bertram Wolfe.

As a moralist, Cohen expressed during the 1920s and 1930s a sense of humanity's limitations that was to come much more into vogue during and after World War II. He was perhaps the least progressive and least optimistic of the social thinkers of his generation who called themselves "liberals." Consistently, he warned his contemporaries of the inevitability of tragedy, the permanence of evil, and the precariousness of human life itself.

As one of the founders of the discipline of philosophy of science, and as one of the early twentieth century's most careful commentators on the metaphysical, moral, and methodological implications of the scientific endeavor, Cohen contributed powerfully to the expansion of "scientific culture" in the United States, and to the closer scrutiny of that culture by philosophers and social scientists. He tried to expose the limitations of the proverbial "scientism" of the period, and yet he was devoted to the search for a more authentically scientific basis for social policy. Much of his career was spent in attacking what the next generation would agree to call the "excesses" of behaviorism, positivism, and crudely Baconian empiricism. He was the foremost critic, from within, of the naturalistic movement Morton White has called "the revolt against formalism."[7] In the years since Cohen's death, more and more attention has been paid to the problems in the cultural relations of science that he helped to identify.

Cohen's career thus flows at several important points into the intellectual history of the period immediately following his own, and this fact brings into bold relief the break in continuity implied by his inability to retain a following. Cohen thus invites our attention for reasons that are more distinctly historical than would be the case with John Dewey, for example, or Albert Einstein, or any other thinker whose work continues to speak to the present.

Historical studies of politicians, artists, and prophets often seek to demonstrate an extensive pattern of relationships between the personality of their subject and whatever activities of the subject render him or her worthy of study. Attempts of this sort are contrastingly rare for philosophers and scientists, whose creative work we seem more willing to separate sharply from their personality. No doubt the realm of scientific, and even technical, philosophical discussion has a more tightly determined structure than do those of politics, art, and prophecy; the

parameters within which personality can express itself through science
or philosophy are correspondingly smaller. Yet the opportunity is always there in some measure, and Morris Cohen, for one, took the full-
est possible advantage of it.

Cohen's emotional capacities and incapacities are strikingly prominent in his choice of metaphors, in the structure of his arguments, and
in his formulation of problems. This is the case even in his most formal
metaphysical writings. He is one philosopher whose career was clearly a
vehicle for his personality; the Morris Cohen that other intellectuals responded to, admired, argued against, and chose finally to ignore was a
social and psychological being as well as a philosophical one. Whatever
may be said in defense of the separation of philosophy from personality for the purposes of studying other careers, a historical inquiry into
Cohen's career is obliged to trace the interplay between his psychosocial
drives and the forms of thought made available to him by the cultural
environment he encountered.

The inquiry can proceed more smoothly if certain basic facts are put
on record at the outset. Born in the Russian city of Minsk, Morris
Cohen emigrated to New York with his family in 1892, when he was
twelve years old. He grew up in the Brownsville section of Brooklyn
and on Manhattan's Lower East Side; he attended public schools, including the College of the City of New York, from which he was graduated in 1900. After completing a Ph.D. at Harvard—where he roomed
with law student Felix Frankfurter, destined to be his lifelong friend—
he unsuccessfully sought employment as a teacher of philosophy. He
at first had to settle for a position in mathematics at City College, a post
he had held before beginning doctoral studies. After five years of waiting, Cohen's transfer to the Department of Philosophy was arranged by
Harry Overstreet, a new chairman, who persuaded City College to overcome its reluctance to allow a Jew to teach philosophy. Cohen then
quickly established himself as one of the most popular and forceful
personalities on the faculty. He was actively involved in the internal

politics of the institution and of its Alumni Association; some of his conflicts with President Frederick B. Robinson during the 1920s—over compulsory R.O.T.C. especially—became part of the permanent folklore of St. Nicholas Terrace.

Despite the reality of ethnic discrimination, Cohen became a prominent figure in American philosophy and cultural criticism by the middle of the 1910s. If there were some who sought to exclude him, others welcomed him. In 1916 Randolph Bourne, for example, praised Cohen, along with Frankfurter, Horace Kallen, and Walter Lippmann, as leaders of the new generation of "Jewish intelligents" whose "clarity of expression" and "masterly fibre of thought" could "hardly be over-valued."[8] Oliver Wendell Holmes, Jr., was also excited by Cohen, whose early articles the Justice had had privately bound for his own convenience.[9] The *New Republic* recruited Cohen in 1914, its very first year of existence, and made him a frequent contributor and editorialist.[10] He read papers regularly to the annual meetings of the American Philosophical Association, many of whose members were impressed with his knowledge of mathematics and physics. When the United States entered World War I and the circle of radical students at Columbia University looked to their cultural heroes for guidance, Cohen's views were noted as carefully as were those of Isadora Duncan, Max Eastman, John Dewey, Thorstein Veblen, John Reed, and Floyd Dell.[11]

Throughout the 1920s and 1930s he contributed frequently to the professional journals of philosophy, to law reviews, and to popular journals of opinion. He was the first editor of the writings of Charles Peirce (*Chance, Love, and Logic*, 1923). Eventually he published more than a dozen books, including *Reason and Nature* (1931) and *Law and the Social Order* (1933), works that confirmed his reputation as an authority on philosophy of science and philosophy of law.[12] Cohen was also a major contributor to the *Encyclopedia of the Social Sciences* (1929-1937) and one of the founding editors of *Philosophy of Science* (1934), *The Journal of Symbolic Logic* (1936), *Jewish Social Studies* (1939), and the *Journal of the History of Ideas* (1940). He was president of the Eastern Division of the American Philosophical Association (1929-1930), and its sixth Carus Lecturer (1944). A leader in the mobilization of Jewish intellectuals against anti-Semitism after 1933, Cohen was the chief founder of the Conference on Jewish Relations. Although primarily identified with City College, he was also, for many of the same years, a mainstay of the teaching program at the New School for Social Research. He taught at the University of Chicago from 1938 through 1941.

Cohen was married in 1906 to Mary Ryshpan, with whom he had three children in the years immediately following marriage. Felix S. Cohen had a distinguished career as a government lawyer in Washington prior to his death in 1953 at the age of 46. Leonora Cohen Rosenfield became a historian and critic of French literature; Victor William Cohen became a physicist. The Cohens lived on 181st Street in Washington Heights, close enough to the City College campus at 135th Street to enable Morris to walk home along the Hudson River when the weather and his health permitted. But his health was often poor, and he worried about it continually. When he was in his early fifties, people who met him often assumed him to be at least a decade older. He depended greatly upon his wife, and when she became seriously ill in 1941, his own health deteriorated very badly. Cohen's career was effectively terminated by a stroke early in 1942. He survived as an invalid for five additional years.

This book has been strengthened by the critical suggestions of Henry F. May, John P. Diggins, Robert W. Gordon, Samuel Haber, Nathan G. Hale, Jr., Carol Hurlburt Leonard, Thomas C. Leonard, Laurence A. Schneider, Martin J. Sherwin, and Ronald G. Walters, all of whom read all or part of the manuscript at one stage or another. I am grateful to my colleague Lewis C. Perry for an especially detailed and helpful critique, and to Lewis S. Feuer for helping me to identify and to correct significant omissions and errors. My greatest debt is to my wife, Joan Heifetz Hollinger.

I want also to thank the many former students and friends of Morris Cohen who took time to talk with me, or to write in response to my queries. I have acknowledged them by name in the notes. For other favors I wish to thank Vicki Nygren, John Henry Schlegel, and Daniel Wilson. I am grateful to Leonara Cohen Rosenfield for permission to quote from her father's papers and to W.W. Norton & Company and Chatto and Windus for permission to quote from Adrienne Rich's *Snapshots of a Daughter-in-Law*.

NOTES

1. *Vanity Fair* XX (1923), 48, 96.

2. Morris Freedman, "The Jewish College Student: New Model," in Elliott Cohen, ed., *Commentary on the American Scene* (New York, 1953), 282.

3. Paul Salter and Jack Librome, "Dewey, Russell and Cohen: Why They Are Anti-Communist," *New Masses* XII (1934), 22-23.

4. Harold J. Laski to Oliver Wendell Holmes, Jr., September 26, 1923, in Mark De Wolfe Howe, ed., *Holmes-Laski Letters* (Cambridge, Mass., 1953), I, 545; *New York Times* (January 31, 1947), 22.

5. The quoted phrases are those of Irwin Edman, "Morris Raphael Cohen—A Tribute," *City College Alumnus* XLII (1947), 5. Cf., as other representative examples, Felix Frankfurter, "As I Remember Morris Cohen," *City College Alumnus* LIV (1958), 3-6, and Robert Bierstedt, "The Wise and Witty Morris Cohen," *Saturday Review of Literature* XXII (1949), 25.

6. See the symposium, "Why I Am Not a Communist," *Modern Monthly* VIII (April 1934).

7. Morton G. White, *Social Thought in America: The Revolt Against Formalism* (New York, 1949).

8. Randolph Bourne, "The Jew and Trans-national America," in Carl Resek, ed., *War and the Intellectuals* (New York, 1964), 132. Bourne's essay was originally published in *Menorah Journal* II (1916), 277-284.

9. See esp. Holmes to MRC, March 9, 1916, in *Portrait*, 315.

10. Walter Lippmann, letter to author, June 22, 1972. Cohen's first contribution, "Intellectual Leadership in America," was signed "Philonous." *NR* I (November 14, 1914), 16-17.

11. Joseph Freeman, *An American Testament* (New York, 1936), 94-95.

12. For a bibliography of Cohen's writings see Martin A. Kuhn, ed., *Morris Raphael Cohen: A Bibliography* (New York, 1957).

MORRIS R. COHEN AND THE SCIENTIFIC IDEAL

On his one hand he might have a precipitous, pine-clad declivity, falling away into the mists; on the other sheer rock might rise, with masses of snow, in monstrous, Cyclopean forms, all domed and vaulted, swelling or cavernous. He would halt for a moment, to quench the sound of his own movement, when the silence about him would be absolute, complete, a wadded soundlessness, as it were, elsewhere all unknown. . . .

On the island of Sylt he had stood by the edge of the thundering surf. In his white flannels, elegant, self-assured, but most respectful, he had stood there as one stands before a lion's cage and looks deep into the yawning jaws of the beast, lined with murderous fangs. He had bathed in the surf, and heeded the blast of the coastguard's horn, warning all and sundry not to venture rashly beyond the first line of billows, not to approach too nearly the oncoming tempest—the very last impulse of whose cataract, indeed, struck upon him like a blow from a lion's paw. From that experience our young man had learned the fateful pleasure of toying with forces so great that to approach them nearly is destruction. What he had not then felt was the temptation to come closer, to carry the thrilling contact with these deadly natural forces up to a point where the full embrace was imminent. Weak human being that he was—though tolerably well equipped with the weapons of civilization—what he at this moment knew was the fascination of venturing just so far into the monstrous unknown, or at least abstaining just so long from flight before it, that the adventure grazed the perilous, that it was just barely possible to put limits on it, before it became no longer a matter of toying with the foam and playfully dodging the ruthless paw—but the ultimate adventure, the billow, the lion's jaw, and the sea.

Thomas Mann

Thomas Reed Powell knew his guest to be a cautious and contemplative man, proverbially detached and unadventurous. The host was not surprised when Morris Cohen, in California that summer of 1937 to teach at Stanford, declined an invitation to visit Yosemite National Park. "You seem to enjoy only things of the mind—you do not crave experience," Powell observed knowingly, not suspecting that his friend would be troubled by a comment so thoroughly in line with Cohen's frequently expressed sense of himself. Yet Cohen had to reassure himself that night: "staying home is also an experience," he wrote in his diary.

Seeing the earth and sky around here is fascinating if you have the energy to enjoy the elements. It is only when we are exhausted that we need the stimulus of novelty. There is enough novelty in the constant changes of the sky, clouds, and diverse aspects of the scenery around us.

Why should he "tire" himself, he asked, and why suffer "the dizzy feeling" attendant upon looking "down from great heights" simply to see sights he could "well imagine without going there"?[1]

More than the charms of Palo Alto restrained Cohen, who felt impelled to justify as an "experience" the "nonexperience" of staying home, and he attributed to himself an abundance of the very energy he feared the trip would drain. Having disassociated himself from the need for novelty—it was a consequence of "exhaustion"—he cited the novelty of the passing clouds as a reason for not bothering with Glacier Point, the grandeur of which he could "well imagine" anyway. Such confusions and contradictions were not characteristic of Cohen, in private or public. Here was a case where his words simply refused to work together: on one level he feared that Yosemite was too much, that he, honestly, would prefer to sit at home and look at postcards; yet another part of him found this attitude so unacceptable it had to be concealed, even from himself, beneath a cluster of false emotions.

In earlier years Cohen had been less overtly ambivalent and defensive about his fears of overextension, his forebodings of dizziness and disintegration, and his affection for the cloister. These sentiments were as prominent as ever when Cohen reached his fifties, but by then he was more conscious of the limitations his temperament had apparently imposed upon his life. "I am certainly not happy," he confessed to himself, and pondered the "paradox" that he who now felt so unfulfilled had devoted his career to teaching "the lesson of peace" through the renunciation of "irrationally passionate drives."[2] The lifelong tension between Cohen's asceticism and his yearning for the enjoyments rejected by asceticism was brought nearer the surface by the inevitable realization, in middle age, that most of his life was behind him. Cohen was also affected by the accumulation, over the years, of complaints against his "negative" orientation, of charges that his "antiseptic" style—an adjective even he used to describe himself[3]—prevented him from making more creative contributions to his culture.

In his most self-aware moments, Cohen acknowledged that the "key" to his life was "an intense self-absorption which stands in the way of disintegration." And the quiet dreams available to a person of this temperament, he implied in his diary, were a poor substitute for the "overflowing energy," the "vitality and flare" of William James or George Santayana, philosophers he knew to be more creative than himself. Cohen had "no bold strokes" and was caught up "in constant brooding and returning to the point of departure." At best, he could claim for himself "a tenacious clinging to truth." Sometimes he carried these reflections to the point of self-mortification, especially when speaking of the works of Santayana, a hero whom he had never met: "the great, sheer abundant, and overflowing vitality of Santayana by contrast to the thin, readily fatigued and exhausted me."[4]

Cohen saw himself as a "desert," in which a few wells and "oases" could be induced to flow now and then, but only with great difficulty. The metaphor of the desert was but one part of an interlocking system of metaphors Cohen used throughout his life, not only in his diaries, but in his public, formal writings as well, and above all in his autobiography *A Dreamer's Journey*. Life's potentialities were represented by bodies of water that threatened, alternately, to "flood" or to "dry up." The "rivers" and "currents" of life were persistently and naturally dangerous and unstable. The use of these particular images to represent this complex of feelings has an obvious derivation from the Old Testament and has long been a convention in Western culture. Still, their appeal to Cohen was unusually compelling: this system of metaphors was firmly grounded in his sense of his own life. It was a convenient way for him to express the apprehensions he had about overextension and disintegration.

Cohen described the most cataclysmic social event of his life—immigration and secularization—as the breaking of a great dam, and the gushing forth of a prodigious flood.[5] An excess of violent water was the most frightening of dangers: one must build dikes and dams to channel "the fitful floods of human passions and impulses."[6] Man was a tiny, embattled figure, floating on a vital but unpredictable expanse of water: "we are but straws on life's currents," he would say, so many ships, each "without a rudder," likely "to be wrecked by the storm."[7] Even when Cohen tried to be cheerful, to argue against too dour a fatalism, he let hope find its way through a watery waste, quoting from Shelley:

Many a green isle needs must be
In the deep wide sea of misery,
Or the poor mariner, worn and wan,
Never thus could voyage on.[8]

Cohen's mariner sometimes found his way beyond the rivers to the sea, which, while it could represent misery, as in Shelley's lines, was more often for Cohen a threat—and a promise—of annihilation. The ocean came to his mind when he spoke of the death of Thomas Davidson, the hero of his youth; and on the day Cohen's mother died in Brooklyn, he twice walked to the Atlantic shore and back.[9] He sometimes spoke wistfully of eternal stability through submission to "the mysterious tides deep and mighty beyond our power to change."[10] Hence the sea, the ancient symbol for peace-as-death, was simultaneously attractive and repulsive, something to be looked forward to and yet resisted heroically, as in the most widely quoted sentence Cohen ever wrote: our beloved reason is "a pitiful candle light in the dark and boundless sea of being," but it is all we have, "and woe to those who wilfully try to put it out."[11] Counterposed to the sea was an opposite attraction, and repulsion: the absolute aridity of the desert. Here at least there were no "treacherous currents," no "fitful floods." There was something permanently safe about it; and he often characterized his teaching career as an effort to lead his students into a desert and leave them there.[12] Carlyle had once said this of Arnold's cultural criticism, as a bitter complaint, but to Cohen the desert was not without attraction. He described even his own "soul" as a desert, whose "oases" and "wells" were held in steady check by tenacious self-absorption. The danger here was that one would become too self-absorbed, too rooted in the desert of inertia. And, indeed, Cohen sometimes admitted that he was "obsessed" with the fear that his mind was "drying up," that his "oases" had ceased to flow.[13]

The wisdom that makes life livable, Cohen wrote early in his career, requires of us a "measured straining in opposite directions," like that of the coachman going downhill: "we urge our horse down . . . yet put the brake on the wheel."[14] Even when he thus stepped outside of his system of aquatic metaphors, Cohen depicted man in a precarious situation, caught between inertia and stampede, struggling not to reform life but only to balance it, to keep it from careening downward, from dashing its flesh against unknown hazards. Danger lies in letting go, duty in the "measured straining" that allows for safe, steady movement. Life's problem, then, is to restrain oneself from doing easy, dangerous things, and to force oneself to perform difficult, necessary acts.

The dynamic tension between total abandon and total restraint was a permanent feature of Cohen's personality and a propelling force behind many of his efforts as a teacher and as a philosopher. These efforts, in the context of the specific terms of philosophical discourse, are the raw materials of his career, and their details will be taken up in their place. Here it can be noted, however, that Cohen developed a philosophy of history based on the tension between "fear" and "freedom," that he aimed in metaphysics, jurisprudence, and philosophy of science to reconcile the static order of "logic" with the contingent order of "history," and that, in general, he was almost pathologically devoted to the eradication of "extremist" threats to a "balanced" world view. Simply to find and defend the virtuous middle way, he insisted, was a difficult, uncomfortable, even heroic act, for all pressures were toward one polar extreme or the other, whether the context was moral philosophy, politics, or the daily control of one's impulses. Profoundly sensitive to the chaotic potential of indiscriminate, immediate experience, he distrusted the concrete, the sensual, and the active; he almost instinctively adopted roles of detached criticism and avoided those of creative involvement. There were important exceptions to Cohen's reluctance to risk going out on a limb, but his career was predominantly an effort to get men to distrust their hopes and give more heed to their fears.

These patterns in the character and career of the adult Cohen had their origins in certain pivotal experiences of his early childhood in Russia. The patterns were also influenced, importantly, by such general phenomena as the social disorganization attendant upon immigration and secularization, the dynamics of ethnic relations in America, and the cultural legacy of East European Jewry; but these larger developments—which will also be taken up in their place—acted upon an already formed basis that was quite distinct. Indeed, it was not every child who, already at the age of ten, hovered at a distance from his playmates and murmured that their games of the moment were "not in accordance with the Torah."[15] The individual circumstances of Cohen's early upbringing established in him certain needs and capabilities which influenced, in turn, the way he absorbed and responded to more general social forces.

The only record of this childhood is in the early chapters of *A Dreamer's Journey*, a product of the same unhappy middle age that made Cohen ambivalent about his own personality and achievements.[16] Not surprisingly, a sense of subdued pain pervades the book, especially the descriptions of his apparently dreary, lonely childhood. Autobiographies, even when written by relatively cheerful persons, are said to concentrate on the sad and traumatic aspects of childhood at the expense of the joyful and the routine. Yet, in particular cases, the conventions of the genre may serve to express, not to conceal, a person's most formative experiences. Uncorroborated autobiographical accounts of childhood do validate themselves, partially, when they contribute to an explanation of the subject's lifelong habits of thought and feeling. In this view, the salient fact about *A Dreamer's Journey*'s roughly drawn picture of young Morris and his family is its plausibility—in the context of everything else known about Cohen's life. Much of the information contained in his recollections falls into patterns Cohen recognized only obliquely, if at all, but the patterns themselves are so convincing that one is reluctant to argue with his intuitions about what childhood experiences were worth remembering.

He was "a very sickly child,"[17] scorned as a weakling and a half-wit, afraid of his own father, suspicious of other children, and the victim of a sequence of minor hurts and frights. As an infant, he crawled out of the house and was frightened by "a pig licking my hand—a terror that I have never forgotten."[18] As soon as he could walk, he got lost.[19] Once old enough to join in "the usual boys' adventures," he was intimidated when run over and almost crippled by a moving buckboard upon which he had tried to leap.[20] When he tried to play games with other children, "some child or other would manage to hurt me so that I would run crying into the house."[21] Among young Morris's greatest pleasures was walking to school in the company of the teacher's assistant, who would "guard against anyone teasing or hitting" his charges.[22] The early chapters of *A Dreamer's Journey* describe scattered moments of happiness, but these are all but obscured by vivid recollections of suffering and grief.

Cohen professed not to remember feeling fright when, at the age of seven, he was told that Russian soldiers had plundered a Jewish inn near his home and killed all the Jews present,[23] but such events affected the general atmosphere in which he grew up. The surviving adults of the local community could scarcely escape awareness of the possibility of sudden, arbitrary persecution and death. *A Dreamer's Journey* sheds little distinctive light on the intensification of anxieties within the Pale of Settlement during the 1880s, but there can be no doubt that Morris's personal traumas took place in a setting of wide-spread social trauma. While he was humiliated by his friends and teachers, he saw his own family, and other economically deprived Jews, battered from pillar to post by hostile magistrates. It was, of course, the tightening of Russia's anti-Semitic policies that gave impetus to the massive emigration of the period; indeed, the Cohen family's decision to move to the United States was made final after Morris's mother became involved in a legal battle with a corrupt police official, with attendant harassment. "The police would knock at our windows in the middle of the night, wake us up," and sometimes compel Morris's mother to "go at once to police headquarters."[24]

This tense atmosphere may have been conducive to the development of some of Cohen's personal traits, but many others grew up under the same general conditions and yet developed personalities substantially different from his. The same can be said of Morris's experience in the heder, where he was subjected to a succession of arbitrary, sometimes cruel teachers, whose vindictive discipline marked his memory for life.[25] If these very common experiences contributed significantly to the formation of Cohen's character, it was because his personal orientation was peculiarly receptive to such impressions. Hence what matters most about Cohen's Russian childhood are the experiences that were more distinctly his: his frailty, his relative isolation from other children, his tendency to cling to the memory of being caressed by a pig on his first "adventure," and, above all, his relationship with members of his immediate family.

Cohen's father, Abraham Cohen, is an obscure figure in *A Dreamer's Journey*, perhaps because he was almost never at home. When his son Morris was three, the elder Cohen went to America, hoping to earn the capital needed to establish himself and his family more firmly in Minsk. Three years later he returned, only to depart again after a few weeks, this time with Morris's two elder brothers, leaving Morris and his younger sister Florence alone with their mother.[26] Abraham Cohen visited home several more times before Morris reached the age of twelve, when the entire family moved to New York, but these visits were disasters as far as Morris was concerned. His father persistently ignored and humiliated him. He inflicted a series of mental injuries on the boy—the details are not recorded—capped by one "unusually severe derogatory remark" that led Morris to run away from home, for a day. "My relations with my father," Cohen summarized, "were not on the whole happy."[27]

Cohen's mother, Bessie, welcomed him home after he had run away, as she regularly comforted him when abused by friends, neighbors, or other members of the family. She, almost alone among the figures memorialized in the early chapters of *A Dreamer's Journey*, was never the agent of Morris's pain and suffering.[28] Many accounts of shtetl life depict fathers as aloof and mothers as active and loving, but in the literal absence of his father, Morris was thrown all the more completely upon his mother as a source of support. So firmly etched is Cohen's picture of his mother as protector and provider that Bessie Farfel Cohen has served scholars as a classic example of the "indulgent" mother of the East European tradition. This type is "a retreating figure of shelter," say two anthropologists, "a most desirable warm figure just out of reach, a poignant symbol of tenderness."[29] Cohen always identified his mother with the actual fulfillment of desires, rather than with the mere promise of gratification, but the hint of distance and "retreat" noted by the anthropologists was concretely present in one pivotal episode in Morris's childhood: his mother sent him away from her when he was seven years old, to live with her own parents for a period of three years. With little money and, in effect, without a husband, Morris's mother earned her living as a vendor of bakery goods and produce on the streets of Minsk; she had no time to care for Morris, reports Cohen in his autobiography, so she sent him to his grandparents in the village of Neshwies.[30]

If Morris perceived this act of his mother as a rejection, he never acknowledged it, and he never let the feeling impair his expressed image of her as his affectionate protector. Even when he criticized her, indirectly, in his adolescent diaries, his complaint was against her permissiveness: the sixteen-year-old Morris chose to attribute his adolescent confusions to a childhood during which he had been under "loose control," and sometimes "without any monitor" at all.[31] Whether or not these comments masked other resentments against his mother, Cohen's "complaints" were at least consistent with his praise for his mother as one who satisfied, rather than thwarted, his childhood desires. Whatever injury Morris may have received because of his mother's absence, her otherwise bountiful responses enabled him to minimize the hurt.

The years in Neshwies might not have been so influential in the development of Cohen's personality were it not for the character of his grandfather, Hirsch Farfel, whose bearing toward Morris was diametrically opposite to that of Morris's mother. "My grandfather," Cohen recalled, "belonged to the stern old school that did not encourage the outward expression of affection." Yet he was attentive to the boy; Morris's grandfather won his affection by caring about him in ways that his own father apparently did not. His grandfather, however, beat him, often "unmercifully and unjustly," Cohen recalled, and subjected him to humiliations "beyond measure."[32] It is an index of Hirsch Farfel's severity that when Morris's mother had been a young girl, he once threatened to cripple her to make her less attractive, in order to prevent her possible seduction at the hands of soldiers encamped nearby. On another occasion his beatings drove the girl into a pond, where she was saved from drowning herself only by the intervention of a group of Christian monks.[33] Morris chafed under the sharp and arbitrary discipline of his grandfather, who "constantly warned" him against getting into mischief with other boys, and coerced him instead to spend more time at his studies. Cohen always remembered his grandfather as a model of extreme "renunciation," of otherworldly asceticism. For the old man, what mattered was not the body, nor the emotions of living people, but "the life beyond" and the religious practices that prepared one for it.[34]

The study of the Torah helped fill Morris's social and emotional vacuum. Under his grandfather's influence, he became increasingly devoted to religious studies, and this devotion, in turn, created a sustaining bond between him and his grandfather. At the age of ten Morris was determined to begin Talmudic studies, but there was no one in the tiny village of Neshwies qualified to provide such instruction. Hence Morris was able to use this ambition to justify his desire—based, in fact, not only on piety, but also on his loneliness and his resentment against his grandfather's discipline—to return to Minsk.[35]

Morris was back with his mother, then, after an interlude of three years during which time he had seen her only on her infrequent visits to Neshwies. He was under the influence of the two dominant figures of his childhood not simultaneously, but alternately: first mother, then grandfather, and finally mother again. The two functioned not in a complementary relation, but as alternating, contrasting, total environments. Morris's grandmother was sickly and was not a factor in his development during the years in Neshwies.[36] And in Minsk, mother was all. The apparent roles of Neshwies and Minsk, of grandfather and mother, can be seen most clearly in one brief incident which can serve as an emblem for Cohen's upbringing.

When Morris was about eight years old, his mother paid one of her rare visits to Neshwies. While all were seated for the midday Sabbath meal, Morris, "in the enjoyment of the unusual pleasure" of his mother's company, became "a little hilarious." Suddenly grandfather "slapped my face with a force that almost stunned me," and that made Morris feel "humiliation" before his mother. The boy left the house, vowing to drown himself, but he hesitated at the well long enough to be overtaken by his mother. She "affectionately took me by the hand and walked with me back to the house. Never in my life has the expression of affection given my heart a more soothing and sweeter happiness."[37]

Long deprived of his mother's love, Morris celebrated its return by letting go. But the happy laughter went too far and had to be violently rejected. Resentment took form as a fantasy about a watery death: the absoluteness of his grandfather's restraint would be answered by the child's total immersion in the well. If liberation was so treacherous, better to remain contained, or to rush headlong to the sea; let the "oasis" be plugged up forever, or turn itself into an ocean.

Yet the abortive drowning drew out again the maternal affection that had turned Morris's head in the first place. "To my dying day," Cohen pledged in *A Dreamer's Journey*, "the memory of her will always be entwined with the picture of that walk hand in hand."[38] And it was mother who led Morris across the waters of the Atlantic and helped him survive the "flood" of immigration and secularization, while grandfather remained in Neshwies, a distant, detached, mute, yet undeniably judicial presence whose opinions about Morris's new life were to inspire the boy's earnest speculation.[39] Mother and grandfather, then, endowed Morris not only with the tension between total abandon and total restraint, but also with certain capabilities for living with this tension: grandfather became the model for Cohen's critical style, for his fierce lashing out against the excessive, the nonsensical, the vain, and the romantic, while mother became a model for brave endurance, for "tenacious clinging" amid the turbulent and centrifugal forces of which she was simultaneously a symbol. Explicitly, Cohen described her as, like himself, "tenacious"; implicitly, he identified her with the heroine of his only effort in belles lettres, a "female victim" who held herself together stoically while being brutalized by a sequence of hostile and arbitrary external forces.[40] Alternately, then, the adult Cohen would seek "positively" to reassert old truths in danger of being pushed aside by upheavals, and would aim "negatively" to expose and to disarm the hasty, foolish conjecture. By achieving control over these impulses, he attained a measure of personal integration and transformed some of the tensions of his childhood into mutually supportive modes of behavior.

NOTES

1. Diary, August 25, 1937, in *DJ*, 267-268.
2. Diary, July 4, 1938, and undated note of about 1939, in *DJ*, 274.

3. E.g., MRC, "Philosophy in the Modern Curriculum," *City College Quarterly* XVII (1921), 8 (*FL*, 413); MRC, "Address," in *Tribute*, 80; *MHH*, 213.

4. Diary, October 22, 1936, in *DJ*, 266; undated note in *DJ*, 270.

5. *DJ*, 95.

6. MRC, "Rule Versus Discretion," *JP* XI (1914), 215 (*LSO*, 267).

7. *KSD*, 93; Diary, May 4, 1898, in *Portrait*, 21; MRC, review of Felix Adler, *An Ethical Philosophy of Life*, in *NR* XIX (1919), 254 (*FL*, 79).

8. Quoted in *DJ*, 49.

9. *DJ*, 115; Diary, November 3, 1936, in *DJ*, 282.

10. *KSD*, 93.

11. *RN*, 165.

12. MRC, "Address," 74; *DJ*, 146.

13. Diary, February 14, 1935, and August 19 and November 30, 1936, in *DJ*, 262, 271.

14. MRC, "The Place of Logic in the Law," *Harvard Law Review* XXIX (1916), 639 (*LSO*, 183).

15. *DJ*, 42.

16. Since most of *DJ*, as it appeared in 1949, was put together by Felix Cohen out of his father's fragmentary notes, sometimes "scattered and cryptic" (see Felix's "Epilogue," *DJ*, 289), it should be emphasized that the early chapters of the volume were composed by the elder Cohen himself. He wanted to record his impressions of the Old World, and of adjustment to the New, for the benefit of the new generation, represented for him by his first grandchild, Gene Maura Cohen, to whom *DJ* is personally addressed (*DJ*, xiii; Mr. and Mrs. Harry N. Rosenfield, conversation with author, Washington, D.C., May 15, 1971). Although he hoped to extend the narrative to cover his entire life, Cohen died before he had written about his adulthood in a sustained fashion. In order to complete the volume, Felix Cohen drew on preliminary drafts and notes and also upon the scattered, random autobiographical comments published by the elder Cohen in a variety of contexts over a period of nearly forty years.

17. *DJ*, 17, 21.

18. *DJ*, 16.

19. *DJ*, 16.

20. *DJ*, 20-21. Cf. *DJ*, 43: "Once . . . I nearly drowned by allowing myself to float on a current [in a river near the heder] which carried me beyond my depth."

21. *DJ*, 21.

22. *DJ*, 22.

23. *DJ*, 29.

24. *DJ*, 51-53.

25. *DJ*, 22-23, 30, 37-38.

26. *DJ*, 18, 23.

27. *DJ*, 42-43.

28. *DJ*, 43.

29. Ruth Landes and Mark Zborowski, "Hypotheses Concerning the Eastern European Jewish Family," in Norman Kiell, ed., *The Psychodynamics of American Jewish Life: An Anthology* (New York, 1967), 35.

30. The circumstances of Morris's move to Neshwies are ambiguous: on the one hand, it was poverty that forced his mother to be away from home all day, yet on the other, it was the money sent from America by her husband that enabled her, in 1887, to pay her own parents to care for her child (*DJ*, 18, 23).

31. Diary, August 19, 1897, in *Portrait*, 16.

32. *DJ*, 29; Diary, June 24, 1935, in *DJ*, 282.

33. *DJ*, 11.

34. *DJ*, 29-31, 39-40.

35. *DJ*, 36, 44.

36. *DJ*, 29.

37. *DJ*, 36-37.

38. *DJ*, 37.

39. *DJ*, 58.

40. See *KSD*, as discussed below in Chapter 9.

The Stoic freedom in which wisdom consists is found in the submission of our desires, but not of our thoughts. From the submission of our desires springs the virtue of resignation; from the freedom of our thoughts springs the whole world of art and philosophy, and the vision of beauty by which, at last, we half reconquer the reluctant world. But the vision of beauty is possible only to unfettered contemplation, to thoughts not weighted by the load of eager wishes; and thus Freedom comes only to those who no longer ask of life that it shall yield them any of those personal goods that are subject to the mutations of Time. . . . To abandon the struggle for private happiness, to expel all eagerness of temporary desire, to burn with passion for eternal things—this is emancipation, and this is the free man's worship. And this liberation is effected by a contemplation of Fate; for Fate itself is subdued by the mind which leaves nothing to be purged by the purifying fire of Time.

Bertrand Russell

Despite his doubts about the "physical appearance and careless dress" of the young Russian Jew who had determined to become a teacher of philosophy, Felix Adler arranged in 1904 for the Ethical Culture Society to finance Morris Cohen's graduate studies at Harvard. Cohen was among the most promising of the intellectually ambitious immigrants Adler had encountered on Manhattan's Lower East Side, where German Jews shared with gentile reformers and philanthropists responsibility for Americanizing the "new immigrants" from eastern Europe. Any hint of the "reeking and snarling" that Henry Adams claimed to see in Jewish immigrants was an embarrassment to the cultivated, established Jews of Adler's class and generation, so it was only after searching scrutiny of Cohen—but twelve years removed from the shtetl—that Adler presented him to Harvard as a successfully uplifted immigrant, a sound enough risk to be entrusted even with the founding of a Harvard branch of the Ethical Culture Society.[1]

Cohen had been well prepared. He had assisted Adler at the offices of the Ethical Culture Society, the organization Adler himself had founded more than a quarter-century before. The "ethical movement," as its partisans have always preferred to call it, had proved especially attractive to American Jews of German origin, and by the turn of the century it was appealing also to immigrants of Cohen's background. The movement claimed to occupy "that common ground, where we may all meet, believers and unbelievers, for purposes in themselves lofty and unquestioned by any." "Diversity in the creed, unanimity in deed," was the motto of what Adler liked to call this "practical religion from which none dissents."[2] These general aspirations had a specific meaning for many immigrants: Ethical Culture stood for aloofness from the peculiarities of the Jewish tradition, especially as that tradition survived in Russia and Poland. Cohen became nominally affiliated after Adler took a personal interest in his affairs, but his actual involvement in the movement was brief and minimal. In later years he was to send his daughter Leonora to the Ethical Culture School, and he and his wife were to remain close friends of several leaders of the society, including

John Lovejoy Elliot; but Ethical Culture was important for the young
Cohen chiefly as a kind of finishing school, and as a respectable label he
could apply to himself in a world that required religious identification
of one sort or another.[3]

Even before receiving the benefits of Adler's patronage, Cohen had
begun to prepare himself for an American adulthood. He had won
medals for his exemplary performance in the public schools of New
York; he was a graduate of the College of the City of New York; and
his life had long centered around a yet more reliable agency of accul-
turation, the Educational Alliance, the great settlement house at East
Broadway and Jefferson Street. At the Alliance Cohen was already a
teacher in the "Breadwinner's College," a night school designed, as he
put it, to teach Jewish working people "to become public-spirited,
generously cultured, pure and high minded."[4] Moreover, Cohen had
been originally "discovered," and then nurtured both socially and intellectually, by Adler's old friend and ally Thomas Davidson, one of the
Lower East Side's most dedicated and renowned evangelists of respect-
ability.

Adler was the only Jew—Russian or German—in the American Philosophical Association, and his chair at Columbia was something of a
thing apart, having been created specifically for him through an arrangement made by the university with Jewish philanthropists.[5] He and his
carefully chosen protégé understood that persons of Cohen's ethnic
and religious background simply did not become teachers of philosophy
in the United States. Hundreds of Jewish immigrants from eastern
Europe had won places for themselves in technical professions such as
medicine and law, but colleges and universities did not entrust to Jews
such morally crucial roles as the teaching of philosophy.[6] Philosophy
was then taught as a comprehensive moral and intellectual endeavor,
as an inquiry into the religious, ethical, and social questions whose
answers made up the marrow of American culture. But Cohen was content neither to take on a technical role for the society at large, nor to
perform a moral and religious function for "his own people," in a

parochial context. He would be neither an amateur nor a "Jewish" philosopher; he proposed to make his living doing the real thing, hopefully in New York City, almost within sight of the Statue of Liberty, symbol of the promise that the world would be his once he chose his calling and exerted enough effort.

The promise was not entirely fraudulent, even as it applied to Russian Jews interested in philosophy. Why was Cohen the one to prove this? How did his emotional energies become so compellingly engaged by the effort to make a career in philosophy? And how, as a social being, had he become capable of this particular ambition in the first decade of the twentieth century? How, in other words, did the general process of cultural accommodation—East European Jewry with America—interact with the process of Cohen's personal growth to produce the earnest and demanding youth Adler sent to Harvard?

The relationship between traditional Jewish attitudes toward learning and the existence in the United States of free public schools is perhaps the central factor in the accommodation of East European Jewry with American culture. It was as if the steam engine had somehow been invented without anything to roll on, and after years of waiting and generating steam had suddenly been positioned on a railway track with no terminals in sight. Connected originally to the need for authoritative interpretations of religious law, the scholarly ideal subsequently flowered among the Jewish laity, and by the nineteenth century a point had been reached where learning was regarded as an intrinsic, positive good.[7] The American social order, in contrast to the Russian, offered both social mobility and an available, indeed compulsory, system of public education. "We would study hard, develop our minds," said Joseph Freeman of the circle of friends in which he grew up in the Williamsburgh section of Brooklyn, "and through them rise to higher rungs of the American ladder" than those of "our fathers, who were tailors, grocers, storekeepers, salesmen, brokers on the pettiest scale imaginable." Freeman and his friends "wanted to know everything," and one of their number "began to read through the entire Encyclopedia, but broke down at 'Crustacea.' "[8] As sociologist Marshall Sklare observes, the Russian Jews were "free at last," and they expressed their freedom by going to school so passionately that "secular education assumed the place that Jewish education had occupied" before emigration. Religious training became the marginal enterprise secular learning had been within the Pale.[9]

Under the influence of his grandfather, Morris had learned to feel "pride at attaining the heights of pious study." Happy in the company of books and scholars, Cohen easily mastered his lessons in the heder and had begun Talmudic studies in a yeshiva shortly before his departure from his native Minsk. He had also begun to read secular works in Yiddish, and he brought to America a bookish disposition that transcended religious piety and, indeed, survived it.[10] Once in New York, Cohen's religious attitudes changed quickly.

The family assumed that young Morris would soon join his father and brothers "in some phase of tailoring," and gave him "no incentive and little opportunity" to continue studies in Hebrew and the Talmud. The Cohen household on Suffolk Street, while under the strict ordinance of religious law, had no religious books. Morris "devoured" what few Yiddish books he could find "as one famished for food."[11] Had he wanted to become a rabbi, the family might have supported his scholarly interests, but his tastes became increasingly secular after his declaration of agnosticism at the age of thirteen. This drift away from orthodoxy partook of the syndrome described by Nathan Glazer: trained in the law and ritual, but not in theology, many Jewish immigrants were peculiarly vulnerable to the influence of adamant and intellectually rigorous skepticism.[12] Within a few months of his arrival in America, Cohen heard his father fumble a challenge to justify his belief in God and Judaism: "I am a believer," was all Abraham Cohen could say. Thereafter Morris participated in religious rituals only because his family made it a condition of his remaining at home.[13]

If Morris's rejection of Jewish religious practice was far from unique, it did place him, decisively, on one side of a barrier that existed between two kinds of intellectually oriented boys in his neighborhood: those who were considering the rabbinate, and those who were not. The seriousness with which this distinction was taken is indicated, for example, by Mordecai Kaplan's recollection that when he and Cohen met on an East Side street in 1893 or 1894, their differences in this particular respect quickly led them to see that they did not have enough in common to pursue a friendship. Kaplan was then already in a preparatory class at the Jewish Theological Seminary. (He would eventually lead the Reconstructionist Movement in Judaism.) Although Kaplan and Cohen attended City College together for five years, they never spoke with each other again.[14]

Cohen's first year in Primary School 92 was chiefly devoted to learning English, but once he mastered his new tongue he astonished his teachers with his intelligence and drive. He won prizes for his compositions and for his ability to do difficult problems in arithmetic; so quickly was he promoted through the grades that his father was persuaded to allow his youngest son to remain in school for a third year, 1894-1895, during which he skipped yet another grade and found himself suddenly eligible to take the examination for entrance to the College of the City of New York.[15] Cohen not only passed the examination in the spring of 1895, but won a gold medal for the best performance of any student from the Norfolk Street Grammar School. He ran home, giddy and incredulous, to his mother:[16]

My mother at that time was bed-ridden, and when I told her that I had passed the examination and was thus admitted to college, a flood of tears came into her eyes. . . . When one of my aunts remonstrated with my mother, "you cannot afford to send your boy to college," she replied, "If need be I'll go out as a washerwoman and scrub floors so that my Morris can have a college education."

This description of the scene, provided by Cohen many years later, sounds today so mythic, and is so perfect a rendition of the legend of Jewish immigrants and public education, that we must remind ourselves of the authenticity of the experiences that gave rise to the legend.

When little Morris had been called a half-wit by neighbors in Russia, Bessie Farfel Cohen insisted that "some day they will all be proud that they have talked to my Meisheleh,"[17] and now her ambitions for the fifteen-year-old Morris won out against her husband's eagerness to have the boy "in the shop": for her son's education, this mother vowed to rise from her sickbed and do hard labor.[18] Thus supported, Cohen took C.C.N.Y.'s five-year course of study, a combined high school and college program, which he completed on schedule in 1900.

Cohen's education in the grammar schools and at City College was important for its content as well as its form. Not only did these institutions provide Cohen and his mother with an opportunity for the fulfillment, in the abstract, of their tradition's scholarly ideal; New York's schools transferred to Cohen the same culture they were designed to pass on to the children of native stock, a culture novel to students of Cohen's background in many, but not all, respects. The petit bourgeois elements in the Jewish tradition, described by Nathan Glazer and other sociologists, made it possible for Jewish youth to embrace the official values of self-reliance, thrift, diligence, and restraint more quickly and thoroughly than could non-Jewish immigrants.[19] Cohen at sixteen treasured his copy of Benjamin Franklin's *Autobiography*, an influence on his moral development rivaled only by the writings of the Victorian self-help publicist Samuel Smiles.

Cohen consciously modeled his diary on Franklin's suggestion that self-improvement depended upon keeping a close record of one's moral behavior; the diary itself was studded with maxims from Smiles's writings, sometimes copied from *Thrift*, at other times assimilated into Cohen's own aphorisms. Much good has resulted from the hard work imposed by poverty, Cohen mused; without work, "life would be a plague, for indolence is the worst of all maladies." Cohen was certain that "by steady industry" he would become famous, and would even raise himself "to the level of authors." Assigned to write an essay on Franklin, Cohen took the lessons of the assignment with utter seriousness: he resolved to his diary to be more resolute in making and following resolutions, decided to "keep a separate book for special resolutions," and for days afterward castigated himself for his laziness.[20] To whatever extent Cohen was heir to a tradition of social solidarity and interdependence, Franklin and Smiles drew out of him instead the equally traditional loyalty to prudence, industry, and self-control, and then connected the latter set of values to a distinctly individualistic sense of responsibility and enterprise.

Cohen's teachers introduced him also to Great Authors, the men of letters whose portraits, in the form of the popular card game "Authors," entered even those American living rooms too remote from "Culture" to have standard editions of the Anglo-American canon. It was no accident that when Cohen and his friends formed a discussion group, it was called "The Bryant Literary Society." The year before Cohen entered City College his teachers led him through Francis Turner Palgrave's *Golden Treasury of Best Songs and Lyrical Poems in the English Language*, which brought Cohen into contact with late-Victorian literary culture at its most proud and genteel: "Poetry," declared Palgrave's preface, "gives treasures 'more golden than gold,' leading us in higher and healthier ways than those of the world, and interpreting to us the lessons of Nature." In addition to Palgrave's selections from Wordsworth, Scott, and Byron, Cohen read the prose of Emerson and Carlyle, and he was inspired by English literature in general to an intellectual "awakening" that was advanced at City College, where he listened admiringly to his English professor's oral readings of Matthew Arnold.[21]

"At that time," Cohen said in *A Dreamer's Journey* about the 1890s, "there were a large number of . . . literary clubs on the East Side, generally named after some well-known poet or writer such as Longfellow, Tennyson, Emerson, Irving, and the like."[22] Indeed, the works of these authors were so much in demand that libraries complained of their inability to stock sufficient copies.[23] Insofar as familiarity with Anglo-American literature and history was part of the program of "Americanization," it was an aspect the immigrants were especially eager to undergo: curious to learn about their new environment, young people like

Cohen absorbed the period's vaunted "literary culture" to the extent of
acting it out in their clubs. Cohen and his friends organized contests
among themselves for prizes in composition, address, and debate. So
seriously did Jewish youth take the style and content of American literary life that teachers and settlement workers were often overawed by
the intellectual intensity and good taste of their upright and studious
charges.[24]

The readiness with which Cohen and his contemporaries took up
secular literary culture is partially explained by the prior influence
upon them of the *haskalah*, the "Jewish enlightenment" that had
brought some of the ideas and sensations of Western literature into
eastern European Jewish experience during the nineteenth century.
While still in Minsk, Cohen read the fiction of Nahum Meir Shaikewick
and Mendele Moker Seforim, who presented in Yiddish many of the
themes of popular German and Russian stories. The secular romances
of the *haskalah* authors expanded the range of emotions that could be
legitimately expressed, heightened their reader's sensitivity to the
limitations of life within the Pale, and promoted a generalized humanism and rationalism as an antidote to the severity of the Biblical tradition as it had been maintained through centuries of diaspora.[25] Shaikewick, the "Dumas of Yiddish literature," led Cohen to seek out Yiddish
translations of the *Arabian Nights* and of the romances of Beauvais, and
accustomed him to the heroic and romantic conventions operative in
the literature he would soon read in English.[26]

Indeed, the animated intellectual life of the Lower East Side is partially to be understood as an explosive flowering, under novel, urban
conditions, of the *haskalah* and of its liberal counterparts beyond the
realm of letters. East European Jewry had been stirred by socialism and
was moving toward a political as well as a literary "emancipation" prior
to emigration; but this Jewish society, so long as it remained in Russia
or Poland, was essentially a scattered, small-town population with only
tenuous connections to the liberal metropolis of Vilna. It was suddenly
transformed into the fully urban Yiddish ghetto of New York, with one

of the highest population densities in the Western world. Here on Manhattan, then, took place the physical consolidation of a culture: connections were more intimate and direct, communications more rapid. New
ideas and responses to experience could travel with unprecedented
rapidity and, in short, all the classic sociological features of urban life
were present. Yet this physical consolidation occurred simultaneously
with ideological dissolution: the East European Jews were confronted,
abruptly, with a plenitude of invitations to break old traditions and
take up new ways of life. Hence, if East European Jewry was experiencing urbanization internally, it was experiencing, in its external relations, cultural cross-fertilization, and even cultural attack.

It was under these conditions that Jewish children sought out and
consumed, at the very earliest opportunity, the epics of Western imagination. It was here that Jacob Epstein would, of his own accord, spend
day after day in a park with Hugo's *Les Miserables*, Dostoevski's
Brothers Karamazov, and Whitman's *Leaves of Grass*; here that Joseph
Freeman read a Hebrew translation of Cooper's *Last of the Mohicans*
eight times; here that Mary Ryshpan would determine to model her
own character on that of George Eliot; and here that Morris Cohen,
while waiting for the first term of public school to begin, would closet
himself with *A Child's History of the Civil War* and Dumas's *Count of
Monte Cristo*.[27] It was here also that the Yiddish theater and the debates between socialist theoreticians reached the pitch described by
the journalist Hutchins Hapgood, whose *Spirit of the Ghetto* gave
added currency to the fashionable idea that the streets of the East Side
were filled with working-class Spinozas.[28] Even Henry James took
notice of the ferment and was tempted to propose a toast "in tribute
to an intellectual people," but the impulse was stilled, in his case, by
the portentous "swarming" of the ghetto, which made him feel trapped,
as in an aquarium beneath "innumerable fish, of over-developed
proboscis," who "were to bump together, forever, amid heaped spoils
of the sea."[29]

By the time Cohen entered City College at the age of fifteen, he was ready to respond favorably to the liberal education C.C.N.Y. tried to provide. Cohen's actual course of study was primarily technical and scientific, but the moral impact of the college was substantial: the college represented to Cohen the practice of "liberal education as opposed to dogmatic indoctrination." C.C.N.Y. was in fact a very authoritarian institution in the 1890s, but it still afforded a greater range of intellectual freedom than had previously seemed to Cohen to be compatible with formal education. The relative openness of discourse and tolerance for cultural diversity contrasted sharply with the atmosphere he had found in the grammar schools, the yeshiva, and the heder.[30]

Important as public education was to Cohen's development, the decisive cultural influences of his youth came from and through the Educational Alliance. Public schools were, after all, aspects of the New World to which immigrants were trying to adapt. The Alliance, founded in 1891 by well-to-do members of New York's Jewish community, was designed as a bridge between the Old World and the New. It was here that the visiting H.G. Wells was pleased to be marched into "a big class of bright-eyed Jewish children," each of whom waved "two little American flags" while singing patriotic songs.[31] The Alliance saw itself unabashedly as "an institution for the Americanization of the foreigner," as a "center of sweetness and light, an oasis" in the East Side's "desert of degradation and despair." Notoriously alien from some of the older immigrants because of its reluctance to sanction the use of Yiddish, the Alliance concentrated on the young, who made up most of the 6,000 persons per day who attended its classes or otherwise participated in its program.[32] Many of these young people were, as Cohen himself noted in a 1902 issue of *The Alliance Review*, torn between the old and the new and bewildered because "the old generation" could do so little when called upon to justify Jewish traditions and religious practices "on the basis of modern science and culture." Cohen, who had himself participated in religious rituals without believing in them for several years, complained of the "pernicious" moral effect of being "forced to play the hypocrite."[33] Cohen, and others less preoccupied

than he with keeping things "balanced," looked to the Educational
Alliance for cultural guidance and stability.

At the Alliance, instruction in American history and government led
to classes in millinery, dressmaking, and other trades, all amid a flurry
of music lessons, concerts, discussion groups, lectures, and calisthenics.
To carry out its work, the Alliance mobilized not only a small army of
uncelebrated teachers and functionaries—such as Edward King, who, as
leader of the "Comte Synthetic Circle," first drew Cohen into the orbit
of the Alliance in 1898—but also a battery of more distinguished spokesmen for "Culture," including Thomas Davidson, the most important
figure in Cohen's youth.[34]

Like Theodore Roosevelt in politics, Thomas Davidson in education
embodied the robust gentility and "practical idealism" so central to
what middle-class Americans at the turn of the century wanted to pass
on to their children. Ostentatiously vigorous, cultured, and clean,
Davidson apotheosized the ideals of the Educational Alliance, and its
directors could have found no one more devoted to saving working-class
Jewish immigrants from pessimism, parochialism, and political radicalism. The masses are "unintelligent, narrow, sordid, envious, and unhappy," Davidson believed, and hence potentially prone to "popular
uprisings and the overthrow of our free institutions."[35] Like so many
educators of the period, Davidson believed the best defense against
"violence and barbarism" was "Culture," which was, as Henry May has
said, "not so much a way of describing how people behaved as an idea
of how they ought to behave and did not."[36] Davidson saw Culture
as preparation for all personal, domestic, social, and political relations;
only a truly broad education could enable the breadwinners to "enter
into lofty personal relations, and to live clean, tasteful, useful, self-
respecting lives." On the one hand Davidson thrust Dante into the
hands of his pupils—in Italian, whether they knew the language or
not—and on the other he led them to "body culture," to "health,
strength, grace, and dexterity":

What is more unbecoming than high or stooping shoulders, a sidelong or rolling gait, a slow, ungainly movement of hands and feet, a general looseness and feebleness of the whole frame? And these things are not only unbecoming, but they also go far to unfit their victims for skilled labor and efficient work.[37]

Before Davidson began to lecture at the Alliance in 1898, he had spent most of his fifty-eight years blustering about the learned circles of America and Europe with all the gusto of Roosevelt's journeys to the Wild West and the Congo. A notorious intellectual adventurer, Davidson embraced successively a number of religious and philosophical enthusiasms, ranging from the "commonsense" orthodoxy of his Scottish upbringing to the Rosminian cult of Domodossola, Italy.[38] Though never attached to a university faculty, he was for a while a leading member of the proud St. Louis Hegelians, and he was acquainted with a number of American philosophers, including Josiah Royce, who referred to him as "that noisy fellow." Davidson's eclectic learning and rustic style appealed to William James, who corresponded with him for many years[39] and whose memorial essay remains the most frequently quoted sketch of Davidson's character. The great value of Davidson, said James, was the example he set as "a knight-errant of the intellectual life," subservient to "no tribal idol." Davidson showed "how a life devoted to purely intellectual ends could be beautifully wholesome outwardly, and overflow with inner contentment."[40]

"Extreme was his need of friends," James had also said of Davidson, and this trait may have contributed to the extreme solicitousness manifested by the bachelor Davidson toward Cohen and others who attended his class at the Alliance in the winter and spring of 1899. Wearing his learning grandly, and dropping the names of the eminent men who were his friends, Davidson so impressed his young listeners with his position in the world that Cohen was dazzled to receive the lecturer's personal attention. After a class discussion in which Cohen had participated, Davidson clasped the youth's shoulder and said, "You have a fine mind. You ought to cultivate it."[41]

Cohen and Davidson grew closer during the spring of 1899, and

Davidson was so eager to have Cohen among the East Siders who were
to spend the summer of 1899 with him in the Adirondacks that he
made the impecunious scholar his guest, in return for the performance
of odd jobs. Davidson's Essex County retreat, Glenmore, was the site
of his "Summer School of the Cultural Sciences," where he promised a
combination of solid study and serious conversation with "reinvigorat-
ing rest and abundant and delightful exercise."[42] In its decade of existence the Summer School drew such distinguished academic talent as
Hugo Munsterberg, William James, and John Dewey, and in 1899
Davidson was joined by the young philosopher Wilmon Sheldon and the
United States Commissioner of Education, William T. Harris. Cohen
talked with these visitors, climbed mountains, chopped wood, studied
Latin, and read Hume, Kant, and Tennyson. Most important were his
conversations with Davidson himself, who by the end of the summer
had become like "an affectionate father."[43] This very concept was for
Cohen, until that point in his life, a Platonic idea, for the father (and
grandfather) he knew was anything but "affectionate." This relationship continued during 1899-1900, when Cohen lectured on world history under Davidson's supervision at the Educational Alliance, and
during the following summer, when Cohen—by then indisputably
Davidson's favorite—was again part of the East Side's contingent in the
Adirondacks. Davidson died suddenly at the end of that second summer at Glenmore, but by then Cohen had been so inspired that he was
to make an annual pilgrimage to visit Davidson's grave at Glenmore for
the next forty years.[44]

   Standing before his co-workers at the Alliance in 1901, a year after
Davidson's death, Cohen eulogized his cultural father in terms that reveal what he had become under Davidson's galvanizing influence. Cohen
spoke exclusively in the idiom of Culture: he praised Davidson for
preferring "the great streams of reality" to the "petty muddles of the
day," for his heroic conviction that "only sheer sloth and cowardice
keep us from trying harder to solve our problems," and for seeing that
the way "to lift the people above their degrading and vicious lives" was

to offer them, through sound education, "an inspiring outlook on life." Cohen approvingly quoted Davidson's reference to "a little knot of earnest Jews" who through their educational endeavors might turn the world upside down if they saw themselves in Lowell's lines: "how weak an arm may turn the iron helm of fate." With Davidson's inspiration, Cohen and his followers would help the breadwinners of the world "to lead simple upright lives," to perform their "duties," to be secure in their understanding "of the great institutions under which we live." Perhaps Davidson's greatest legacy, Cohen concluded, was his conviction that the old and the new could be balanced, that the "tragic relation between the older and younger generations" could be transcended by reverence for the past and loyalty to the future, a stance Cohen illustrated with some of Tennyson's most reassuring lines:[45]

Not clinging to some ancient saw
  Not mastered by some modern term;
  Not swift nor slow to change, but firm:
And in its season bring the law;

That from Discussion's lips may fall
  With Life, that, working strongly, binds—
  Set in all lights by many minds,
To close the interests of all.

Cohen tried to fill Davidson's role—literally—at the Educational Alliance, where he made himself the custodian of Davidson's ideals and traditions. Cohen's own career began with his hero's death: he led the other "Davidsonians" in the development and expansion of the "Breadwinner's College," an attempt to carry out Davidson's mission, "judging ourselves," as Cohen expressed it, "by the standard by which he would have judged us."[46] As the administrator and most dedicated teacher in the program for night-school instruction of working people, Cohen inaugurated his professional life with an explicit attempt to model himself on Davidson. Hence Davidson's importance to Cohen's development went beyond his role as the supreme exemplar of a set of values, and a tone, that the entire process of "programmed" Americanization had prepared Cohen to adopt as his own. As Davidson's anointed, Cohen

was in a position to take over and, through his ambition and his leadership, to attract the attention, eventually, of his next benefactor, Felix
Adler.

Although it is not possible to determine what would have happened
to Cohen had he not been drawn so firmly into the orbit of Davidson
and the Educational Alliance, Cohen was aware of the opportunities
offered by the Lower East Side for some very different kinds of experience. Some of the brittleness of the adult Cohen's commitment to
"high culture" may have derived from the awareness that many Jewish
youths of the 1890s had absorbed these other, less refined aspects of
East Side life, and from a related sense that his own hold on his chosen
life was weak. The "sharp Jewish kid" who signed on with a local Tammany leader, for example, got into a rather different life than the one
Davidson presented to Cohen. Samuel Ornitz's *Haunch, Paunch, and
Jow* is a vivid fictional portrait of exactly this social type, the youth
who begins as an especially crafty combat strategist in street fights with
the "Micks," stumbles upon ways to extort "protection" money from
vandal-wary merchants, and is enlisted by the district's Irish political
boss to help extend Tammany's control over Jewish voters. Ornitz's
protagonist eventually becomes a lawyer for the Bosses, and finally a
corrupt judge; cynically, he keeps his own constituency in line by at-
tending the synagogue regularly and by ostentatiously sponsoring Jewish philanthropies.[47]

Ornitz describes what was obviously an extreme case, and one that
required a temperament very different from Cohen's. Yet what needs
to be underlined is that the young Cohen grasped onto Culture while
physically surrounded by the same vice and squalor central to the story
Ornitz tells, and to the similar interpretations of East Side life presented
by Michael Gold's *Jews Without Money* and Abraham Cahan's *The Rise
of David Levinsky*.[48] At the age of seventeen Cohen worked in a poolhall operated by his brother Samuel, and patronized by gangsters, gam-
blers, drunks, and, according to Samuel Cohen's own recollections,

"pimps and dope fiends who . . . conducted some preliminary business in our place and made contacts there."[49] Cohen's autobiography does not detail the Bowery panorama of brawls, prostitutes, and official corruption, but it must be remembered that he wrote *A Dreamer's Journey* with his young granddaughter in mind. Even when inside the poolhall, Cohen seems to have strived mightily to screen out the immoral life around him: he would hide himself so completely in a book that customers, observed his brother, would "tease him about his constant reading and they would apologize in the most elaborate manner for disturbing him in order to buy something." In these surroundings Cohen read—in snippets, over the course of about a year—Gibbon's *Decline and Fall of the Roman Empire*, a work that remained more vividly impressed upon his memory, he later insisted, than anything he studied that year at City College.[50]

Perhaps young Morris was too much an introvert for the wild life of the Bowery to have ever posed a real alternative to the life represented by Gibbon, Davidson, and the Educational Alliance. Still, what remains to be explained is the peculiar intensity with which Cohen actually pursued Davidson's mission. Without the special, intimate relationship Cohen developed with this elderly, generous, and perhaps lonely man, one doubts that it would have been Cohen who, at the age of twenty-one, had the audacity to pick up Davidson's fallen banner, and one doubts also that Cohen would have been able in the next two decades to concentrate his energies so successfully on the effort to become a philosopher. This unusual friendship, therefore, demands closer scrutiny in the specific context of the development of Cohen's personality in his teens and early twenties.

Three and half years after Morris Cohen arrived in America, he began to keep a diary. The very idea of keeping a diary was one of the chief topics for discussion: the sixteen-year-old Cohen saw the project as a means of steadying himself, restraining unwanted impulses, and goading himself to behave appropriately. By forcing himself to write down his thoughts, by recording systematically his efforts to "be good," he might keep himself "under a restraint." The difficulty, he mused, was lack of control in his earlier life; it was here that Morris criticized his mother, implicitly, for leaving him "without any monitor." Now, "unsteady" at sixteen, he yearned for some "system" to which he could subject himself, some instrument of "moral government" to save him from temptations unnamed—except for "idleness"—but apparently very compelling.[51] Hence Benjamin Franklin's self-directed program of moral improvement was ideal: it was systematic in spirit, and was certainly a strategy of "tenacious self-absorption."

In fact, the diary was anything but systematic; the "steadying" function was to be performed, apparently, by the simple act of writing down his resolutions, his reflections on their importance, and a miscellany of his activities in school and at home. And Cohen's adolescent confusions, while they had a particular character, were not strikingly unusual: these notebooks were produced by an extremely self-conscious, serious youth who regularly counted the number of books in his possession, doted on his triumphs in school and in streetcorner discussions, and doubted that he had the inner strength required to achieve the greatness about which he frequently fantasized.[52]

If the diaries leave the impression that Cohen, in his late teens, was largely nonsocial, concerned solely with his books and his essay contests, this sense is resoundingly confirmed by the recollections of others. Cohen took ponderous books along to social affairs. Gibbon may have remained in the poolroom, but a volume of Schopenhauer was in Cohen's pocket even on weekend picnics. When the threat of intimate social interaction loomed, the book was there to be read.[53] When girls were introduced into the literary society, Cohen admitted to his diary that he had not been able to "hide" his "adversion toward the 'ladies.' "[54] He was known to his peers as a "brain" who didn't talk to girls. His first conversation with Mary Ryshpan, who was later to be his wife, proceeded as follows: the two happened to be near one another as they left a lecture hall, and Mary asked, "What did you think

of the talk?" Cohen replied, "To answer your question would take
volumes that only the learned would read."[55]

The Cohen of this period served as the prototype for the supercilious,
passionless superbrain in *Unquiet*, the novel written by Joseph Gollomb
more than thirty years after he and Cohen had together attended City
College and frequented the Educational Alliance. Gollomb's character,
"Moey Cohen," was the "mental prodigy" in the circle of Lower East
Side youth depicted in the novel. Characteristically snide and always
"too intellectual," Moey Cohen "skipped grades by twos and threes,"
then became increasingly aloof from friends his own age as he took up
"associating with adult intellects." In Gollomb's novel, Cohen's leadership of the "Breadwinner's College"—Gollomb did not bother to change
its name either—was extravagantly pretentious and partook of ego-
mania. When Gollomb's obviously autobiographical hero, David Levitt,
abandons the college in order to follow his own career, Moey Cohen
vilifies the defector: "We'll survive your loss, but someday we'll remind
you what King Henry said, 'Go hang yourself, brave Crillon, we won at
Arques and you were not there!' "—a phrase that the real Cohen actually used in a speech of 1909 to castigate defectors from the college.[56]

About the time Morris first met, and rebuffed, Mary Ryshpan, he
tried to spell out, in his diary, the loneliness and the obliquely understood sexual desires masked by his Olympian detachment. "My mental
and physical organism," he noted,

needs another half, a magnetic opposite to cooperate with, but this
other half I think (from my scanty experience) utterly impossible to
exist in the opposite sex. . . . I would like to open my mind to someone
who could read into its deepest recesses. . . . But even when this conception of my other half, my magnetic opposite, my poetic supplement
is strongest and most attractive . . . I cannot get myself away from the
belief that love is a delusion and that my nature, my incessant intro-
spection and weak character, renders me incapable of loving and being
loved.[57]

No woman, then, could make the required entry, but some "magnetic"
presence was needed to open him up and draw him out. This passage

from Cohen's diary becomes especially significant when viewed in the light of the actual course taken by Morris's relationship with his wife-to-be.

By twenty-three, Cohen was less skeptical about women as candidates for his "poetic supplement," but his letter of proposal began haltingly, with the grave observation that marriage might take him "from the larger needs of the world," and hence the impulse to marry ought, perhaps, to be stifled. Then, dramatically, Cohen changed the mood, and implored Mary to sweep him out of his sexual inertia: "I ask you to take me—take me to your self, to your love, your sympathy, your faith . . . take me and inspire me."[58]

Soon after the engagement, Morris left New York to begin his graduate study at Harvard. He was scarcely out of town before he addressed a strange request to his fiancée. He asked that she go to his house and open a "little drawer" in his desk where she would find a collection of his private papers. He demanded that she "examine every one of those scraps with a truly psychologic microscope." Mary took the matter much less seriously, but Cohen persisted, and he agonized over her reactions. He was impatient to be judged yet not to be judged; Mary protested at one point, "you ask for what is impossible when you say that I should not come to *any* conclusion about the things in the little drawer." It is not clear now what the precious cache contained—perhaps Cohen's adolescent diaries—but the correspondence between the two refers repeatedly and cryptically to the drawer. The episode was an emblem, in turn, for their entire correspondence during the three years between betrothal and marriage: the recurrent issues were how well Mary did or did not see inside Morris, how gifted Morris was or was not.[59]

As the wedding approached, Cohen's enthusiasm was guarded, to say the least. He ponderously assured his fiancée that if they did actually go through with the marriage, he would proceed with a full knowledge of his responsibilities, and with "a determination to fulfill them." She frankly complained of her suitor's lack of ardor, and he had to assure her of his interest. When it appeared that unexpected financial help from a relative might enable them to marry sooner than they had planned, Morris was not displeased, but he suggested that the "training" of waiting another year "ought to be valuable" for them both.[60] Wait they did, and in the meantime Cohen complained of depressions, moodiness, and nervousness; in February of 1906 his health broke down so completely that he spent a month in "rest cure" at Watkins Glen, New York. From there Cohen wrote his betrothed to suggest that when they did get married, they hold the ceremony in the sickroom of her father, then confined to his bed. The idea of this sickroom wedding so energized the ailing Morris that he offered to take the very next train home, should Mary's father indicate an interest.[61]

Cohen's fantasy of marriage in a sickroom was actually quite in keeping with his semiconscious aspirations: the head of the new family was to be a weak and sickly man of indefinite lifespan, much in need of being looked after and looked into. The bedfast father-in-law was, therefore, not so alien as a model for the groom. Years later, when Cohen was an established family man, the most sanguine thing he could say about the institution of marriage was that it was not a "bed of roses," but rather one of "suffering."[62]

As it happened, then, Cohen's prediction as an adolescent that no female would be able to see inside him fully, and draw him out, was not so far from the truth. It was Thomas Davidson whom he was to revere for having

got hold of me when my soul was parched . . . [He] opened the wells of life within me, and caused living waters to flow forth. I stopped brooding . . . and went in, with all my might and main, into Davidson's work.[63]

Cohen wrote these words in 1909, a decade after Davidson had taken hold of him—literally, by the shoulders—after a discussion group, and announced that anyone whose eyes were set as far apart as Cohen's simply had to be intelligent.[64] Davidson invited Cohen to visit him at home, but "shyness or other reasons" delayed this visit until a day when the two met accidentally on the street near Davidson's apartment on Stuyvesant Square. Led up to the apartment, and engaged by Davidson in bookish chit-chat, Cohen was then asked about himself with a solicitude that touched the youth deeply. After this experience, Cohen rushed to the next scheduled meeting of Davidson's class "with the ardor of a young swain going to woo his inamorata."[65]

Cohen strained the conventions of polite discourse in search of ways to express his feelings about Davidson. He doted on the phrase "my beloved teacher" when addressing letters to his new idol, and made a point of assuring him "that every time I use the phrase, I do so with an increased meaning." When Davidson, a political conservative, seemed annoyed at Cohen's intention to study the works of Karl Marx, Cohen was cut deeply by the rebuke: "And now, my most beloved teacher, with my eyes full of tears, I do most earnest[ly] beseech you not to let these sad misunderstandings mar the relations which have up to now existed between us." Years later Cohen fondly recalled being "intoxicated"—a word he almost never used, except to condemn the state of agitation it connoted—by the warmth of Davidson's interest in him.[66]

Cohen was not the first Jewish youth in whom Davidson had taken a special, personal interest. Some years before, in St. Louis, he had adopted Arthur Amson and sent him to study at a European university, only to have the boy die there. Cohen was moved to learn that he had taken Amson's cherished place in Davidson's heart, and that he too might be adopted and sent to Europe under Davidson's auspices. Davidson went so far as to mention this plan to Cohen's parents, whose reactions to the idea of their twenty-year-old son being "adopted" are not recorded. Nothing in *A Dreamer's Journey* implies that the family would have found this inappropriate, and Cohen's own daughter still spoke casually, sixty years later, about the fact that Davidson had "died before he could do anything about" his adoption plan.[67]

Davidson was well equipped to activate and influence Cohen. Intimate and firm in his approach, he spoke with robust authority on every sub-

ject in philosophy, manners, and morals. He mixed his affections with
confident advice, providing his disciple with exactly the sort of guidance
the latter had longed for: discipline and control, but with tenderness; a
love relationship, but with clear injunctions following from it. Davidson
did not hesitate to define the great problems of the new century, nor to
prescribe the approach to these problems appropriate to young people;
he knew what subjects were to be studied, what books were to be read,
what values needed to be affirmed. Cohen stood in awe of his benefactor's "unshaken equipoise."[68]

Under Davidson's impact, then, Cohen was able at last to forsake the
passive idiom, and say of himself that he "went in, with all [his] might
and main." He used this phrase in relation to Davidson not only in 1909,
the year of his actual debut as a participant in professional philosophical
discourse, but again late in life when, sadly, he felt that he had lost
"that free mind, ready to give itself up to any new thought with all its
might and main" that had characterized him when he "first met Thomas
Davidson." In the intervening years there had always been "preoccupying thoughts, even if only in the background of consciousness, and not
the large free force of thought available in the days of my youth."[69]
Hence the passionate entry had been into Davidson's work; the farther
he got into his own work, and the more his own career became separ-
ated from the emotional conditions of its origin in intimacy with
Davidson, the more did Cohen retreat into self-absorption, into the
"brooding" and the not-understood "preoccupying thoughts" that
impeded resolution and creativity.

Cohen's emotional involvement with Davidson, then, seems to have
been intense enough to release an otherwise unused store of psycho-
sexual energy and make possible its sublimation into a career as a philosopher and a teacher. That career was to be the context in which the
tension between inertia and stampede would resolve itself. It was as a
philosopher and a teacher that Cohen would alternately lash out and
cling tenaciously; it was here that his emotional capacities and incapacities would find public expression.Whatever measure of satisfaction

Cohen derived from his marriage, and from his personal life generally, there remained always a compelling residue of anxiety about dry "wells," "magnetic" forces, and "the fitful floods of human passions and impulses." These anxieties took possession of his career in a number of ways, and helped to determine the patterns in which he expended the intellectual energy Davidson had enabled him to draw upon and to focus in the general direction of philosophy and teaching.

NOTES

1. *DJ*, 130; Henry Adams, *The Education of Henry Adams* (New York, 1918), 238. On the attitudes of German Jews toward the post-1880 arrivals from eastern Europe, see Moses Rischin, *The Promised City: New York's Jews, 1870-1914* (Cambridge, Mass., 1962), 95-111, and Peter I. Rose, Introduction to *The Ghetto and Beyond: Essays on Jewish Life in America*, ed. Peter I. Rose (New York, 1969), 6-7.

2. Felix Adler, speech of May 15, 1876, quoted in Henry Newmann, *Spokesmen for Ethical Religion* (Boston, 1951), 6. Ethical Culture awaits a scholarly study. A recent historical sketch by an apologist for the movement is Howard Radest, *Toward Common Ground: The Story of the Ethical Societies in the United States* (New York, 1969).

3. *DJ*, 129-130; *Portrait*, 71; Max Grossman, "Morris Cohen, Felix Adler, and the Ethical Movement," *Ethical Outlook* XLIX (1963), 121-125; MRC, "The East Side," *Alliance Review* II (1902), 455.

4. MRC, "Some Ideals and Characteristics of Thomas Davidson," *Alliance Review* I (1901), 261.

5. The members of the American Philosophical Association were listed annually in *PR*, e.g., XIX (1910), 183-187. On Adler's position at Columbia see John Herman Randall, Jr., "The Department of Philosophy," in Columbia University, *A History of the Faculty of Philosophy* (New York, 1957), 120-121.

6. Rischin, *Promised City*, 71-73; Oscar Handlin, *Adventure in Freedom: Three Hundred Years of Jewish Life in America* (New York, 1954), 98.

7. Mark Zborowski, "The Place of Book-Learning in Traditional Jewish Culture," in Margaret Mead and Maria Wolfenstein, eds., *Childhood in Contemporary Cultures* (Chicago, 1955), 118-141; Marshall Sklare, *America's Jews* (New York, 1971), 58.

8. Joseph Freeman, *An American Testament* (New York, 1936), 28.

9. Sklare, *America's Jews,* 19-20, 158.

10. *DJ,* 30-36, 44, 46.

11. *DJ,* 69, 72.

12. Nathan Glazer, *American Judaism* (New York, 1957), 70.

13. *DJ,* 69-70, 72.

14. Mordecai Kaplan, letter to author, July 9, 1974.

15. *DJ,* 70-72, 79-80, 82-83.

16. *DJ,* 84-85.

17. *DJ,* 21.

18. For the role of this incident in the folklore of the Lower East Side see, for example, Morris Freedman, "The Jewish College Student: New Model," in Elliot E. Cohen, ed., *Commentary on the American Scene* (New York, 1953), 281.

19. Nathan Glazer, "Social Characteristics of American Jews," in Louis Finkelstein, ed., *The Jews: Their History, Culture and Religion* (3rd ed., New York, 1960), 1694-1735, esp. 1718.

20. *DJ,* 85; Diary, January 14 and 20, and February 19, 1897, in *Portrait,* 8-10; Diary, January 4, 5, 6, and 7, 1897, Cohen MSS.

21. *DJ,* 85-86, 91; Francis Turner Palgrave, *The Golden Treasury of Best Songs and Lyrical Poems in the English Language* (New York, 1880), preface. The influence of Palgrave's *Treasury* is also noted in other memoirs, e.g., Freeman, *American Testament,* 46. Palgrave, incidentally, had been born with the surname of Cohen. For a succinct discussion of the role "great literature" played in American society around the turn of the century see Henry F. May, *The End of American Innocence* (New York, 1959), esp. 30-31.

22. *DJ,* 86.

23. Rischin, *Promised City,* 209.

24. *DJ,* 86-87; Rischin, *Promised City,* 199-200.

25. *DJ,* 48-49; Meyer Waxman, *A History of Jewish Literature from the Close of the Bible to Our Own Time* (New York, 1936-1941), III, 308-309; VI, 486; Yudel Mark, "Yiddish Literature," in Finkelstein, *Jews,* 1208-1210; Simon Halkin, "Socio-Historical Implications of Modern Hebrew Literature," *Historia Judaica* X (1948), 3, 6-7; Irving Howe, "Introduction to Yiddish Literature," in Irving Malin and Irwin

Stark, eds., *Breakthrough* (Philadelphia, 1963), 278-300; Jacob Katz, *Tradition and Crisis: Jewish Society at the End of the Middle Ages* (New York, 1961), 260-275. Cf. S.M. Dubnow, *History of the Jews in Russia and Poland from the Earliest Times until the Present Day*, trans. I. Friedlaender (Philadelphia, 1916-1920), II, 125-138, 206-242, 324-335.

26. *DJ*, 46.

27. Jacob Epstein, *Let There Be Sculpture* (New York, 1940), 4, 8; Freeman, *American Testament*, 24; *DJ*, 72-74, 97.

28. Hutchins Hapgood, *The Spirit of the Ghetto* (New York, 1909).

29. Henry James, *The American Scene* (New York, 1906), 131-133.

30. *DJ*, 90. Cf. Willis Rudy, *The College of the City of New York: A History* (New York, 1949), 128-129, 159-161, 193-195.

31. H.G. Wells, *The Future of America* (New York, 1906), 148.

32. David Blaustein, "From Oppression to Freedom," in Miriam Blaustein, ed., *Memoirs of David Blaustein: Educator and Communal Worker* (New York, 1913), 34-44; Rischin, *Promised City*, 101-102; Paul Abelson, "The Education of the Immigrant," *Journal of Social Science* XLVI (1906), 163-172.

33. MRC, "The East Side," 452.

34. *DJ*, 96-97.

35. Thomas Davidson, "The Higher Education of Breadwinners," in William Knight, ed., *Memorials of Thomas Davidson* (Boston, 1907), 90-91.

36. May, *Innocence*, 30; the phrase "practical idealism" is discussed in *Innocence*, 9-19.

37. Davidson, "Higher Education," 92-93; Thomas Davidson, *The Education of Wage-Earners* (Boston, 1904), 69-70. For Davidson's insistence that his East Side charges master Dante in Italian see Louis I. Dublin, "Thomas Davidson: Educator for Democracy," *American Scholar* XVII (1948), 205.

38. Herbert W. Schneider, *A History of American Philosophy* (2nd ed., New York, 1963), 391-395; Joseph Blau, "Rosmini, Domodossola, and Thomas Davidson," *Journal of the History of Ideas* XVIII (1957), 522-528.

39. Ralph Barton Perry, *The Thought and Character of William James* (Boston, 1935), I, 731-761.

40. William James, "A Knight-Errant of the Intellectual Life," *McClure's Magazine* XXV (1905), 3-11.

41. *DJ*, 104-105. Another account, complementary to Cohen's recollections, of how Davidson took the Educational Alliance by storm can be found in A.J. Kovar, *Thomas Davidson: Pioneer in Adult Education* (New York, 1950).

42. Prospectus for the "Glenmore School," presumably written by Davidson, in Knight, *Memorials*, 60; *DJ*, 106.

43. *DJ*, 108.

44. *DJ*, 114; *Portrait*, 50, 52.

45. MRC, "Characteristics of Davidson," 259-261, 291, 293. The lines are from "Love Thou Thy Land."

46. *DJ*, 119-121; MRC, "Characteristics of Davidson," 259-261, 291-293.

47. Samuel Ornitz, *Haunch, Paunch, and Jow* (New York, 1923).

48. Michael Gold, *Jews Without Money* (New York, 1930); Abraham Cahan, *The Rise of David Levinsky* (New York, 1917).

49. Samuel S. Cohen, "Recreational Enterprise on the Bowery: Two Jewish Intellectuals Keep a Poolroom," *Commentary* XIV (1952), 484. Cf. the references to prostitution in Epstein, *Sculpture*, 6; Gold, *Jews*, 6-9; Cahan, *Levinsky*, 125. For Ornitz's treatment of sex on the East Side see *Haunch*, 53-54, 67, 69, 128-129, 134, 142-143.

50. Cohen, "Recreational Enterprise," 481; *DJ*, 91.

51. Diary, January 1, 3, and 20, April 1, August 2 and 19, and October 26, 1897, in *Portrait*, 5, 7-8, 11, 15-17.

52. E.g., the first entry in the 1897 diary, in which Cohen refers to "love of books," not only for what they contain, but "for themselves," as his own "principal characteristic." His "next principal characteristic" was his "great desire to be good" and his "impotency to comply with this desire." See *Portrait*, 5-7. The excerpts from these diaries printed in *Portrait*, 5-24, are fully representative of the five notebooks dating from 1897, 1898, and 1899, now in the Cohen MSS.

53. *Portrait*, 26.

54. Diary, August 28, 1897, in *Portrait*, 22.

55. Mary Ryshpan, quoted in *Portrait*, 26.

56. Joseph Gollomb, *Unquiet* (New York, 1935), 164, 193, 285, 288, 366, 400-401, 404, 410, 436. The existence of this novel was brought to my attention by a footnote in Lewis Feuer, "The Political Linguistics of 'Intellectual,' 1898-1918," *Survey* LXXVIII (1971), 161. Gollomb was born in St. Petersburg in 1881, emigrated at the age of ten, and graduated from City College in 1902. For Cohen's speech of 1909 see the draft quoted in *Portrait*, 62.

57. Diary, undated entry of 1898, in *Portrait*, 23-24.

58. MRC to Mary Ryshpan, undated letter of 1903, in *Portrait*, 29.

59. MRC to Mary Ryshpan, October 1904, and Mary Ryshpan to MRC, October 24, 1904, in *Portrait*, 30. Leonora Rosenfield concludes that the adolescent diaries were in the drawer (*Portrait*, 3 and 30).

60. MRC to Mary Ryshpan, April 6, 1905, and May 1905, in *Portrait*, 38, 40.

61. See Cohen's letters to Mary throughout October and November 1905, in *Portrait*, 42-43. The "bedside" suggestion is in MRC to Mary Ryshpan, February 27, 1906, in *Portrait*, 43.

62. MRC to Harry Schlochower, June 28, 1929, in *Portrait*, 46.

63. Note of 1909, in *Portrait*, 54.

64. *DJ*, 104.

65. *DJ*, 104-105. Cf. Diary, November 1, 1900, in *Portrait*, 52: "I never loved anything before I met my beloved teacher. He opened my heart...."

66. MRC to Thomas Davidson, June 9 and 17, 1900, in *Portrait*, 63; *DJ*, 105.

67. *DJ*, 112-113; *Portrait*, 52.

68. MRC, "Characteristics of Davidson," 292.

69. Undated note in *DJ*, 270.

That 'all things flow' is the first vague generalization which the unsystematized, barely analysed, intuition of men has produced. It is the theme of some of the best Hebrew poetry in the Psalms; it appears as one of the first generalizations of Greek philosophy in the form of the saying of Heraclitus; amid the later barbarism of Anglo-Saxon thought it reappears in the story of the sparrow flitting through the banqueting hall of the Northumbrian king; and in all stages of civilization its recollection lends its pathos to poetry. Without doubt, if we are to go back to that ultimate, integral experience, unwarped by the sophistications of theory, that experience whose elucidation is the final aim of philosophy, the flux of things is one ultimate generalization around which we must weave our philosophical system.

Alfred North Whitehead

The American Philosophical Association, meeting at New Haven in
1909, heard twenty-nine-year-old Morris Cohen scold "our younger
philosophers" for abandoning some of philosophy's traditional obligations, including "the old ideal of culture."[1] Cohen began his public
career at a time when generational conflict within the guild was especially acute, and he found himself closer to the oldsters than to most
of his own contemporaries. Already secure in the Western and Anglo-
American traditions that Cohen was striving to make his own, many
young, native-born Protestants were searching in philosophy for adventures that were of little interest to him. Cohen introduced himself to
his peers by criticizing the nature of their revolt against their elders.

He cast his remarks of 1909 in the form of caveats against the transition from a "metaphysical" to a "scientific" approach to philosophy.
By carving out a rigidly specialized area within the larger sphere of
knowledge, philosophers, he warned, were on the verge of abandoning
the claims to comprehensiveness that gave philosophy its enduring appeal. By making philosophy "into a modest special science, dealing
with definite problems and giving definite answers," Cohen observed,
some thinkers hoped to make philosophical discussion "scientific."
Cohen thoroughly endorsed this scientific ideal insofar as it implied
"logical rigor," strictness of method, and the elimination of prejudicial
and arbitrary opinions, but he warned that eagerness to attain the
measure of certainty requisite to science might lead philosophers to
avoid the difficult yet important task of synthesis.[2]

"Let philosophy resolutely aim to be as scientific as possible,"
Cohen urged his listeners, but he reminded them what they were to be
scientific *about*: philosophy was about "life," he declared unabashedly.
The method of the discipline could never be smaller than the object,
and the mission of philosophy was to provide "a working view of the
universe and of man's place in it." This goal restricted the independence
of philosophy, for it could not turn its back on "other" sciences and
and try, like them, to indulge in its own private parochialism. The
philosopher's role, said Cohen, was performed by Matthew Arnold and

other critically oriented men of arts and letters, as well as by trained philosophers. Philosophy was above all else an enterprise of "system-building"—Cohen almost apologized for using the unpopular phrase—whereby "the present anarchic tendency" toward overspecialization might be "controlled in the interest of sanity."[3] Science itself, no less than sanity, was threatened by the new "scientific" philosophers who, Cohen complained, ignorantly equated science with "immediate empiricism," the crude belief that the scientist achieves knowledge by merely observing the objective particulars within the range of his perception. These philosophers were even more parochial in their assumption that the scientific ethos is one of flux instead of fixity: Cohen laughed at the fashion according to which one praised some things as *experimental, functional,* or *dynamic,*" and consigned others to "the lowermost depths from which no power can rescue" them by characterizing them as *"static."*[4]

Cohen had defined the "antiformalism" now proverbial to historians of the period[5] and had identified many of the drives that made his contemporaries so different from both himself and the older generation. The generational conflict became evident in the ensuing discussion, when Ralph Barton Perry of Harvard, a recognized leader of the insurgents, rose to assure Cohen that system-building was permissible so long as one thing was kept straight: this activity had nothing to do with scientific method. Perry's offer of a loaded peaceful coexistence—let the metaphysicians be, so long as they know their place—was then rejected by the venerable George Trumbull Ladd of Yale, whom Cohen had just singled out as an exemplary practitioner of system-building. Ladd declared bluntly that there was "no breach between science and philosophy."[6]

Ladd's confidence that classical philosophy's relation to science was not problematic, that one could be "scientific" and continue to do the same old sort of philosophy, was a manifestation of the fuzzy, genial tolerance that made the older crowd seem so tedious to the zealots who had recently founded the *Journal of Philosophy, Psychology and Scien-*

tific Method to counter the traditionalism of the *Philosophical Review*, until then the association's uncontested oracle.[7] Cohen had correctly named John Dewey and J.F.E. Woodbridge as leaders of the new wave, and he had quoted their work to prove that they had indeed made dynamism and concreteness as central to their outlook as wholeness and harmony had been to that of their elders.

Cohen might have felt more at home with his own age group had he come to intellectual maturity thirty or forty years earlier, and had he grown up with the likes of Ladd. Philosophy in the late nineteenth century often aimed to provide a sense of integration and stability, which Americans very much needed during the unsettling process of secularization, and to ease the psychic distress attendant upon the Civil War and the Darwinian controversy. Nowhere, in fact, was the obligation to satisfy the need for order and consolidation taken more seriously than among academic philosophers. They felt privileged to ignore industrialization, urbanization, political conflict, and the other social sources of these needs, while they worked conscientiously on the more abstract issues that they, in particular, had been given to resolve: What, if any, were the unifying principles in reality as a whole? What was the relation between our (presumably) permanent moral values and the physical order as revealed now by the ethically neutral methods of natural science? After Darwin, how could one be sure that human life was not a process of random flux, devoid of rational structure?[8]

What these philosophers had to offer was called "idealism," essentially the doctrine that behind the temporal changes we observe in phenomena, there exists a universal mind, or spirit, rational and moral in its constitution, within which contingency and evolution have their being. Taking as their technical equipment the metaphysics of Kant or Hegel, the American idealists used the suprasensuous "ultimate reality" of classical idealism as a sponge; whatever seemed threatening in their intellectual environment could be absorbed within it. This "all-embracing benevolence," as the method of the idealists has been termed,[9] enabled those who employed it to accept with good cheer not only Darwin, but anything science might come up with, for both the process of biological evolution and the enterprise of science were manifestations of that rational and moral entity called Reality. That this vision was not incompatible with intelligent thinking is proven by the example of Josiah Royce, whose work continues to instruct philosophically long after the writings of Ladd, George Holmes Howison, Borden Parker Bowne, and Jacob Gould Schurmann have been shelved alongside early editions of Baedeker, guides only to the tastes of a distant and charming era.

The idealists and their counterparts in other professions performed their tasks so well that fragmentation was routed, at least psychologically. Their heirs feared no loss of moral values, or of intelligibility, in a contingent and plural universe. Cohen's account of the preoccupations of his colleagues was therefore not inaccurate, generated though it was by sensitivities peculiar to him. Many of the young believed themselves strong enough, and the water safe enough, to break away from the moorings Royce and Howison had built. Among such reckless companions, Cohen was ill at ease.

Cohen had been introduced to the philosophical profession by Felix Adler. Although Adler had first met Cohen at Glenmore before the turn of the century, his influence as an intellectual and vocational model did not become important until about 1903, when Cohen, who had by then distinguished himself as principal of the Thomas Davidson School at the Educational Alliance, turned up in Adler's classes at Columbia. Cohen was then making his living as a mathematics instructor in the high-school division of City College, but he was enrolled simultaneously as a graduate student in philosophy at the university. After Adler had tried unsuccessfully to obtain a fellowship for Cohen, he took him on as an aide at the Ethical Culture Society, where the youth prepared a series of papers for Adler's seminars on the comparative study of religious ceremonies.[10]

Adler created an environment in which the most grandiose of idealism's spiritual and synthetic aspirations were paramount. Adler was
himself an institution, with branches at the Ethical Culture Society and
at Columbia University; his formal philosophical work was intimately
connected with his practical religious activities. When Cohen entered
his orbit, Adler was well advanced toward the completion of the metaphysical system outlined in 1918 in *An Ethical Philosophy of Life*,
which sought to provide the technical foundations for Ethical Culture.[11]

Cohen pursued a distinctly Adlerian path at Harvard. While studying
Kant under the direction of Josiah Royce, he organized and lectured
before classes of Boston's "breadwinners," led the activities of the
Cambridge Ethical Culture Society, and served Adler as "a sort of ambassador" to the capital of American academic gentility. Although
Cohen read a great deal of philosophy during his two years at Harvard,
he was so frequently ill, so preoccupied with thoughts about his impending marriage, and so depressed and lonely generally, that his Harvard experience was much less pivotal in his intellectual development
than one might expect.[12] Royce certainly reinforced Cohen's prior
loyalty to Culture, and proved to Cohen that this loyalty could express
itself through acts of mind more rigorous and technical than those of
which Felix Adler or Thomas Davidson were capable. William James,
too, solidified the sense of philosophy's mission that Cohen was eventually to articulate in 1909, for James, while in many ways the prophet
of the new trends that Cohen feared and disliked, was then in his most
"popular" phase, eager for his teachings to satisfy the spiritual cravings
of the age.[13] Yet neither these nor any of Cohen's other Harvard
teachers (Hugo Munsterberg, George H. Palmer, and Crawford H. Toy,
among others) altered the sense of vocation he had developed under
previous influences.

Cohen brought to Harvard not only the legacy of his relationship with
Adler, but the prior and more compelling sense of the philosopher's
calling he had derived from Davidson. Cohen had quickly sensed that
Davidson's dialectical capabilities were limited,[14] but what mattered

was the nature of Davidson's mission as a philosopher and a teacher. Never intimidated by technical obstacles, Davidson held forth the promise of heroic and comprehensive intellectual achievements; he imbued Cohen with his enthusiasm for a projected "Encyclopedia of Philosophy that should do for the twentieth century what the Brothers of Sincerity did for the tenth, and Diderot and d'Alembert did for the eighteenth." Even at the end of his career, Cohen insisted that everything he read "somehow or other gets fitted into that scheme."[15] Moreover, Davidson passed on to Cohen the sense that teaching philosophy was a means to affect the entire complexion of a student's life; no one embodied more than Davidson the late-nineteenth-century image of philosophy as the all-encompassing moral and intellectual discipline.

The "conservative" professional stance Cohen took in 1909 was prepared also by his experiences with the Socialist Labor party, which had begun even prior to his contacts with Davidson. Hoping to produce "more active and intelligent propaganda" for the party prior to the election of 1896, Cohen and a group of friends "read Marx's *Das Kapital* and other socialist classics." Simultaneously, Cohen was reading John Stuart Mill in his classes at City College. His attempt to resolve the contradictions between the two led him to Hegel, and other philosophers, and inspired his interest in doing philosophy.[16] His diary of this period was pointedly entitled "Notes of a Boy Philosopher."[17] To be sure, Cohen did not develop a remotely realistic sense of what it meant to be a philosopher until he met Davidson, nor did he, until then, begin to have the reinforcing experiences that enabled this early ambition to grow. And Cohen's own "Marxism," although he later enjoyed referring to it as the starting point for his career, is revealed by his diaries to have been a romantic venture and an expression of abstract allegiance to the political forces seeking to mitigate "the misery of the East Side." It was a commitment with a minimum of intellectual significance, like the militantly Republican or Democratic postures struck by adolescents in other social groups. Cohen fantasized about becoming a socialist "orator," but at the same time he quoted Samuel

Smiles; he once pondered the question of whether or not Smiles was a socialist.[18] Still, Cohen's first excitement for "philosophy" was stimulated by that calling's most extended social and cultural relations.

Cohen's New Haven address was an emblem for, as well as an introduction to, more than a dozen papers he would produce during the following few years, addressed to a great range of problems in metaphysics, ethics, jurisprudence, and philosophy of science. Many aspects of these papers are to be understood only in the context of what was going on in these fields, but taken as an aggregate, they reveal a basic orientation that transcended the various specific contexts in which they were written. For Cohen, the problem of the age was to hold onto what was valuable about the inherited philosophical traditions of the West while moving toward new insights; his philosophy took form as a defense of certain wise, tried-and-true axioms that a hasty but well-meaning generation was threatening to ignore, or to destroy; a dialectic of "threat" and "defense" quickly established its control over Cohen's philosophical writing.

"The laws of logic and mathematics do hold of nature,"[19] Cohen adamantly insisted in opposition to any implication that the intelligibility of the world was imposed on it by the order-craving minds of men. That men would lose their all-too-precarious grasp on what he, for one, believed to be the innate logical structure of the world was Cohen's most compelling and persistent fear. Indeed, he brought to philosophy an acute sensitivity to the loss of coherence, a sensitivity that was to inform most of his subsequent work, especially in metaphysics.

So, too, did he bring a sense that the moral order of the universe was authentically "there," though it might be obscured by the valid but unsteadying insight that there was no God holding it together. No one was to be more adamant than Cohen in making the distinction between "is" and "ought," and few were as convinced as he that his own generation was pathologically determined to ignore it.[20] In the same vein, Cohen looked to disinterested "reason" for the discovery of truth and of ethical obligations; he perceived threats to classical rationalism as attacks on the very possibility for rationality and sanity, and, by implication, as attacks on logical truth and moral values.[21] Finally, Cohen was concerned to defend the superiority of comprehensive, cosmopolitan perspectives over parochial, fragmentary outlooks on experience. He was peculiarly sensitive to the pitfalls of looking at a thing in its most immediate, detailed, and local aspects. He saw immediacy as a threat to valid experience, not an avenue toward it; he aimed, through suspended judgment, to keep things at a distance until they could be completely understood and controlled.[22] He had, after all, resisted marriage on the grounds that it might take him from "the larger needs of the world."

It is not surprising that someone with Cohen's personal and social experience should bring to philosophy a disposition best defined as a set of cautions, nor is it surprising that his cautions should be organized as a defense of such classical sources of stability as disinterested reason, suspended judgment, logical order, and the autonomy of the "ought" from the world of actual existence. Other persons, too, agreed with these basic values—indeed, many of Cohen's contemporaries saw them as boring truisms, not at all threatened by the currents of the age—but the leitmotiv of Cohen's career was the fear that these cosmic anchors were about to be washed away by a turbulence quietly building up within the intellectual and emotional preferences of the twentieth century.

If there was a certain consistency among the values Cohen hoped to defend, so, too, did the multiple threats to those values manifest an implicit kinship. Man's access to the logical order of things was impaired by a passionate impulse to plunge into the flux of concrete, temporal, historical experience by means of various "nominalist," "vitalist," and "mystical" world views; his grip on the moral order was loosened by an ostensibly "scientific" desire to look upon human and ethical experience in the indicative, without the prior constraints of moral prescriptions; his ability to reason was diminished by an interest

in "intuition" and "self-expression" that served only to single out for
emphasis and adulation those elements in experience least susceptible
to rational comprehension and control; and his cosmopolitanism was
destroyed by the desire to enjoy the particular atoms of contingent experience that happened to be immediately within reach. In all, it was
the world of "history" that threatened to pull the world of "logic"
down, to bend it and entangle it in physical matter, or, perhaps, to dissolve it smoothly into a whirlpool of particulars.[23]

"The intellectual world was . . . divided for me into two camps,"
Cohen said of his college days; there was the "panlogism" he found in
Hegel, and to some extent in Marx, against the antithetical "atomism"
of Mill.[24] Later, at Harvard, Cohen found himself caught between
Royce and James, who, while they in effect cooperated to push Cohen
further toward his New Haven affirmation of philosophy's spiritual
mission, worked against each other in almost every other respect. Only
George Santayana, of Harvard's philosophers, was sufficiently independent and formidable to have broken the polarity between these two
notorious adversaries, but Santayana was on leave throughout Cohen's
two years at Harvard. Hence Royce, as the great prophet of logic, was
monolithically opposed to James, who Cohen felt had "never gotten
beyond Mill."[25] Cohen argued frequently with James, who, somewhat
ironically, was much more attentive to him personally than was Royce,
whose philosophical ideas were the more palatable. James was destined
to become Cohen's lifelong exemplar of passionate, wrongheaded irrationalism. The one figure over fifty years of age that Cohen criticized
in his New Haven address, James appeared more than twenty years later
in the first chapter of *Reason and Nature* as the representative of the
ideas Cohen most wanted to destroy. Characteristically, Cohen had been
marked most deeply by the graduate teacher who most repelled him;
James's earthy, pluralistic attack on idealism gave courage to the empiricist and pragmatist revolts that Cohen associated with the age's undue
emphasis on the realm of "history." Sitting in James's lecture halls at
Harvard, Cohen tried in his own mind to "annihilate" James "logically."[26]

In this context, it is surprising that Cohen did not follow up his New Haven address by affiliating with idealism. Generationally dated as the idealist tradition was in so many ways, some young men did adopt it, including G. P. Adams (b. 1882), G. Watts Cunningham (b. 1881), and W. E. Hocking (b. 1873). And "affiliation" was exactly what was asked of Cohen, implicitly, by the social environment of the profession. This was preeminently the age of alignment, an era of cooperative manifestos, organized movements, and almost compulsive classification according to groups and schools. Never before or since has participation in a movement been more imperative for American philosophers.[27]

Yet Cohen quickly developed a reputation for being above the factions, or somehow between them. His New Haven critique of the insurgents was followed by more detailed complaints, but he tried to make peace by insisting that the most valuable points made by the new "scientific philosophers" were simply a working out of *Royce's* ideas.[28] One of Cohen's attempts at brokerage was resisted by a "realist" who warned his own colleagues against "reformed Kantians . . . bearing gifts."[29] In time, he came to describe himself as "a stray dog among the philosophers."[30] One wonders how much this obliquely arrogant, yet self-effacing characterization was a response to the anti-Semitism with which Cohen had to contend. Did he want to join one of the philosophical fraternities, only to get a cool welcome? Was the self-imposed, often postured independence of his entire career the result partially of subtle, unrecorded rebuffs received as a young man? In any event, Cohen was unable to obtain a teaching job in philosophy until five years after completion of his degree, when, in 1911, thanks to the initiative of Harry Overstreet, he was allowed to move from the mathematics to the philosophy department at City College.[31] And the next Russian Jew to begin a career in philosophy—Jacob Loewenberg—tried persistently to conceal his ethnic and national origin, and was successful in doing so at Wellesley during the early years of World War I.[32]

The idealists had no monopoly on anti-Semitism, but they had several traits that undoubtedly prevented Cohen from fashioning a more complete solidarity with them. While officially cosmopolitan, American idealism was materially parochial: it was well understood by both its proponents and its critics to be a means of affirming the goodness and wholeness, not only of being in general, but of American society and the Christian religion in particular.

Logically, it has always been possible for an atheist or revolutionary to accept Berkeley's analysis of knowledge or Kant's transcendental method, but in social fact the American idealists were religionists and patriots. Santayana's now-clichéd description of them as the embodiment, in philosophy, of "the genteel tradition" was largely sound as a cultural analysis, however limited it may have been as a philosophical critique.[33] Among their greatest achievements was the proof that evil did not exist; even Royce was not free from the felt need to prove that what appeared as evil was, in the final analysis, a species of good.[34]

Cohen was more offended by idealism's lingering Christian theism than were many of his otherwise more "insurgent" contemporaries; he held even Davidson at fault for not renouncing supernaturalism in all its guises.[35] Cohen's doctoral thesis was largely controlled by an interest in reformulating Kant's ethics without making use of the God concept.[36] Having rejected Judaism for modernity, Cohen was impatient with "moderns" who smuggled their own ancestral theology into their philosophy; he saw supernaturalism of any sort as an embarrassing weakness on the part of its victim.[37]

The good cheer idealists managed to mix with their sobriety was also a stumbling block for Cohen: great as was his faith in deductive logic, he was socially and psychologically protected against its use to prove that God was in his heaven and all was right with the world. The "job" done on evil and contingency by the idealists had an absoluteness, a final completeness, that both attracted and repelled Cohen. Eager as he was to replace precariousness and sin with something good, safe, and permanent, he retained a sense that life's treachery was too endemic to be so fully eradicated. He preferred the Faustian struggle against fate, the stoic defiance of inevitable pain and death popularized in this period by Bertrand Russell in "A Free Man's Worship."[38] Cohen would always retain some of the sensibility of Hugo and Dumas, and of the other Romantic authors whose work had moved him in his childhood and early youth. And back beyond even this influence, there were the Yiddish novels that taught, in Irving Howe's phrase, "the virtue of powerlessness, the power of helplessness," and the "sanctity of the insulted and the injured."[39] To Cohen, the metaphor of the "frail" boat "likely to be wrecked by the storm" would have a permanent significance.[40]

Idealism, despite his affinities for it, appeared to Cohen as an extreme outlook, which must of necessity be balanced against an opposing extreme. Insofar as he identified idealism with "logic," he found it too aloof from the realities of "history." Lacking a firm sense of where to stand between Royce and James, between panlogism and atomism, between permanence and flux, yet knowing that the second, more dangerous half of these dichotomies was an authentic part of existence with claims that were not to be denied, Cohen made it his habit to define philosophical issues in terms of the reconciliation of such extremes. While "history" and "logic" were the most basic concepts in tension, so, too, did the mental balance the physical, and the altruistic, the egoistic.[41] Cohen posed always as a centrist, as one who knew that the North Pole—his favorite example—was useless without the South Pole.[42] He was certainly not the first philosopher to believe his own views were more "balanced" than those of his contemporaries, but few thinkers have gone to remotely comparable lengths to define each field of discourse in terms of two monolithic, abstract extremes, each of which could be dismissed through the reductio ad absurdum. In this way, the dialectic of "threat" and "defense" in Cohen's papers was made to operate in a special way: threats took the form of disequilibrium in the relations between polar extremes, and defenses consisted in reestablishing balance, not simply in a general way, but specifically between polarities.

Hence Cohen cast his defenses of an innate logical order and of natural law in the form of attacks on extremists who would go so far as to banish permanence and value from the universe. He was quick to divorce himself from the die-hard mechanists who denied contingency in physics, and from the rigid formalism of the natural-law theorists of the nineteenth century, but he railed against the more "modern" philosophers of physics and law for throwing out the baby with the bath, for foolishly substituting chaos and nihilism for an overly brittle morality and rationality. "Against the blind worship of the dogma of universal and absolute change, it ought to be sufficient to point out that change and constancy are strictly co-relative terms," he would fume. "The belief that the world consists of all change and no constancy is no better than the belief that all vessels have insides but no outsides."[43]

Cohen's career began with tensions, not with the unilinear revolt against Royce that Morton White and others have correctly identified as the primal growing-up experience for most of Cohen's philosophical contemporaries.[44] Threatened by the new and skeptical of the old, Cohen was caught between generations and between countless polarities. His personal predisposition to see a given environment in terms of opposing, inadequate extremes was reinforced by his confrontation with Royce and James, and then with a profession in which his difficulties in finding a home were not entirely of his own making. He looked earnestly for ways to mediate between idealism and realism, panlogism and atomism, permanence and change, ought and is, logic and history, grandfather and mother; he felt himself almost alone in the face of a range of anarchic enthusiasms and sterile absolutisms. Both sets of enemies functioned, in different ways, to impair man's capacity to discriminate and integrate; Cohen's problem was to combat these enemies without imposing on life an order too brittle, or too amorphous. He was like one caught between Arnold's fears and Mill's principles: unable because of Mill's liberalism to endorse Arnold's program, yet unable because of Arnold's insights to relax under Mill's open-mindedness.

Cohen could at least remain free of entangling alliances: he set out to be the kind of philosopher he felt was most needed, one who would speak out "in the interests of sanity" and balance, and who, armed only with life's most tried-and-true regulations, would "police the intellectual realm."[45] What remains to be asked here is how these two interlocking aspirations—to hold the line and to impose sanctions on those who did not—sought fulfillment through a commentary on the scientific ideal.

At the 1904 Congress of Arts and Sciences in St. Louis, everything from the selling of insurance to the doing of metaphysics was classified, along with physics and geology, as a "science."[46] This was the great age of American scientism, when it seemed that the advocates of every doctrine or plan of action felt obliged to justify themselves in the name of science. Moralists who hoped for a more sober, disciplined, and tightly unified society preached the "scientific" virtues of self-abnegation, restraint, and docile obedience to "facts."[47] Moralists who aimed for a more liberated, active, and pluralistic society urged a stance of "scientific" open-mindedness, iconoclasm, and experimentation.[48] If the scientific ideal was formulated and used very differently, depending upon the ideological and psychological orientation of a given speaker, there was no doubt that most contributors to critical discourse wanted the banner of science to fly over their work. The apparent success with which scientists of the nineteenth century had pursued their search for knowledge made it seem that the methods and ethos of science would of necessity produce impressive results when transferred to previously nonscientific endeavors. This hope was to suffer many disappointments in the twentieth century, but it was still robust when Cohen came upon the scene.

Although science appealed to Jewish immigrants undergoing secularization for many of the same reasons it appealed to Americans of other backgrounds, it had a special meaning for persons like Cohen. Science was unquestionably a central element in the Western tradition these newly emancipated immigrants were seeking to absorb, but it also had one significant distinction that made it especially attractive. Science aimed, by definition, to enter a dialogue with the most universal and timeless segments of experience. Science sought truth of a sort that would command assent from persons of any national, religious, or ethnic background; it was concerned with propositions that were in no way culture-bound. As such, science differed from literature, which, while often containing insights that seemed to apply to the entire human species, was nonetheless shot through with cultural particularity. A Jewish agnostic of the turn of the century could be enthusiastic, within limits, about Milton, but Milton was irreducibly English and Protestant; and even James Fenimore Cooper was clearly a product of a particular time and place. Science, by contrast, focused on what was least particular in the entire range of human experience; science thrust aside, in effect, those aspects of the Western tradition that served as barriers between nations, religions, provinces, and individuals. Science was potentially the basis for a fully secular ideology that would exclude no one from full participation in modern life.

This appeal was especially strong to those, like Cohen, who rejected both Judaism and Zionism. A sharp distinction can be made between Cohen's social type and that of his contemporary, Horace Kallen. Kallen, a Zionist, retained an unequivocally parochial tie to the Jewish tradition.[49] Religionists and Zionists, even when sensitive to the ways in which secular liberalism promoted tolerance and equality, were not as adamantly universalist as Cohen, whose rejection of Jewish particularism was—especially in his youth—absolute. To Kallen, the Jewish tradition remained a vast if sometimes vague presence that could stabilize and guide; to the Voltairean Cohen, the tradition simply did not function in this way. Certainly there were many Zionists and religionists interested in science—including Kallen—but they did not have as much invested in contemporary discourse about the nature of science. Cohen's dependence on science was greater than Kallen's, and greater than that of most native-born Americans, because Cohen acknowledged no other cultural arbiters. Whatever unacknowledged influence his

Jewish background exercised over him, Cohen's conscious deliberations required a fully secular, universalist touchstone. The scientific ideal was compellingly available to serve this need. Hence it was much more crucial for Cohen than for Kallen that science be properly defined, that it become the embodiment of the "right" social values, that it be structured in such a way as to enable it to organize culture on terms that one could personally accept.

It was in this context that Cohen became unusually sensitive to the assumptions about the nature of science that informed learned and popular discourse in the 1910s. This sensitivity was heightened by the fact that others were attempting to justify many disturbing threats to his basic intellectual and moral commitments by placing them under the banner of science. In his New Haven address, for example, Cohen cited as an instance of what he most disliked about the new ethos in philosophy an article in which John Dewey identified the philosophy of "immediate empiricism" with the method of science.[50] What Cohen most feared was the identification, through the influence of Dewey and James especially, of "science" with the realm of "history" at the expense of the realm of "logic." The very universalism of science—so vital to Cohen's interest in it—was de-emphasized by the unnerving tendency of the pragmatists to see science as an access to immediate, material, atomistic reality, rather than as an access to the universally valid laws of which any given experience is but a representative example.

Fortunately for Cohen, the traditional ideology of science contained ammunition for rationalists as well as for empiricists. He was able to draw upon a sizable arsenal of characterizations of science that served his own purposes very well. The version of the scientific ideal Cohen put together stressed science's mediating role: science would balance pure reason and pure experience. By bringing "reason" and "nature" together, science transcended both the debilitated rationalism that remains "too high" and "too long" above the tumults of life, and the doomed romanticism that immerses itself in indiscriminate immediacy.[51] Thunder peals, he quoted Tennyson, "Wherever Thought hath wedded Fact."[52]

Science was hence the supreme balancer for Cohen: it was the embodiment of his general conviction that polar extremes could be mediated, and it was the agency whereby the specific tensions most troubling to him could be kept in a state of equilibrium. Cohen's science would keep directly in touch with material, sensual reality, yet would escape the immediate and the parochial through the universal and the cosmopolitan. Science recognized the vitality of "tempestuous" waters, yet it would try to chart them in order that man might have some light between his "two eternities of darkness." Science was a device to keep experience under control without foregoing it; it was a builder of protective, but not repressive, structures. It was supremely a distinction-making enterprise, a mitigation of temporal flux, an approach to the world founded on the ancient truths that A is A, A cannot be non-A, and non-A cannot be A.[53] Finally, science was a mode of containing unwanted or feared impulses. Cohen wanted thought to "wed" fact but to abstain from all other adventures; science's "great service" to humanistic learning, for example, was its "discipline," its "rigorous self-control in the presence of intellectual temptation." Cohen instructed the "scientific Ulysses" to resist "voluptuous" temptations in order to proceed patiently, logically, methodically, and arduously toward truth.[54]

NOTES

1. MRC, "The Conception of Philosophy in Recent Discussion," *JP* VII (1910), 409 (*SPS*, 47).

2. MRC, "Conception of Philosophy," 402-403, 409 (*SPS*, 37-38, 47).

3. MRC, "Conception of Philosophy," 405, 408-409 (*SPS*, 41-42, 46-47).

4. MRC, "Conception of Philosophy," 402, 408 (*SPS*, 37, 46).

5. The phrase was popularized by Morton G. White's influential book *Social Thought in America: The Revolt Against Formalism* (New York, 1949).

6. Walter B. Pitkin, "The Ninth Annual Meeting of the American Philosophical Association," *JP* VII (1910), 40.

7. The sudden appearance at this time of intense factionalism on largely generational bases has been widely noted. The atmosphere is intelligently discussed by John Passmore, *A Hundred Years of Philosophy* (2nd ed., London, 1966), esp. 260-265. Cf. May Brodbeck, "American Philosophy, 1900-1950," in Brodbeck et al., *American Non-Fiction, 1900-1950* (Chicago, 1952), 57-67.

8. The American idealists await a modern, historical study informed by a perspective on the American social setting. The best synthetic account of English idealism as an episode in the history of philosophy remains J. H. Muirhead, *The Platonic Tradition in Anglo-Saxon Philosophy* (London, 1931). Cf. Herbert W. Schneider, *A History of American Philosophy* (2nd ed., New York, 1962), 375-430. An excellent brief treatment is in Arthur E. Murphey, "American Philosophy in the Twentieth Century," in William H. Hay et al., eds., *Reason and the Common Good* (Englewood Cliffs, N.J., 1963), 215-222. On idealism generally, see H. B. Acton, "Idealism," *Encyclopedia of Philosophy* (New York, 1967), IV, 110-118. On the cultural role of academic philosophers in mid- and late-nineteenth-century America see D. H. Meyer, *The Instructed Conscience* (Philadelphia, 1972). On the generalized need for stability and unity in the United States of this period see especially Robert Wiebe, *The Search for Order* (New York, 1967); R. Jackson Wilson, *The Quest for Community* (New York, 1968); John Higham, *From Boundlessness to Consolidation* (Ann Arbor, 1969); and George M. Fredrikson, *The Inner Civil War* (New York, 1965). Cf. the interesting study of British intellectuals, Shirley Letwin, *The Pursuit of Certainty* (Cambridge, Eng., 1965).

9. Murphey, "American Philosophy," 222.

10. *DJ*, 110, 114, 128-130.

11. Felix Adler, *An Ethical Philosophy of Life* (New York, 1918).

12. *DJ*, 131-134.

13. See, e.g., William James, *Pragmatism* (New York, 1909).

14. *DJ*, 108-109. Cf. undated letters of early 1900 exchanged by Cohen and Davidson, in *Portrait*, 58-59.

15. *DJ*, 109.

16. *DJ*, 166-167.

17. Diary, April 2, 1897, in *Portrait*, 11.

18. Diary, January 20, 1897, in *Portrait*, 8, and January 21, 1897, in Cohen MSS.

19. MRC, "The Present Situation in Philosophy of Mathematics," *JP* VIII (1911), 546. Cf. MRC, "Mechanism and Causality in Physics," *JP* XV (1918), 365-386, which was read before the American Philosophical Association in 1911.

20. MRC, "Jurisprudence as a Philosophical Discipline," *JP* X (1913), 225-226 (*RL*, 140); MRC, " 'Real' and 'Ideal' Forces in the Civil Law," *Ethics* XXVI (1916), 347-358 (*LSO*, 248-258); MRC, "Jus Naturale Redivivum," *PR* XXV (1916), 761-777; MRC, "History vs. Value," *JP* XI (1914), 710 (*RN*, 379).

21. MRC, review of John Dewey, *Essays in Experimental Logic*, in *NR* VIII (1916), 118-119 (*PL*, 208-214); MRC, "The New Philosopher's Stone," *NR* III (1915), 338-339 (*FL*, 403-407).

22. MRC, "Philosophy," in Paul Monroe, ed., *A Cyclopedia of Education* (New York, 1913), IV, 685-696; MRC, "Jurisprudence," 227-228 (*RL*, 143); cf. MRC, review of A. T. Ormond, *The Concepts of Philosophy*, in *Ethics* XIX (1909), 385-389.

23. See esp. MRC, "History vs. Value," *passim* (*RN*, 369-385).

24. *DJ*, 168.

25. *DJ*, 132.

26. *RN*, 3; *DJ*, 132; Diary, November 1, 1904, in *Portrait*, 74.

27. Passmore, *Hundred Years*, 260-265.

28. MRC, "The New Realism and the Philosophy of Royce," *PR* XXV (1916), 378 (*SPS*, 133).

29. William P. Montague, "Unreal Subsistence and Consciousness," *PR* XXIII (1914), 56.

30. *DJ*, 174.

31. *DJ*, 135-139. Jewishness continued to be viewed as a consideration relevant to the professional evaluation of candidates for teaching appointments throughout the 1920s and even into the 1930s. The atmosphere is revealed, for example, in private remarks made about Cohen in 1922 by Arthur O. Lovejoy, one of the most liberal academics of the period, and a figure who often championed Cohen within the profession. Lovejoy had been asked by the University of California to nominate candidates for the Mills Professorship at Berkeley. Yet even Lovejoy, who urged California to build a diverse department keyed by "a large measure of disagreement among its members," felt obliged to preface his advocacy of Cohen, in particular, with the observation that

he did not know whether "Cohen's Jewish origin and associations would be regarded as an element of ineligibility." Lovejoy went on to extol Cohen's abilities, and to observe that no one else known to Lovejoy had "read, digested, and remembered, the current literature of philosophy so nearly universally as Cohen." Lovejoy concluded that "on the side of the amenities," Cohen would, perhaps, be "a little less eligible" than other candidates. Lovejoy to Henry R. Hatfield, April 1, 1922, University of California Archives, The Bancroft Library, Berkeley.

32. See J. Loewenberg, *Thrice-Born: Selected Memories of an Immigrant* (New York, 1968), esp. 111.

33. Santayana's "The Genteel Tradition in American Philosophy" is in the collection *Winds of Doctrine* (New York, 1913), 186-215.

34. E.g., Josiah Royce, "The Problem of Job," in Perry Miller, ed., *American Thought: Civil War to World War I* (New York, 1954).

35. *Portrait*, 60.

36. MRC, "Kant's Doctrine as to the Relation between Duty and Happiness" (Ph.D. dissertation, Harvard University, 1906). For a detailed analysis of Cohen's dissertation see David A. Hollinger, "Morris R. Cohen and the Scientific Ideal" (Ph.D. dissertation, University of California, Berkeley, 1970), 57-74.

37. E.g., MRC to Mary Ryshpan (January 1905), in *Portrait*, 33. Cf. *Portrait*, 25.

38. "A Free Man's Worship," was widely read in America in two collections of Russell's work, *Philosophical Essays* (London, 1910) and *Mysticism and Logic* (New York, 1917), 44-54. For Cohen's attitude see MRC, "Philosopher's Stone," 338-339 (*FL*, 405-407); Oliver Wendell Holmes, Jr., to MRC, September 10, 1918, in *Portrait*, 318; and, for a later qualification, MRC, "Amor Dei Intellectualis," *Chronicon Spinozanum* III (1923), 18 (*FL*, 318-319). Cf. MRC, review of Robert Michels, *Political Parties*, in *NR* VIII (1916), 304 (*FL*, 160-161).

39. Irving Howe, "Introduction to Yiddish Literature," in Irving Malin and Irwin Stark, eds., *Breakthrough* (Philadelphia, 1963), 289.

40. MRC, review of Felix Adler, *An Ethical Philosophy of Life*, in *NR* XIX (1919), 254 (*FL*, 79); MRC, review of Paul Elmer More, *Platonism*, in *NR* XVI (1918), 143 (*FL*, 74); MRC, "The Distinction between the Mental and the Physical," *JP* XIV (1917), 261-267 (*SPS*, 90-98). Cf. MRC, "The Idealist Tradition and Josiah Royce," *NR* XX (1919), 148-150; MRC, review of Ormond, 385-389; MRC, "New Realism and

Royce," 382 (*SPS*, 137); MRC, "Josiah Royce," *NR* VIII (1916), 264-266.

41. MRC, "Distinction between Mental and Physical"; MRC, "Forces in Civil Law."

42. *DJ*, 170.

43. MRC, "Jus Naturale," 773-774; MRC, "Mechanism and Causality." Cf. MRC, "History vs. Value," 716 (*RN*, 385); MRC, "Rule versus Discretion," *JP* XI (1914), 208-215 (*LSO*, 259-267); MRC, "Logic in the Law," *Harvard Law Review* XXIX (1916), 622-639 (*LSO*, 165-183); MRC, "The Subject Matter of Formal Logic," *JP* XV (1918), 675 (*PL*, 18).

44. Morton White, *Science and Sentiment in America: Philosophical Thought in America from Jonathan Edwards to John Dewey* (New York, 1972), 220.

45. MRC, "Conception of Philosophy," 409 (*SPS*, 47); MRC, "New Realism and Royce," 214 (*SPS*, 132).

46. George Haines IV and Frederick H. Jackson, "A Neglected Landmark in the History of Ideas," *Mississippi Valley Historical Review* XXXIV (1947), 201-220.

47. E.g., John M. Coulter, *The Mission of Science in Education* (Ann Arbor, 1900), 13, 18-19, 27; John M. Coulter, "Practical Science," *Science* n.s. XXXI (1910), 886.

48. E.g., Walter Lippmann, *Drift and Mastery* (New York, 1914), 150-151, 154, 158, 161-163, 165, 169-170, 173; Randolph Bourne, *Youth and Life* (New York, 1913), 19-20, 232-233, 238-241, 243-244.

49. For Kallen see esp. Horace Kallen, *"Of Them Which Say They Are Jews"* (New York, 1954).

50. John Dewey, "The Postulate of Immediate Empiricism," *JP* II (1905), 399; MRC, "Conception of Philosophy," 402 (*SPS*, 38). Cf. Ralph Barton Perry, "Recent Philosophical Procedure with Reference to Science," *JP* I (1904), 171-174.

51. MRC, review of More, 143-144 (*FL*, 74).

52. MRC, "Jurisprudence," 232 (*RL*, 147).

53. MRC, review of More, 143-144 (*FL*, 74); MRC, "Qualities, Relations, Things," *JP* XI (1914), 627.

54. MRC, "Philosopher's Stone," 338-339 (*FL*, 405); MRC, review of Benedetto Croce, *La Filosofia di Giambattista Vico*, in *PR* XXXIII (1914), 369 (*SPS*, 212); *DJ*, 171; MRC, review of Henry Crew and Alfonso De Salvio, trans., Galileo, *Dialogues Concerning Two New Sciences*, in *NR* XI (1917), 85 (*FL*, 418).

The Walrus and the Carpenter
  Were walking close at hand:
They wept like anything to see
  Such quantities of sand:
"If this were only cleared away,"
  They said, "it *would* be grand!"

"If seven maids with seven mops
  Swept it for half a year,
Do you suppose," the Walrus said,
  "That they could get it clear?"
"I doubt it," said the Carpenter,
  And shed a bitter tear.

Lewis Carroll

Inside the classroom or out, "all of us were students of Morris Cohen," insisted Justice Felix Frankfurter in 1958, when dedicating the Morris Raphael Cohen Library on St. Nicholas Heights.[1] Frankfurter expressed a widespread sense of the terms on which his old roommate had interacted with his age. Cohen's role as a teacher far transcended the performance of instructional duties at City College; he was felt to be a distinctly professorial, didactic, and even schoolmasterly presence in other contexts as well. And nowhere was this image more prominent than within the professional subculture of American philosophy; the *Journal of Philosophy's* portrait of him in 1925 deserves to be quoted in full:

The Association is fortunate in having cherished for some years a faithful and watchful guardian who, under no illusions about the possibilities of our refractory material, has chided us for our failures and commended our progress, loyally keeping our best interests at heart even when compelled to point out our worst mistakes. It would have been very easy for Professor Cohen to grow discouraged and leave us to our own devices; but without a trace of impatience or cynicism he has continued to watch over our wanderings. Perhaps he can find some slight consolation in the knowledge that his annual papers, brilliant, clear, and pertinent, are universally looked forward to as criticisms of proved and unvarying worth.[2]

It was Cohen the schoolmaster whose approval was sought, and who for nearly twenty years was the most frequently quoted participant in the American Philosophical Association's annual meetings.[3] In 1931 the *Journal of Philosophy* reported typically that "Professor Cohen spared none of the speakers for their shortcomings." He "ridiculed the ineffable philosophy" of one symposiast, "censured" another "for not doing justice to the philosophical significance of symbolic logic," and discoursed at length on the merits and deficiencies of a third.[4] By his later years, the association was increasingly populated with persons who had studied with him at City College,[5] but his reputation as the house critic antedated this development, and one must look for its source, to some extent at least, in Cohen's own sense that teaching and doing philosophy were different phases of the same activity. Indeed, Cohen's entire career

as a public sage, as a professional philosopher, and as an undergraduate
teacher manifested a consistent style and tone best understood if examined first, and most fully, in what might be called his natural habi-
tat: the classroom.

Cohen's eminence as a teacher of undergraduates was partially the
result of his having been at the right place at the right time. City College was one of the most important institutions of higher education in
the United States during the 1910s, 1920s, and 1930s because of its
distinctive role in the lives of thousands of bright and intellectually
ambitious immigrants and their sons, especially those of Jewish origin.
By virtue of its location in New York and its public status, the college
attracted many students who could not or would not attend schools
that were more expensive, more distant from home, or more discrimina-
tory on the basis of race, religion, and ethnicity. Often faced with more
applicants than it could accept, the college could choose the most
promising students, and the result was a remarkably intelligent and
eager student body. By every account, Cohen was the dominating moral
and intellectual force on the campus; he stood out to the extent that
alumni were known to refer to him, and him alone, as "our teacher."[6]
Obviously, others were also "at the right place at the right time," but
none attained a legendary status comparable to Cohen's. What, beyond
quick intelligence, did Cohen have to offer that others did not? And
why were City College students so responsive to him, even to the point
of making him a cultural hero?

Ernest Nagel tried to answer both of these questions in 1927, when
Nagel was but four years out of City College himself. The occasion was
a testimonial dinner in Cohen's honor held at the Hotel Astor, and the
subsequent publication of the evening's proceedings by "The Youth
Who Sat at His Feet." The virtual "idolatry" of Cohen was to be explained, said Nagel, by the exemplary fashion in which he upheld and
practiced the life of the mind: "We, who have been taught to prize the
majesty of the intellectual life have found in Morris R. Cohen the living
symbol of our ideal." Quoting the priestess Diotema, Nagel observed

that the "beauty of the body" was often worshiped, while this beauty was in fact a mere "haunting anticipation" of spiritual beauties "incomparably superior"; similarly, Nagel explained, Cohen's admirers could be forgiven for succumbing to the same temptation, mistaking the tangible expression of mind—Morris R. Cohen—for the intangible ideal of intellect.[7]

For the more than 1,000 guests at the Astor that night, Cohen had earned his status as the supreme symbol for intellect, and "intellect" was a quality sincerely respected in that setting. Yet Cohen was a symbol for more than intellect. The dinner at the Astor was organized as a show of strength against the highly authoritarian president of City College, Frederick B. Robinson, who was known to be looking for means to dismiss, or discipline, his popular professor of philosophy. Cohen had sided with student "radicals" in their attempt to do away with compulsory courses in military science, and had opposed many other policies of the administration. Robinson's well-known contempt for Cohen was resented by some of those who understood that Cohen was an unofficial representative of, and symbol for, Jewish students and alumni. So clearly was Cohen identified as the spokesman for a particular constituency that the *Manufacturer's Record*, in 1925, cast its editorial on "Teaching Treason in American Colleges" in the form of an anti-Semitic attack on Cohen, personally: Cohen was one of the "Russian Jews" who had never "learned to think as an American," and who used their growing influence in American colleges to eliminate military science and thereby serve the interests of "that Jewish government that is Soviet Russia."[8] East European Jewish immigrants and their sons were able to see Cohen "as one of themselves," commented one alumnus many years later, "whose foreign accent" resembled that of their own parents, and "who seemed despite all obstacles to have pried open the doors to the sacred world of science and scholarship."[9]

Cohen's wife Mary, and Max Grossman of the class of 1916, a lawyer, organized the Astor dinner partially as a demonstration to Robinson, and to the trustees, of how formidable Cohen's support was.[10] The strategy of the pro-Cohen faction was to drop as many names as possible. At the dinner, whose ostensible purpose was to commemorate Cohen's twenty-fifth year on the staff at City College, letters of congratulation were read from Felix Adler, Roscoe Pound, Benjamin Cardozo, Walter Lippmann, Alvin Johnson, Albert Einstein, and Justice Holmes. The toastmaster was Felix Frankfurter, then a professor of law at Harvard. Speakers included John Dewey, J. F. E. Woodbridge, and Bertrand Russell.[11] President Robinson himself appeared, thereby providing an incentive for the others to express fully their respect for the guest of honor. After listening to the tributes, Robinson rose to criticize Cohen, indirectly, through the terms he chose to "praise" his notoriously insubordinate employee. Robinson observed that the "immature students" of City College might be greatly endangered if they were exposed to "skepticism and doubt." What they needed, instead, was "guiding influence" toward things "wholesome and good." Robinson implied that Cohen—who had in fact made skepticism and doubt his public posture—was of great value to the college because he provided a wholesome influence, because he helped to "instil ideals of loyalty and devotion . . . national, state, and parental." Robinson depicted Cohen's course in legal philosophy as a means to inculcate in young men the need for the "subordination" of "the individual will" to the "controlling law of the community."[12]

The adulation of Cohen that evening served obvious political and ethnic functions, yet there is no reason to doubt the basic sincerity of most of what was said at the Astor and in the additional tributes collected for the published version of the proceedings. The specific points made about Cohen's teaching were consistent with one another, and they established the patterns followed in later years by admirers who were under no obligation to defend Cohen against a hostile administration.

The appreciation of Cohen, as a genre, had two interlocking themes. The first was embodied in Nagel's remarks, as quoted above: Cohen is thanked for reinforcing certain very general values, especially the "life of the mind" itself. The second theme emerged the most clearly in Max Grossman's preface to the printed version of the *Tribute to Morris R. Cohen, Teacher and Philosopher.* Cohen's style, said Grossman, was akin to "the surgeon's sharp knife," the bite of which the student learned to forgive when "there came the realization of the profound earnestness of this seeker for genuine ideas." Or, Grossman continued, Cohen's impact could be compared to a bracing splash of cold water "at the fountainhead" which "cleared the mind of cobwebs and musty ideas."[13] Repeatedly, in 1927 and in later years, City College "Old Boys" insisted that they had been slashed, stabbed, scrubbed, and seared for their own good.

Nagel noted the "pain" inflicted by Cohen's "ruthless logic."[14] Sidney Hook recalled how "painful" it was to be impaled by Cohen on the horns of a dilemma, "but it was a bleeding quite salutary for the soul." To watch "the bright blue rapier of his dialectic leaping, parrying, and thrusting," Hook said of his teacher, to watch him "cleave through a knotty tissue of irrelevancies" was an experience "both inspiring and chastening." The experience left an enduring, beneficial scar, Hook added, the "mark of Cohen." It was worn by Cohen's students

in their manner if not on their brow. Sometimes they were not popular with other members of the faculty—they stressed the importance of giving reasons, raising doubts, challenged time-worn dogmas, interrupted the full-flowing periods of rotund rhetoric and were deaf to all arguments from authority. For they had been trained by the Socratic method.[15]

Most of Cohen's students chafed under the master's "tyranny," noted recent alumnus Joseph P. Lash in 1931, but "they glory in it next term when they see newcomers subjected to the same scathing bath of logical objections."[16] Delighted as students were with Cohen's "rapierlike wit," they "lived in dread of becoming the butt of his sallies," admitted two old grads shortly after Cohen's death; "Cohen could sometimes be an intellectual bully." "We were often resentful," explained Jules Kolodny ('32) and William Isaacs ('25), until we realized that "we were being prepared to search for facts, to weigh evidence . . . and to think things through."[17] Cohen's "fire," added another nostalgic former pupil, "branded you for the rest of your life."[18] Cohen's "student-baiting," added another, amounted to a "whetstone" against which students' minds could be ground until sharp.[19]

This pattern in the rhetoric of appreciation gives credibility to the sense of Lewis Feuer ('31) that Cohen "played on the masochism" of many of his students.[20] And Louis Schneider ('35) observes that "Jewish students in the midst of a most anxiety-evoking depression had their streak of sadism too"; they admired Cohen as the "master of a logical scalpel which could deliver deep and rather cruel cuts." They would imitate Cohen as a pastime, "hacking up an opponent with a display of Cohenian logic."[21]

Cohen was also remembered for flashes of personal warmth, manifest especially in his relations with students who made honest and humble, even if unsuccessful, efforts to do philosophy well. After a session in which he had been especially hard on a student, Cohen was sometimes known to seek out the student and, with his arm around the shoulders of the all-but-sobbing youngster, explain that no personal offense was intended by his method of instruction.[22] At other times Cohen would agree to spend his lunch hour going over text passages that had puzzled those of his students who demonstrated a real eagerness to learn.[23] When alone with a student whose intellect and attitude he respected, Cohen was capable of carrying on straightforward, intellectually honest conversations, as when walking home along the Hudson with Ernest Nagel. Yet Nagel ('23) recalls that whenever the two were joined by a third party, the atmosphere changed abruptly, and Cohen would theatrically play one student off against the other.[24] Cohen sometimes responded helpfully when asked for advice, but he often chose to make his petitioner tremble; Benjamin Nelson ('31) overheard the following exchange, which he regards as characteristic:[25]

Student: "Professor Cohen, should I go farther in philosophy?"
Cohen: "Absolutely not!"

Student: (shocked, and for a moment silent)
Cohen: "Only a jackass could ask such a question."

Even those who were fortunate enough to receive Cohen's warmth, and who remember him as the finest and most remarkable teacher they have ever known, tend to come back to what Sidney Hook ('23) calls Cohen's "persistent cruelty."[26] One former student who regards Cohen as "an incomparable teacher," and a "great man" whose image is "still burningly alive" for him, explains that no matter what one's stance toward Cohen, "it is not possible to forget his acerbity."[27]

That Cohen fulfilled a compelling psychological and moral need for many young Jewish males is hardly to be doubted. There were of course no women to be seen; City College was not yet coeducational. What Meyer Liben ('34) describes as "the problem of Total Maleness" certainly made the atmosphere more combative; so exclusively did Liben remember City College as a man's outfit that years later, when he saw "a girl wearing a C.C.N.Y. sweatshirt," he experienced a "curious feeling, in the gray area between amazement and incredulity." How different things might have been with females around, muses Liben: Is the Kronstadt Rebellion "the kind of thing you'd want to talk about with girls?"[28] The atmosphere, recalls another alumnus, was "not unlike that of a yeshiva."[29] And the sociologist Marshall Sklare, in his survey of the relation of public education to American Jewish history, designates Cohen, in particular, as the "secularized counterpart of the *rosh yeshiva*."[30] To those in need of a schoolmaster of a certain type—emancipated, yet unmistakably one of the tribe; severe, yet obliquely loving—Cohen was a nearly perfect answer.

Whatever the ultimate sources of its appeal to students, Cohen's classroom method was essentially to state questions and to criticize the various answers offered by the pupils he called upon. This style of teaching has often been called Socratic, both by Cohen himself and by many of his former students,[31] but what actually went on was not always the careful reasoning characteristic of the dialogues recorded by Plato.

Cohen's wit and showmanship often kept the galleries rapt, sometimes at the expense of a student. B. H. Haggin ('21) recalls as typical the following exchange between Cohen and a student who was then captain of the water-polo team:

Cohen: "Mr. Menkes, tell us about Epictetus."
Menkes: "Well, he believed . . ."
Cohen (interrupting): "You don't know what he believed. Sit down."

"I write as one who was lucky enough not to be humiliated myself by Cohen," insists Haggin, but as one who noticed that those he humiliated were not always "guilty of the contradiction, the easy or thoughtless answer that Cohen, like Socrates, was obliged to deal with ruthlessly."[32] Lewis Feuer has vivid recollections of Cohen ridiculing students who had given answers that were not only sincere, but perfectly accurate.[33] Paul Goodman ('31), who would yield to no one in his respect for Cohen, admitted nonetheless that Cohen's Socratic method was, indeed, "fraudulent."[34] However, if Cohen's manner did not always conform to the Socratic ideal of systematically leading a student to think out the implications of a proposition and of its alternatives, if he sometimes put aside dialogue in the interests of one-man theater, his attempts to serve the Socratic ideal functioned at least to implant that ideal in the minds of even those who found Cohen's own performance deficient. Goodman, for example, claimed that he had always tried, as a teacher, to succeed where Cohen had failed.[35]

Everyone knew what the *rosh yeshiva* had to offer: the Torah and the Talmud. What Cohen had to offer seemed so negative, by contrast, that his most extravagant admirers often strained to reassure themselves that his teaching had "positive" aspects. Cohen "was more concerned with a method and a technique for dealing with problems than with the answers themselves," explained some.[36] Yet Cohen did have "answers" of a certain order, and these were manifest in the very general values—such as the superiority of "mind"—that his students felt him to symbolize. Meyer Liben recalled Cohen's "remorseless voice of reason," which taught that if we fear thought and intelligence, we are but deluded and perishable brutes, but if we love and pursue thought, we need not be ashamed of our ignorance. . . . [We] might even help keep alive the fitful light our teacher so passionately cherished, might even make something of ourselves in the world where irrationality was at a premium.[37]

Such reflections may seem too general to reveal anything, but they are not to be dismissed as merely banal—they do help identify a crucial element in Cohen's teaching. The oft-repeated claim that Cohen "never made disciples"[38] ignores his considerable role in cultural transferal.

Even his most sophisticated students seem to have been stunned and inspired by Cohen's ability to put them directly in touch with great segments of the Western intellectual tradition. Cohen introduced his students to a prodigious range of sources, and he used a variety of historical and social contexts to illustrate the authenticity of classical philosophical dilemmas. He achieved this effect even in standard philosophy courses such as logic and metaphysics, but most of all in philosophy of law and "philosophy of civilization." The latter course, which extended over several semesters, introduced students to many of the problems pursued in the social sciences and in philosophy of history; here, more than anywhere else, Cohen transferred to his pupils the broad concerns that energized Western scholarship and science. The basic text was Santayana's *Life of Reason*, the systematic study of which became a crucial experience in the lives of many City College boys.[39]

The reading assignments and the topics for study engaged students, in many instances, as firmly as Cohen's celebrated classroom style. If they were ready in any event to be challenged by Santayana, it was Cohen who led them to sit down and actually confront *The Life of Reason*. Cohen's "civilization" course was the core of a liberal-arts education; it served to identify a body of literature and a set of questions. Cohen did not formulate a set of "manageable" problems for his students; instead, he tried to convey the grandeur and seriousness of difficult and unresolved questions. Reading Buckle and Huntington on the role of climate in history, his students were made to feel that they, though puny undergraduates, were truly living the life of the mind, and on an ambitious level.[40]

Cohen used his position to mobilize and deploy what Arnold would have called "the best which has been thought and said in the world."[41] His students were eager, as he had been a generation before, to enter the world of secular intellect if given a little encouragement; he now extended their cultural horizons toward his own principled cosmopolitanism. Cohen's approach to his assigned readings was not, however, Arnoldian. He rarely showed reverence for a great text. F. H. Bradley's *Appearance and Reality* was for many years required reading in Cohen's metaphysics course. So thoroughly did he cut Bradley's views to tatters that the protest was often heard, "If the book is so devoid of merit, why did you make us buy it?" Cohen's response was that *Appearance and Reality* was one of the greatest books ever addressed to the problems of metaphysics.[42] And, indeed, he chose to hold this particular volume in his hand in 1927 when he posed for the oil portrait that was presented to the college at the Astor dinner.[43] It was characteristic of him to attack works he liked, and to do so from an "independent" perspective that he managed to persuade even his cleverest students was not to be reduced to one classical position or another. The same assault was performed on books Cohen disliked, with yet more devastating effects.

The approach was decidedly not one of "problem solving," according to which a given answer to a problem would eventually be recognized as superior to others and defended against its rivals; Cohen was "critical" in a narrower sense. He employed discursive intellect to attack, but rarely to justify. Energetically pursued, this approach shocked the bulk of the students, who assumed that texts were sources of insight, to be studied and integrated with what the instructor said. If this overbearingly negative use of critical intelligence led some of them to despair and cynicism, they have remained silent, for Cohen had exactly the opposite effect on those who have made their feelings public. Most left Cohen's classroom convinced that viable answers did exist, if only one could extend logical analysis a bit farther, if only one could achieve a more comprehensive perspective than had been available to such hapless victims of Professor Cohen's criticism as F.H. Bradley.

The ability of Cohen's students to keep this faith undoubtedly derived largely from hopes and energies developed long before they encountered Cohen, but the faith was reinforced by Cohen's classroom use of what he elsewhere called the "principle of polarity." This term emerged in his formal metaphysical writings in the early twenties; it denoted Cohen's belief that the world ultimately consists of a series of polarities, of "opposites" that require each other in order to be understood. Cohen's attempts to formulate and defend this idea in the context of metaphysical discourse will be taken up presently; what needs to be stressed here is his practice of introducing students to a variety of contrasting claims about a given question. "The most important thing I got from Cohen," Paul Goodman recalled shortly before his own death in 1972, "was the practice of taking everything into account, of avoiding one-factor analysis."[44] Cohen's students read antithetical arguments about a problem and were then led to criticize the narrowness of each; the inadequacy of a thinker often turned out to be a function of parochialism. The most successful thinking thus became equated with cosmopolitanism, and the price of its achievement was heroic self-restraint: the supreme moral act of mind was to suspend judgment until everything had been considered.

The land of "suspended judgment" was of course the "Desert of Freedom" in which Cohen would leave students after freeing them from the "Egyptian bondage" of false and incomplete ideas. "I had faith that they would enter the Promised Land without me," he said.[45] Yet it was the best-kept secret of Cohen's teaching career that he had taken his students as close as he could to the promised land where everything is "taken into account." He was perhaps unequaled as an advocate of suspended judgment, as a critic of incomplete solutions, but his own supply of "complete" answers was thin, and he was not much help in resolving his students' choices among the alternative, necessarily "incomplete" theories to which his varied reading lists had introduced them.

Cohen tried to put a virtuous face on the situation: he said he sought to train "the critical and scientific spirit" to attack dogmas, prejudices, and illusions, while stoically restraining himself from "preaching his own convictions."[46] "Knocking logical errors out of young people's heads is not a pleasant occupation," he said, but it was an "important service in the cause of liberal civilization." It was enough, he protested, to have "cleaned the stables."[47] At the Astor dinner in 1927, he spoke proudly of serving as a "logical disinfectant."[48] Elsewhere, he explicitly endorsed the teaching of philosophy as a much-needed "antiseptic."[49]

Yet Cohen was privately ambivalent about the "aridity" of the locale in which he left his students.[50] His use of the desert as a metaphor for the "freedom" he served has a touching, almost pathetic irony, since he, as one of his generation's most insistent critics of laissez faire doctrines, believed that freedom without a means of getting where you wanted to go amounted to sterile inertia at best, and at worst rendered one vulnerable to exploitation.

Cohen, even at the end of his career, simply did not have a set of "problem solutions" to offer his students; the promised land had eluded him, and he was left to lament privately the endlessness of the path he insisted publicly would lead his students to fulfillment. The difficulty was that through a lifetime of use of the scientific intellect, of logic, of the "method of reason," Cohen had not been able to formulate and justify a positive position on the specific issues that defined the terms of discourse among American philosophers. His professional philosophical efforts will be the focus of our attention soon, but it can be noted here that he had no carefully worked-out metaphysics, and no articulate, viable doctrine of the "good" on which to build a moral philosophy. Even his influential critiques of popular empiricism and legal realism never took the form of a systematic philosophy of science and of law. He always knew what was wrong and, in a very general sense, what was right, but the latter tended to wither away whenever he sought to formulate it specifically and defend it in technical discourse. Cohen's claim that he "made no disciples" is valid with reference to the more or less technical questions around which academic discourse was organized, for to such questions he proposed very few answers worked out carefully enough to compel assent from students who went on to graduate school in a given specialty. Yet Cohen did try to do philosophy of this sort, and he would have been glad for disciples; the myth that he tried not to influence his students is given the lie, for example, by the testimony of both Hook and Nagel that when they left City College for graduate study at Columbia, they were certain that Cohen had refuted Dewey's philosophy once and for all.[51]

Although there were elements of self-deceit in his teaching attitudes, the fact remains that Cohen, as a teacher, turned to creative use the limitations that impeded his originality as a thinker. When unable to decide what the "truth" was, when unable, in other words, to perform the act of confident judgment so long "suspended," Cohen did not fake the consummation for the benefit of students. Instead he turned his own covert uncertainty about specifically formulated propositions into an opportunity to affirm those few, precious truths of which he *was* certain. Most obvious among these was the classically "liberal" insight that there is no valid orthodoxy on most questions human beings must face, that a variety of opinions have equally strong, if fragmentary, claims to truth, that pluralism is a natural condition. It is probably impossible to exaggerate the dramatic force with which this outlook was inculcated by Cohen's method of instruction. In the same order of general truths, for Cohen the teacher, were the superiority of cosmopolitanism over any and all parochialisms, the supremacy of the life of the mind and the method of reason, the foolishness of hasty decisions, and the sanctity of truth itself.

Cohen the teacher was very much like Cohen the self-styled "logician" who made no substantive contributions to logic, yet became his generation's greatest advocate of logic.[52] The questions to which he had answers that "took everything into account" were of an irreducibly general nature, and it was in the interests of addressing those questions that he so theatrically refused, in the classroom, to become identified with answers to lesser questions. This distinction between the "answers" Cohen was sure of, and those he was not, helps explain his simultaneously detached and engaged attitude toward teaching. There were times when he played games with a class, trying to keep them guessing as to his own views.[53] This cavalier stance was possible when it made little difference to him which of a series of opinions a student would eventually adopt. The game itself was a means of making a larger point about one of the unstated questions he was actually addressing. When issues of this second type were directly on the line, he played no games; no one was left to guess how he felt about the role of reason in the search for truth, or about the importance of scrutinizing the principles inherited from one's parents.

It would be a mistake to conclude that Cohen's use of the classroom to inculcate liberal values resulted from a decisive inability to use it for anything else. Even if his own creative efforts in philosophy had been largely abortive, there were in the works of Bradley, Russell, and others a number of opinions that he could have chosen to defend as the best available. His failure to do this was not simply a precious refusal to endorse assertions that failed to take everything into account. No doubt he would have swallowed these scruples if his purposes had been strictly to explore with his classes the specific problems of metaphysics, jurisprudence, and so on. But his mission from the beginning had been broader than this. He had made the decision to become a teacher of philosophy while under the influence of Thomas Davidson and Felix Adler. He wanted to deal with questions of moral significance, with "philosophy of life." It was Cohen, after all, who defended "the old ideal of Culture" in 1909, and who set out in the 1910s to "police the intellectual realm" according to safe and sane regulations.[54] There is thus a sense in which the generality of his teaching message was prior to, not a substitute for, specific philosophical doctrines he was never able to formulate. He sought from first to last to affect the culture in which his students would live.

Even when he referred to his having "trained thinkers" and not "made disciples," Cohen revealingly compared himself to two of the late nineteenth century's most sturdy "custodians of culture," Charles E. Garman of Amherst and George Holmes Howison of Berkeley.[55] Like them, Cohen gave his students what he thought they needed most, and what he himself was the most sure of. But Cohen was sure about fewer, and different, things, and his sense of how much needed to be "taken into account" was much more demanding. As he summed up his mission, it was to teach "regard for the weight of evidence," "the habit of admitting ignorance when we do not know," and, above all, devotion to "the critical spirit of free inquiry which is inseparable from the love of truth that makes men free."[56] Cohen was neither the first nor the last undergraduate teacher to serve these goals, but no one did more than he to popularize them, and no one made them seem less platitudinous to students.

As a philosopher and public sage, Cohen alternated between the two modes that defined his classroom teaching: the "tenacious clinging" to what he believed to be true, and the "surgical" cutting away at disease, rubbish, and confusion. Although he was only partially aware of this pattern in his behavior, he had tried from the beginning of his career to transcend it through the creation of viable "answers" to questions more difficult than those answered by his small store of cherished "truths." Cohen's style and tone as a philosophic critic were sharpened by the frustration of these more synthetic, "positive" ambitions; his public career as a whole, like his classroom teaching, drew from the first on his capacities for "tenacity" and "surgery," and he was forced to fall back on them again and again, with renewed demands, when his efforts to find a middle way were frustrated.

Although more than a dozen books were eventually to bear his name, his characteristic genres were the book review and the short critical essay. Many of his books, including his chief contributions to philosophy of science and law, were collections of previously published articles. This was largely true even of *Reason and Nature*, his first, and most important, full-length work, which did not appear until 1931, long after Cohen's reputation was established. The essays and reviews that had created this reputation—some of which were reprinted in *Reason and Nature*—drew upon Cohen's exceptional capacity to identify things he did not like and to articulate clearly what he found repulsive about them.

The standards by which Cohen made his judgments were invariably simple and straightforward: this or that thinker had confused "is" with "ought," had emphasized "flux" at the expense of "logic," or in some other way had violated one of the basic commitments we have seen developed in Cohen's early papers. We have seen, also, how thoroughly these papers are controlled by a dialectic of "threat" and "defense," and how frequently these threats appear in the guise of "extreme" or "imbalanced" claims. Cohen dealt with these errors of philosophers exactly as he dealt with those of his students: the negative judgment was propounded with great polemical force, and frequently with sarcastic wit; then the injunction was given to "take everything into account." Finally, there followed an affirmation of some very general value that the "threat" had challenged.

Cohen was much more at home in a journal of critical opinion than in a systematic philosophical treatise; he was peculiarly well equipped to work in the border area between philosophy and journalism. It is not surprising that he had a brilliant career as a contributor to the *New Republic*, while the other leading philosophers of his generation—C. I. Lewis, George Herbert Mead, and Arthur O. Lovejoy, for example— were better able to concentrate their efforts on the production of the book-length essays for which they are still remembered. Although a number of Cohen's papers in metaphysics and philosophy of science— published, usually, in philosophy journals—were more specialized than his articles for popular consumption, the bulk of his work was composed in the same idiom, regardless of intended audience. In every context he was preeminently a critic, concerned always to clarify the implications of technical work for the most general of moral and intellectual questions.

Cohen's particular style of thought and feeling was also manifest in his personal relations with other thinkers. An argument he once had with the legal scholar Jerome Frank is worth following in some detail for what it reveals about Cohen's approach to informal discourse. Frank was a devoted, and even a fawning, admirer of Cohen,[57] with whom he chanced to be invited to a dinner party at the home of Judge Julian Mack in the spring of 1931. Among the other guests were Benjamin Cardozo, Harold Laski, Thomas Reed Powell, and Felix Frankfurter. In the course of the evening Frank admitted that he had some doubts about one point, at least, in Cohen's *Reason and Nature*, which had been published only a few months before. Hadn't Morris gone too far in denying that a psychological description of a thinker's reasoning can help us to assess the validity of his reasoning? To support this reservation, Frank gave examples of how a person may assert something on the basis of irrational, or in any case unarticulated, premises: Couldn't we better evaluate what such a thinker says if we knew about those hidden premises? Cohen replied that the truth or falsity of an assertion was a matter distinct from that of a person's motivation in making the assertion. Frank and Cohen went back and forth for a while, with the others joining in occasionally. Frank believed afterward that Cohen had never understood his point, and several days later he addressed a twelve-page letter to Cohen, putting forth his own views in detail.[58]

Cohen wrote back that Frank "did not in the whole letter raise any new arguments or say anything which I did not answer (to my mind quite clearly) at Judge Mack's dinner." Cohen insisted that Frank's case would "completely evaporate" if he would recognize the distinctions Cohen made at the Mack dinner, to wit: "the factual truth of any assertion" is a question to be distinguished from "the logical relation between premises and conclusions," and from "the reliability of a man's testimony."[59] In point of fact, these distinctions were slighted in Frank's letter, and most of Cohen's reply reads as a lucid commentary on their relevance to the point Frank had tried to raise. To Frank's insistence that "the unexpressed motives of a thinker deserve much attention," Cohen agreed, insofar as one wants to know about the reliability of a thinker's testimony, but he disagreed insofar as one's interest is in the truth or falsity of what the thinker asserts—the latter can be determined "only by reference to the material content" of what the thinker says. "The moon is in a given place" whether a given person testifies to it or not. This letter, which was to be the first of more than a dozen Cohen wrote to Frank during the following seven months, was destined to be one of his most honest and extensive efforts to speak directly to Frank's concern. But even this letter included barbs that offended Frank grievously and helped create a prolonged argument. "Now Jerry dear, I like you very much," said Cohen, "but I have little patience with your manner of arguing," especially "[your] annoying habit of not giving your opponent . . . the credit for meaning exactly what he says: thus when I say no to a given proposition of yours, you repeat it in different words." The friendship can remain intact "if, recognizing a certain incompatibility in manner of arguing, we can avoid prolonged arguments."[60]

Frank wrote back that Cohen's judgments of his intellect were "brutal" and "unfair," and that the other guests at Judge Mack's would surely dissent from Cohen's characterization of his manner of arguing. "Your fiat puts a stop to further discussions between us," and "I shall never again annoy you by going beyond grunts of approval or disapproval with respect to your views."[61] Cohen was quick to respond that no "fiat" against further discussion had been intended, and that Frank's other interpretations of Cohen's previous letter were similarly erroneous. Cohen reviewed his recollection of exactly who said what to whom at the Mack dinner, and to whose approval. Cohen also apologized for having left Frank with the impression he thought poorly of Frank's mind. "My wife says: 'All your friends are saints,' and I reply, 'They must be to stand me.' "[62]

It takes two to make an argument, and the subsequent intensification of this one throughout the summer and fall says as much about Frank's disposition as about Cohen's. Cohen repeatedly observed that the correspondence was futile, yet he would always tie this observation to another assertion that he had been absolutely right from the beginning about the points at issue. Frank was unable to accept these put-downs and seemed to demand at least a slight concession from Cohen as a price for calling the argument to a halt. Had Frank been willing to forgive Cohen his self-righteousness the matter might have dissolved, as it might have had Cohen, for his part, been willing to wave a flag of truce without simultaneously taking potshots at his foe. The correspondence was obsessive on both sides: Frank, continually referring to the intellectual superiority of his foe (e.g., "I may serve a useful purpose as some of Socrates' stupid fools"),[63] disgorged one ten-to-fifteen-page letter after another entreating and challenging Cohen to grant him a point; Cohen, reminding "dear Jerry" frequently of the warmth of their friendship (e.g., "If I didn't like you so much I would not take the trouble . . ."),[64] made peace virtually contingent on an implicit, if not explicit, admission on Frank's part that Cohen had been philosophically correct. "I can only hope," Cohen said in a tone characteristic of the imbroglio, "that the process of learning logic which you so generously attribute to the reading of my book will continue to the point where you can see the error of your contention."[65]

What Frank wanted specifically was an acknowledgment from Cohen that *Reason and Nature* made too sweeping a claim when it denied (on page 11) that "a psychological description of reasoning as a mental event can determine whether the resulting conclusion is true." Frank was afraid that this dictum would be used by conservative legal philosophers to perpetuate dangerous myths about judicial behavior.[66] Frank wanted to diminish the concealment of "judicial prejudice and incompetence" behind a screen of "specious rationality."[67] Hence he tried to persuade Cohen of the inapplicability, in certain legal situations, of "the distinction between (a) factual truth and (b) reliability of testimony as to facts asserted." Frank had in mind those situations in which a judge, confronted with conflicting evidence, must form a conclusion as to what the "facts" of a case are, and must then report this conclusion as part of the opinion he writes. What had actually happened in the case before the judge was not relevant to Frank's concern; the question he wanted to ask was this: Does the judge's written opinion correctly report the judge's *construction of the facts*, or does that opinion report this construction incorrectly? The situation, then, was one in which what was being *testified* to was the content of a given person's mind, and for this reason Frank believed that the question of *factual truth* was the same as the question of accurate testimony.[68] But for Cohen the relation between (a) the content of a given person's mind and (b) testimony concerning that content, was logically the same as the relation between the moon's location and testimony about that location.[69] Still Frank persisted, believing that he could win the argument by getting Cohen to count this single "exception," and thereby forcing Cohen to concede that *Reason and Nature* made too sharp a distinction between logic and psychology. To Frank's prodigious briefs, Cohen wrote short responses, often contenting himself with returning Frank's missives filled with his own marginalia.

Exasperated, Cohen tried to quiet Frank at the end of August by informing him that Laski and Frankfurter had looked over the early letters of the exchange some time ago and pronounced Cohen in the right.[70] Frank called this an "ex parte" hearing and decided in September to report his own side of the ongoing argument to Frankfurter. This act stimulated Cohen to write his own, renewed apologia to Frankfurter, and led to several rounds of disputation between Cohen and Frank over the propriety of involving mutual friends as mediators.[71] Frank seems finally to have exhausted himself by January 7, 1932; Cohen's note of that date—clarifying yet another "misunderstanding," this time concerning what Cohen had meant in an earlier letter by accusing Frank of an "abuse" of the privileges of private correspondence—is the last item in Frank's file of letters.[72]

The flavor of the discourse Cohen carried on with Frank in this episode was of course quite different from that of the conversations that took place in Cohen's home on Sunday evenings, when a circle of Co-

hen's closest personal friends would gather with their wives to listen to
Morris read his manuscripts.[73] Where he was not seriously challenged,
Cohen could maintain the warmest of relationships. Indeed, most of
Cohen's correspondence with other thinkers was cordial—but trivial.
Nowhere in Cohen's nearly twenty years of correspondence with Justice Holmes, for example, were philosophical issues discussed as seriously as in the Frank episode; Cohen was always deferential to Holmes,
and the two confined themselves largely to exchanging aphorisms and
expressions of admiration for each other's work.[74] Cohen's former
students, not surprisingly, were deferential to him in much the way he
was to Holmes. Indeed, the striking characteristic in the bulk of Cohen's correspondence—as printed in *Portrait of a Philosopher: Morris R.
Cohen in Life and Letters*—is the absence of forthright philosophical
discussion between peers. In the few cases where Cohen was not allowed to have his own way, he reacted much as he had to Frank. In
1936, for example, Cohen and Felix Frankfurter exchanged a flurry of
impatient letters over a point that Frankfurter wanted to challenge, but
the matter was put to rest when Frankfurter cheerfully admitted himself to be "simple" and "naive," while letting Cohen get away with
denying an analogous criticism Frankfurter had offered of Cohen's
character.[75] Another potential antagonism was averted when Judge
Learned Hand acknowledged the possibility that he had stolen an idea
from Cohen.[76]

   Cohen was most comfortable with relationships that were either adversary or deferential; he rarely sustained an intellectual relationship
that did not fall into one of these two modes. When former student
Sidney Hook shocked Cohen with a mildly critical review of *Reason
and Nature*, Cohen's reaction was to thrust Hook back into the classroom, into pupillike deference: "I knew I should never have given you
an A in philosophy of science," he snapped.[77] And John Dewey spoke
for a number of Cohen's generational peers when he complained that
Cohen's chief fault was "his undue fear lest somebody else agree with
him."[78] Cohen was vaguely aware of his tendency to exasperate others

through his swift recourse to an adversary mode; sometimes he reversed himself and apologized, thereby drawing forth, as from Columbia literary scholar John Erskine, for example, the assurance that his table talk was not too aggressive.[79]

The sense that Cohen's style was too negative, and his personality "bleak" and "parched," was shared by many of those who understood and valued highly Cohen's two great strengths: a devotion to the axioms of good sense, and a brilliant talent for finding the flaw in an argument.[80] It was these clearly demarked strengths that defined the terms of his personal interaction with the editors of the *New Republic*, most members of the intellectual community on Morningside and St. Nicholas Heights, and most of the philosophers, lawyers, and jurists with whom he dealt regularly. Cohen's social presence was thus of a distinctive type; it is not enough to say that he was an active and influential animator of discussions,[81] for he performed this role very differently than did William James, for example, or even Thomas Davidson. James and Davidson each had an enormous capacity for enthusiasm, for riding along with, and inside of, a great diversity of ideas; these men functioned as animators in a manner quite different from Cohen's.

Having "braved the muddy realities" of the world, Cohen claimed in *A Dreamer's Journey*, he was denied admission to some "palaces" of philosophy because he "never completely got rid of the out-of-door mud."[82] Continually, Cohen would try to remove it from himself and from others; the task of removing "dirt and manure" he gladly took as his own.[83] He was mildly obsessive about it, and referred so often to himself as "cleaner of stables" that the phrase caught on: it found its way into the title of an article *Time* magazine did on him shortly before his death, and it has been widely quoted by his former students.[84] Cohen's focus of attention, not only in the classroom but in his career generally, was on the "useless rubbish" that got in the way of beginning "to build."[85] He liked to compare his own career to that of the hospital administrator Florence Nightingale, who believed that whatever else hospitals did, they ought not to spread disease.[86]

NOTES

1. Felix Frankfurter, "As I Remember Morris Cohen," *City College Alumnus* LIV (1958), 3-6.

2. J. H. Randall, Jr., "The Twenty-Fifth Annual Meeting of the Eastern Division of the American Philosophical Association," *JP* XXIII (1926), 37.

3. For accounts of Cohen's participation in these meetings see *JP* XI (1914), 59, 337, 344, 346-349; XIII (1916), 100; XV (1918), 177-178; XVII (1920), 94, 96-97; XVIII (1921), 158; XIX (1922), 278-279; XXI (1924), 43, 48-49; XXII (1925), 47; XXVI (1929), 126, 128-130; XXVII (1930), 78; XXVIII (1931), 88-89, 96-97; XXIX (1932), 98-99, 101. The *Journal* discontinued these reports after 1932.

4. Ernest Nagel, "The Thirtieth Annual Meeting of the Eastern Division of the American Philosophical Association," *JP* XXVIII (1931), 88-89, 96-97.

5. The extraordinary number of prominent American philosophers who studied with Cohen at one time or another has been frequently noted by historians of the discipline; e.g., Andrew J. Reck, *The New American Philosophers* (New York, 1968), esp. 122-123, 164, 315.

6. Meyer Liben, "CCNY—A Memoir," *Commentary* XL (1965), 68. Cf. the comment of Abraham Edel, an instructor at City College during the 1930s: "Cohen was *the* teacher of all those City College alumni who went on to become, proverbially, the best graduate students everywhere" (conversation with author, San Francisco, California, August 17, 1972).

7. Ernest Nagel, "Appreciation," in *Tribute*, 98.

8. "Teaching Treason in American Colleges," *Manufacturer's Record* (December 31, 1925), 1.

9. Lewis S. Feuer, review of *DJ* and *SPS*, in *NR* CXX (1949), 21-22. Similar observations have been expressed by Louis Schneider (letter to author, September 24, 1974) and Benjamin Nelson (conversation with author, New York City, June 19, 1974).

10. On the Astor dinner and the circumstances surrounding it see *Portrait*, 101-103. My understanding of these events is also based upon the recollections of Ernest Nagel (conversation with author, New York City, December 31, 1968) and Sidney Hook (conversation with author, New York City, June 3, 1971).

11. About Russell's participation in the event, Sidney Hook (conversation with author) recalls the following. Russell was in New York in the fall of 1927, and was to be approached by Hook and a friend, Morris Bolisuk, on the basis of the rumor that Russell was an admirer of Cohen. When Bolisuk asked Russell to speak at the Astor dinner, Russell's immediate response was, "Who is Morris Cohen?" Russell then asked why he should speak. Bolisuk thereupon offered Russell an honorarium of $50.00, which was accepted as "fifty excellent reasons" to speak. Hook believes the apparently false report of Russell's admiration for Cohen came originally from Harold J. Laski. In fact, Laski's letters to Justice Holmes, during the early twenties, attributed to Russell the view that Cohen was America's foremost philosopher, superior to Dewey, explicitly. See Laski to Holmes, February 11, 1923, January 18, 1924, and December 12, 1925, in Mark De Wolfe Howe, ed., *The Holmes-Laski Letters*, I, 483, 698, 809. Laski's friends were frequently scandalized by his "habit of unscrupulous romancing," as it was termed by Edmund Wilson, whose candid and helpful discussion of the problem is in *The Bit Between My Teeth: A Literary Chronicle of 1950-1965* (New York, 1965), 80-84.

12. Frederick B. Robinson, "Address," in *Tribute*, 53-61.

13. Grossman, "Introduction," *Tribute*, xvi-xvii. *Tribute* was privately printed, but under the personal supervision of publisher Ben Heubsch. See the recollection of Grossman, "Morris Cohen, Felix Adler and the Ethical Movement," *The Ethical Outlook* XLIX (1963), 124.

14. Nagel, "Appreciation," 96.

15. Sidney Hook, "Professor Morris R. Cohen as Teacher," *Tribute*, 90-92.

16. Joseph P. Lash, "Former Student Pens Appreciation of Morris Cohen," *Campus* [student newspaper at City College] (March 20, 1931), 4. Cf. Joseph P. Lash, "Campus Reporter Finds Prof. Cohen Is A Classicist in a Romantic World," *Campus* (October 17, 1928), 1 and 3.

17. Jules Kolodny and William Isaacs, "We Remember Morris R. Cohen," *The City College Alumnus* XLV (1949), 18-19. Cf. Arthur F. Smullyan, quoted in *Portrait*, 95.

18. Harry N. Rosenfield, quoted in *Portrait*, 99.

19. Bertram D. Wolfe, "Mind-Shaker and Mind-Sharpener," Chapter six of an unpublished autobiography, esp. 27.

20. Lewis Feuer, conversation with author, Toronto, Ontario, January 16, 1974.

21. Louis Schneider, letter to author.

22. Many persons recall witnessing such scenes, e.g., Paul Goodman (conversation with author, North Stratford, New Hampshire, July 9, 1972) and Abraham Edel (conversation with author).

23. Paul Weiss, quoted in *Portrait*, 97.

24. Ernest Nagel, conversation with author.

25. Benjamin Nelson, conversation with author.

26. Sidney Hook, conversation with author.

27. Louis Schneider, letter to author.

28. Liben, "Memoir," 69.

29. Benjamin Nelson, conversation with author. Cf. Wolfe, "Mind-Shaker and Mind-Sharpener," 26-28.

30. Marshall Sklare, *America's Jews* (New York, 1971), 159.

31. *DJ*, 144, 148; Hook, "Cohen as Teacher," 91; Richard B. Morris, quoted in *Portrait*, 96; and Robert I. Wolff, "A Tribute from a Student of Physics," *Tribute*, 99.

32. B. H. Haggin, Letter to Editor, *Commentary* XLI (March 1966), 26; B. H. Haggin, letter to author, July 8, 1974. Haggin's letter to *Commentary* was prompted by Liben's uncritical "Memoir," previously cited. Cf. Liben's angry response to Haggin, *Commentary* XLI (April 1966), 16-18.

33. Lewis Feuer, conversation with author.

34. Paul Goodman, conversation with author.

35. Paul Goodman, conversation with author.

36. Kolodny and Isaacs, "We Remember," 18. A similar comment was made by Lloyd Rodwin (letter to author, August 22, 1974).

37. Liben, "Memoir," 68. A similar comment was made by Leo Barnes (letter to author, July 27, 1974). Cf. the editorial published after Cohen's death in *Campus* (February 14, 1947), 2.

38. E.g., *DJ*, 147.

39. E.g., Benjamin Nelson, conversation with author.

40. Of the many accounts I have received of this course, the most helpful were those of Louis Schneider (letter to author), Paul Goodman (conversation with author), Benjamin Nelson (conversation with

author), and Ernest Nagel (conversation with author).

41. Arnold's dictum can be found, for example, in "Literature and Science," in his *Discourses in America* (London, 1885), 643.

42. Benjamin Nelson had such an exchange with Cohen; Paul Goodman overheard another almost exactly like it. Cf. MRC, letter to editor, *NR* L (1927), 20-21.

43. The portrait, by Joseph Margulies, hangs today at City College. It was reproduced as the frontispiece in *Tribute*, and again on the dust-jacket of *Portrait*. The significance of the portrait as a metaphor for Cohen's view of the scholar's role in society has been noted by Gabriel Kolko, "Morris R. Cohen: The Scholar and/or Society," *American Quarterly* IX (1957), 327.

44. Goodman, conversation with author. Cf. the dedication of Goodman's *The Structure of Literature* (Chicago, 1954). Cf. also Paul Weiss, "Persons, Places, and Things," in Institute for Religious and Social Studies, *Moments of Personal Discovery* (New York, 1952), 51.

45. *DJ*, 146-147.

46. *DJ*, 146.

47. *DJ*, 146. Cf. MRC, "Philosophy in the Modern Curriculum," *City College Quarterly* XVII (1921), 9 (*FL*, 413).

48. MRC, "Address," in *Tribute*, 80.

49. MRC, "Philosophy in Modern Curriculum," 9 (*FL*, 413).

50. E.g., MRC to Holmes, March 7, 1934, in *Portrait*, 360; Diary, July 4, 1938, in *DJ*, 274; undated note in *DJ*, 270. Cf. the confession of Paul Weiss that Cohen's effect on him was to quicken thought but to "stop the imagination" ("Persons, Places and Things," 52).

51. Sidney Hook, "Some Memories of John Dewey, 1859-1952," *Commentary* XIV (1952), 252; Nagel, conversation with author.

52. See Cohen's "The Faith of a Logician," in George P. Adams and William P. Montague, eds., *Contemporary American Philosophy* (New York, 1930), I, 222-247 (*SPS*, 3-32).

53. As described, e.g., in *Portrait*, 125.

54. MRC, "Philosophy," *Monroe's Cyclopedia of Education*, 685-696; MRC, "The Conception of Philosophy," 409 (*SPS*, 47).

55. For the use of Garman to represent this type see Laurence R. Vey-

sey, *The Emergence of the American University* (Chicago, 1965), 226-227.

56. *DJ*, 146.

57. See, e.g., Jerome Frank to MRC, April 2, 1931, in Frank Papers, Yale University Library.

58. Frank to MRC, June 4, 1931, Frank Papers.

59. MRC to Frank, July 3, 1931, Frank Papers.

60. MRC to Frank, July 3, 1931.

61. Frank to MRC, July 7, 1931, Frank Papers.

62. MRC to Frank, July 9, 1931, Frank Papers.

63. Frank to MRC, June 4, 1931.

64. MRC to Frank, July 26, 1931, Frank Papers.

65. MRC to Frank, September 18, 1931, Frank Papers. Cf. the unusually testy letters, Frank to MRC, November 5, 1931, and MRC to Frank, December 5, 1931, Frank Papers.

66. Frank to MRC, July 16, August 25, and November 15, 1931, Frank Papers.

67. Frank to MRC, July 16, 1931.

68. This argument is made the most clearly in Frank's eight-page letter of July 16, 1931. Cf. Frank to MRC, September 14, 1931, Frank Papers.

69. Cohen's most forthright answer on the matter of this "exception" is in MRC to Frank, July 26, 1931. Cf. MRC to Frank, September 10, 1931, Frank Papers.

70. MRC to Frank, August 23, 1931, Frank Papers.

71. See esp. MRC to Frankfurter, undated (October 1931); Cohen's notes on Frank's letter to him of December 8, 1931; and Frank to MRC, December 14, 1931, Frank Papers. Cf. Frank to MRC, October 7, 1931, and Frank to MRC, January 6, 1932, Frank Papers.

72. MRC to Frank, January 7, 1932, Frank Papers.

73. *Portrait*, 417.

74. The Holmes-Cohen letters are reprinted in *Portrait*, 313-360. Their chief historical interest is their revelation of Holmes's expressed agree-

ment with Cohen's critique of the twentieth-century historicism with which Holmes, himself, is usually identified. Cf. esp. Morton White, *Social Thought in America* (New York, 1949), 15-18, 59-75.

75. See the exchange in *Portrait*, 268-274. Cf. Cohen's complaint, a few years later, that Frankfurter had let the friendship lapse: MRC to Frankfurter, January 2, 1939, in *Portrait*, 285.

76. Learned Hand to MRC, January 15, 1916, in *Portrait*, 295.

77. Hook, conversation with author.

78. John Dewey, in *Tribute*, 19. Dewey, who was generally patient with Cohen, was sometimes enraged by what he saw as a tendency on Cohen's part to pick an argument over nothing; see, for example, Dewey's curt note to Cohen, May 25, 1922, Cohen MSS.

79. John Erskine to MRC, March 2, 1925, Cohen MSS.

80. These phrases were used, for example, by Lewis Mumford (conversation with author, Amenia, New York, June 21, 1974) and Paul Goodman (conversation with author). Cf. the opinions quoted even by Laski in letters to Holmes, e.g., January 18, 1924, and April 17, 1932, in *Holmes-Laski Letters*, I, 698; II, 1376.

81. Leonora Rosenfield (*Portrait*, 431) correctly refers to Cohen as an *animateur*.

82. MRC, "What I Believe," *Nation* CXXXIII (1931), 128; *DJ*, 174.

83. *DJ*, 146.

84. *DJ*, 146; *Time* (March 11, 1946), 42; Felix Frankfurter, review of *DJ*, in *New York Times Book Review* (March 27, 1949), 1; Wolfe, "Mind-Shaker and Mind-Sharpener," 28; Lloyd Rodwin, letter to author.

85. *DJ*, 146.

86. E.g., *RWJ*, 8.

Philosophy is written in this grand book—I mean the universe—which stands continually open to our gaze, but it cannot be understood unless one first learns to comprehend the language and interpret the characters in which it is written. It is written in the language of mathematics, and its characters are triangles, circles, and other geometrical figures, without which it is not humanly possible to understand a single word of it; without these, one is wandering about in a dark labyrinth.

Galileo Galilei

"If you deny that things are what they are, you annihilate all reason, sanity, and discourse," Morris Cohen warned the twentieth century, which seemed all-too-willing to destroy itself intellectually. Infatuated with the novel concept of universal flux, the popular and academic philosophers of the age were foolishly setting aside the clear and firm identities actually possessed by the objects of nature. As metaphysicians, they were flirting with "a chaos beyond anything in the most insane mind," a world in which "a smile could become a forest fire."[1] What historians of the period have called "the revolt against formalism" was to Cohen a "riot of anarchic mysticism";[2] the leaders of this self-destructive "liberation" would remain Cohen's favorite targets even in the 1940s. His sense of nature's rationality was profoundly outraged by Henri Bergson, William James, Ernst Mach, and Karl Pearson; it was their attack on "reason" that Cohen was most determined to repel.

When early-twentieth-century thinkers considered the perennial question of the nature and sources of intelligibility, they were caught up in the ambiguous legacy of two of the nineteenth century's most notorious conceits. First was the Victorian sense of fact, the faith that scientific knowledge was reliable by virtue of its firm connection to nature. Second was the certainty (found both in the psychological orientation of British philosophy and in the idealism of the Kantian and Hegelian traditions) that "mind" was somehow or other essential to whatever natural order humans had discovered, or could ever expect to discover. These once complementary "halves"—the objective and the subjective— had an ambiguous legacy because they began, at the end of the century, to distribute themselves differently in what had been the sphere of wholeness. Partisans of "nature" and "reality" wanted to extend objectivity, to attribute to the natural order greater independence from "mind"; they found sufficient intelligibility in the concrete and contingent reality of nature to encourage them to scorn as hopelessly abstract the more complete rationality provided in different ways by John Stuart Mill and F. H. Bradley. Their ranks eventually embraced Bergson, Bertrand Russell, and most of the philosophers who called them-

selves "realists," "naturalists," or "pragmatists," including James.
Meanwhile, there developed in other quarters a disposition to ground
concreteness not in nature, but in the consciousness of the observer: in
the formulations of scientists, not in their natural objects, do we find
the regularities of our world, insisted Mach, Pearson, and other presti-
gious scientist-philosophers. Their description of scientific knowledge as
a set of useful fictions led Henry Adams, for one, to conclude that
"Chaos was the law of nature; Order the dream of man."[3]
The two movements had gotten in each other's way in their common
drive for hardheadedness. A sense of order less all-inclusive than what
most of the dying century demanded seemed to satisfy each party, but
their contrasting discontents with abstract equilibrium created for the
new century a set of opposing iconoclasms, each justifying itself in the
name of science, yet disagreeing vehemently over essentials: What
counted as "concrete"? Where was it to be found? How much of it was
"logical"? To what extent could a reality that was concrete but not
logical remain intelligible? These questions had been opened up dramatically just before Cohen entered the discussion. The metaphysical here-
sies of nominalism and temporalism, long kept in their quiet place by
the idealists, had become respectable as a side effect of the growth of
Victorianism's confident heirs, the self-sufficient mind and the self-sufficient fact.

The notion that scientific knowledge has little to do with the actual
structure of nature was hard to ignore in the 1910s, for the assertion
was being made by people in whom great intellectual and moral authority had been vested: physicists and those philosophers who claimed
intimate familiarity with the recent developments in the natural sciences. Pierre Duhem and Henri Poincaré in Paris, Mach in Vienna, and
Pearson in London generally agreed that the statements of scientists,
including Newton, were most appropriately regarded as succinct con-
structions of the mind. Duhem, for example, announced that the bodies
on which the laws of physics are constructed "are formed from abstract
and ideal matter defined by the principles of the cosmology favored by

the physicists"; such bodies are "in no wise similar to the visible and concrete bodies we observe and manipulate every day."[4] These reflections antedated the proposal by Einstein of a viable alternative to classical mechanics; as Charles C. Gillispie has said of Mach, "it was not the laws of Newtonian physics which he questioned, but their existential value; not the principle of inertia, the citadel of classical physics, but its attribution to matter as an intrinsic property independent of measurements and specifications of reference." This disposition was reinforced by the increased recognition around the turn of the century that the explanation of several recent experiments would require a reorganization of all physical theory: when the laws of nature suddenly changed, it was harder to resist the suspicion that they were merely "conventions." Moreover, insofar as the philosophical atmosphere around physics included a vision of "nature"—an entity made so remote by epistemological preoccupations—it was explicitly a vision of radical contingency, and implicitly one of nominalism. One "law" after another was allotted a smaller and smaller dominion, and whatever logical order one professed to find in the physical world had to be of an increasingly sophisticated variety. This was even more the case after Einstein "wrenched the common consciousness" with the relativity of time.[5]

The potentially nominalistic implications of the new philosophy of physics were considerably more disturbing to Cohen than to most of the other American intellectuals who took notice. Cohen wanted to employ scientific knowledge and scientific method as the foundations of a general world view, but the texts of Duhem and Poincaré were more readily assimilated into a religionist's denigration of the pretensions of science. Duhem himself was a devout Catholic, and it became common for American and European Christians to embrace the clichés of science's retrenchment as evidence that religion's role in giving order to the world remained indispensable.[6] Cohen no doubt agreed with the *Nation* that "young minds" might be adversely affected by the image of the physicist "reveling wildly" in the freedom of a discipline that suddenly couldn't tell fact from fancy, but his stake in the reliability of scientific knowledge was too great to let him stop, like the *Nation*, at wistful reminiscences about the days when scientists dealt in "knowledge untainted by human passion."[7] Cohen would show that the examples of physics proved as much as ever that "logic holds of nature"; he would defend the scientific intellect against the charges of "subjectivism," even if the indictment had come in the form of a confession.

Cohen's desire to ground meanings in something outside the subject was shared by the party of Reality, the diverse members of which emphasized the authenticity of whatever intelligibility was found in nature. But this camp in the 1910s was really divided in three, there being so little agreement about the nature of the known. Bergson's "vitalism" depicted the object of knowledge as a temporal flux, which made sense emotionally but not in the limited terms conventionally applied to it by intellect. The "realism" of Russell and G. E. Moore affirmed the objectivity of particular entities of commonsense understanding, logically defined. The "pragmatism" of John Dewey and his followers grounded meanings in contingent, temporal conditions, but retained a view of what was "really there" more akin to the common sense of the realists than to the overt anti-intellectualism of the vitalists. A force behind all three movements was the ubiquitous James, prophet of pragmatism, Bergson's most influential champion in America, and author of the legendary paper of 1904 ("Does Consciousness Exist?") that inspired young American realists in much the same fashion as Moore's more famous "Refutation of Idealism" inaugurated British realism.[8]

Cohen's attitude toward Bergson and all his works was one of simple and absolute antipathy. What most infuriated him about James, even, was the latter's sympathy for Bergson's blunt denial that the formulations of logic could apply to a world in flux. Bergson claimed for every natural event a distinctness so radical that its character would be falsified by the application to it of intellectual categories derived from the experience of other events.[9] Bergson fulfilled the vision of Heraclitus, and there was no surer way to become Cohen's bête noir than to make all reality into an unpredictable, flowing river within which no event could repeat itself.

The enthusiasm of educated Americans for Bergson only made his philosophy seem more dangerous to Cohen, and more in need of refutation. Two years after Bergson visited New York in 1913, Cohen still fumed about the Frenchman's triumphant reception, during which members of the well-to-do public created a then-rare traffic jam around Columbia University, where Bergson was to speak.[10] Journalists hailed him as a guide to a richer, more authentic experience of reality; the young Walter Lippmann thanked Bergson for making available a world beyond science, a world of "fragrance," "rhythm," and "perplexing novelty."[11] When Santayana sought in 1913 to depict the "romantic anarchy" that defined "The Intellectual Temper of the Age," he found at its core the "scatterbrained" school of Bergson.[12]

Although Bergson was not without advocates within the American Philosophical Association,[13] academic philosophers of Cohen's generation were more drawn to pragmatism or realism. These were the colleagues Cohen chastised at New Haven in 1909 for their conception of philosophy; it was *their* interest in the dynamic and concrete that Cohen found excessive, *their* revolt against the nineteenth century—not Bergson's or Pearson's—that Cohen explicitly faulted. Cohen's relationship with the pragmatists and realists was as complicated as his abhorrence of Bergson and Pearson was simple. He accepted the terms of discussion as proposed by the idealists: Would not the pragmatists and the realists rob the universe of its orderly structure? Yet he saw the realists as potential allies in his struggle to establish a rationalistic world view trimmed of the epistemological, religious, and social associations of idealism. Cohen's metaphysics got under way as a simultaneous attempt to refute the positivists and the vitalists, to castigate the pragmatists for a temporalism too close to Bergson's, and to turn the considerable polemical energies of the American realists *from* their preoccupation with the objectivity of particular physical objects *toward* a more explicit affirmation of the objectivity of abstract, logical structures in the texture of nature. What the American realists did and did not say was therefore the technical context in which Cohen formulated his metaphysics.

What *The New Realism* stood for was formidably detailed in a volume of that title authored in 1912 by six young philosophers, of whom Ralph Barton Perry, E. B. Holt, and W. P. Montague were destined to become the most well-known.[14] The exceptional rigor of this volume won Cohen's admiration, and cut an intimidating swath in a field where none but Royce (Peirce, a social outcast, was not really part of the professional community) had so deftly employed logical analysis to root out obscurity. The new realists were determined to destroy idealism as an epistemology: the unifying claim of the collection was the independence of the object from any kind of "mind." As a careful historian of the movement has pointed out, the new realists' defense of this claim amounted to the argument that relations are autonomous objects in the same sense that the knower and the known are distinct entities. Neither the knower nor the known can in any way be "constituted by" its opposite in the "knowledge relation."[15]

Cohen's review of *The New Realism* for the *Journal of Philosophy* praised the relentless antisubjectivism of the contributors and tried to elucidate the metaphysical implications that were overshadowed by the volume's preoccupation with a technical analysis of the epistemological problem. The new realists had in fact said very little about the nature of the known, and what was said differed considerably from philosopher to philosopher, but Cohen brought out their common opposition to Bergson's temporalism and insisted on seeing "nominalism" (a word he admitted was never used in the text) as the most deserving casualty of new-realist metaphysics.

Cohen made the new realists serve his purposes by slighting a distinction they had made between "existence" and "subsistence": the former term described the ontological status of, the sort of "being" enjoyed by, objects of sense; the latter did the same for abstractions. The category of "subsistence" was crucial to the new realists, for with it they could affirm the nonmental character of the "relations" (abstract, of course) that obtained between the knower and the physical objects that constituted the known. The reality Cohen most wanted to be "realis-

tic" about was constituted by the logical abstractions that relate things
and that (in his view, as he made clear very soon) *define* physical objects; hence the conditional objectivity granted to abstractions by the
new realists as a tactic in the defense of the unconditional objectivity of
physical entities was ironically the movement's strongest drawing card
for Cohen. He minimized the distinction between the mathematical and
physical, declared that mathematical entities "certainly have as much
being as physical entities do," and took his would-be allies to task for
not understanding who their real friends and enemies were: when epistemology is put aside, he announced, the new realists were very close
to Royce in their affirmation of the ontological status of abstractions.
The enemy, Cohen said, was "dualistic or psychologic pragmatism,"
according to which "objects of thought" are denied "the ontological
status of objects of sense." He would urge the new realists to give up
their generational revolt and go after the nominalists among their fellow
insurgents.[16]

The cause for which Cohen was trying to recruit the new realists became more explicit in the course of a two-year battle with Arthur O.
Lovejoy in the pages of the *Journal.* The dispute was occasioned by
Lovejoy's casual reference to "the physicist's doctrine" that most of
the sensible attributes of matter are "subjective." Lovejoy had used this
illustration from science to remind the new realists of the classical dilemma of epistemological realism: the problem of error. Some qualities
of an object remain the same however we look at it; they are "primary"
to it. But objects persistently manifest "secondary qualities," characteristics that are perceived differently by different observers. This relativity of secondary qualities "is taken by science as an evidence of their
subjectivity," said Lovejoy, who believed that the relativity of some
kinds of knowledge exposed the new realism as epistemologically
naive.[17] Cohen saw nominalism in Lovejoy's assertion that whatever
may be the status of an object's weight and mass, its color and shape
are functions of a given subject's peculiar relation to that object. What
nettled Cohen into sustained public anger, however, was Lovejoy's use

of examples from *science* to support this implicit nominalism.

Cohen replied that the category of subjectivity was irrelevant to science,[18] and when Lovejoy in turn challenged him to dispense with it in a philosophical account of the role of "secondary qualities" in science or in general,[19] Cohen rejected the distinction between the "qualities" and the "relations" of a thing. He took Lovejoy to task for believing in the "ghost of the ding-an-sich"; he explained that Lovejoy's "qualities"—primary as well as secondary—were ultimately functions of relations.[20] At this point the new realists sensed that Cohen was a dubious ally; he was extending their concept of "relations" too far. Montague called him a "serpent" who would entrap the new realists and drive them into the wilderness.[21] What was becoming of the hard-and-fast objects whose "independence" the new realists had been trying to establish? The realist "craves a world of objects which have each *some* intrinsic and solid character," Lovejoy observed, not a world in which objects "endlessly deliquesce into mere relations to other things, themselves equally characterless and elusive."[22] Just what sort of reality was Cohen trying to be "realistic" about?

Cohen answered that most philosophers, including the new realists, were foolishly "prescientific" in their attempts to make concrete commonsense entities the ground of intelligibility. In the "clarified vision" of science, matter sheds "its isolated self-sufficiency and becomes a vortex or strain in the universal ether, or a group of electric charges." Ontological good sense therefore begins with "the relational structure of things," with the formal, not the material aspects of things. An intelligible "thing" derives its nature from a context or system, from the various relations in which it participates: a banker is a banker so long as he "issues credit or receives deposits," so long, in other words, as he has certain relations with certain other entities. The "thing" that is our neighbor may be a banker, and may have other "qualities" such as being modest or tall, or simply being our neighbor, but these attributes are to be understood as functions of relationships with other, similarly constituted "things." Cohen believed that all "things," including those

made up of what Lovejoy called "primary qualities," were subject to
changing relationships; hence any "realism" that established the "independence" of commonsense entities was still too temporal and too
nominalistic. Cohen's realism would give order to this flux: the "trans-
formations" that "things" experience follow certain invariant "rules,"
he declared, "the objects of pure mathematics and logic." His realism
would therefore be a *logical* realism, a metaphysics that would make
abstractions as "real" as atoms in order that meanings might be an-
chored in a formal yet nonmental stratum of being. The propositions of
logic and mathematics refer to "invariant relations" that constitute, not
simply the mind of man, but "the very heart of the nature of things."[23]

Cohen's attempts to defend and modify the new realism were informed by his reading of Bertrand Russell's *Principles of Mathematics.*
This book made Russell into Cohen's acknowledged "philosophic Al-
lah," in that it gave him a philosophical justification for his vision of
nature.[24] Cohen's "logical realism" derived directly from two aspects
of Russell's work, its Platonic theory of meaning and its demonstration
that logic and mathematics are ultimately the same thing.

When Russell wrote the *Principles* in 1903, he believed that every
meaningful statement was a statement about something, was "denotative." This included statements in logic, for Russell accepted the existence of intangibles as well as tangibles. Thus, to use the favorite example
of philosophers, statements about "the present king of France" are not
prevented from having meaning because France has no king. Rather, it
is understood that "the present king of France" has an intangible *existence*—a Platonic existence—in the realm of essences. As this applies to
logic and mathematics, one can say that "an implication," or "a class,"
exists as an abstraction; it is not necessary to talk about a particular
implication in order to be denotative.[25] By 1905 Russell had simply
"decided," as D. F. Pears has put it, "not to postulate that other
world" where dragons, implications, and the present king of France
reside.[26] Russell was content to justify his decision chiefly on the
grounds of his "sense of reality,"[27] something not shared by Cohen,

who had read the original Russell as a welcome demonstration that logic "constitutes a part of the real world as well as the world of thought."[28] Intelligibility would not be preserved, for Cohen, by some immediately sensible, perhaps abrasive and contingent, set of objects; but now the identity of things could be abstract while remaining "natural" and "real." Such was the promise of Platonism when found in the special company of logic and mathematics, and unencumbered by the epistemological "subjectivism"—as Cohen would say—of the idealists and of Russell's later philosophy.

The importance of the *Principles of Mathematics* in the history of philosophy followed from its argument that logic and mathematics are one. Prior to 1903 it was conventionally held that logic and mathematics were distinct, that mathematical propositions were "synthetic" while logical propositions were "analytic." According to the synthetic-analytic distinction, mathematics was generated by contact with the contingent world; it produced *knowledge* by making potentially verifiable assertions about the world. The propositions of logic, by contrast, were absolutely "necessary," were truths that could be neither confirmed nor denied by contact with anything outside of themselves. Logic, whether or not regarded Platonically, was not taken to be an element of the same world that generated mathematics. Logic was unequivocally a priori, mathematics a posteriori. Russell's demonstration that mathematics reduced to logic suddenly made the technical apparatus of mathematics relevant to philosophical problems formerly pursued without regard to mathematics.[29] Some philosophers then accepted mathematics along with logic as "analytic," and rejected, as Russell himself was to do, the Platonic interpretation of both. Cohen did the opposite; he set out to establish the objectivity, the "denotative" character, of all analytic truths.

The relation of these denotative analytic truths to the reality studied by contemporary physicists was, of course, important to Cohen, for physics had given oblique support to the generalized "subjectivism" and "nominalism" against which he sought to mobilize the new realists more effectively. He tried to indicate his view of this crucial relationship in a paper first presented in 1911, "Mechanism and Causality in Physics."[30] Studded with friendly references to Duhem, Poincaré, Einstein, and other luminaries of both the philosophical and scientific movement against classical mechanics, the paper attacked the ignorance and tender-mindedness of the older physics, according to which the laws of nature control the movement of particles "with absolute accuracy for the smallest atom as well as for the largest cluster." Cohen stoically endorsed the stark modern view which replaced "the classic notion of absolutely uniform causation" with "the more modest doctrine of statistical averages." In his most grandiose maneuver, he praised the most formidable of skeptics, David Hume, for doubting that any single event can cause another event. We can now go even farther than Hume, he insisted, for "modern physics suggests that the laws of nature which do correlate these events are themselves contingent, in the sense that they are known to be true only within the limits of observation, and may perhaps not prevail outside the infinitesimal portion of the universe whose surface we have scratched."[31]

There Cohen was, out in the "dark and boundless seas of being," but before the essay was done he revealed that he had a chart after all. Hume's insight, and modern physics generally, had been wrongly taken by "empiricists" to deny that "the logically necessary relations which hold between mathematical expressions hold of phenomena themselves." What the empiricists deny is in fact the "fundamental assumption" of all science. Cohen would allow Mach to say that a scientific concept is an "expedient," or an "invention," so long as everyone understood that any such "expedient" can fairly represent its object only because relations between the expedient's parts "are precisely those between the corresponding parts of the object represented." Even if the likeness of antecedent situations—so-called "identical" events—are a matter of degree, genuine similarities *do* exist; a "law" of nature is still a law, even if "only statistically true." The nominalists and the subjectivists were simply refusing to look at an obvious "fact"; "after all nature does behave in conformity with logical and mathematical principles."[32]

Einstein did not shake Cohen's faith. In the early 1920s, when so many nonphysicists saw only metaphysical fragmentation in Einstein's theories of relativity, Cohen assured the readers of the *New Republic* that the general theory of relativity established the "absoluteness of the laws of nature."[33] This was by no means an incorrect inference; the most thorough historian of the popular controversy over Einstein has found Cohen to be one of the most sophisticated and careful contributors to the discussion.[34] The term "relativity" had the unfortunate effect, explained Cohen, of obscuring what was really important about Einstein's discovery, which was its revelation that the laws of nature hold absolutely "for all possible systems of measurement." Einstein had given a "deathblow" to the old formalism's sense of space and time as "empty forms or vessels existing independently of, and possibly prior to, their material contents," but the fact that every physical system can now be said to "have its own time and space" does not deprive the theory that explains this diversity of its coherence and reality. Indeed, Einstein's theory "establishes a universal time and space" by providing formulas "for correlating all possible physical systems." The layman should not be bewildered by the "profusion of different rates and places, time rates and velocities," for all "can be readily and simply harmonized" by formulas, "just as we harmonize different accounts in yards and meters, or in dollars and pounds sterling."[35] Cohen thus handled Einstein's views by defining them, in effect, as just one more species of the larger genus of scientific theories that seem to do their job. If one theory better explains nature than another, we adopt that theory, and there is no reason to doubt that it works since nature corresponds to it. Hence the *specific characteristics* of a theory are less important than its status as a viable *theory*: dollars and pounds are both currency, so why get upset when we have to switch from one to the other?

Cohen's discussions of physics were part of his attempt to clarify and defend his claim that nonmental, logical invariants were both intrinsic to nature and compatible with the radical contingency of the physical world. The clarification and defense of this claim was the most specific and sustained goal of all of his work in metaphysics, from these early, halting efforts through the very end of his career. As his debate with Lovejoy and his discussions of physics showed, there was much to be clarified. If the nonmental world includes both permanence and change, both invariant logic and contingent matter, just how are these two modes of being related to each other, and what are the parameters of each? It was all right for a sage to observe that logic and history may "involve" each other,[36] but a philosopher is expected to specify exactly how.

When Cohen set out to do serious metaphysics in the late 1910s and 1920s, he acknowledged two starting points: (1) the classical distinction between abstract form and material content, and (2) the post-Kantian assumption that "material content" is by definition an order of contingency. He of course rejected the Kantian corollary that analytic truths are mental; he tried to make plausible the view that the orders of logical necessity and of material contingency are distinct, yet interdependent and equally intrinsic to nature. The reality mirrored in formal logic is not temporal, he explained; it is the very structure of possibility within which all temporal objects are constituted and transformed. He sought to depict the relation of the logical order to the temporal order in terms of the subject matter of learned disciplines: the truths of any specialized science are "factual" and "material" because they are grounded in assumptions about *certain* objects—objects occupying time and space—while the truths of formal logic are grounded in what we have learned to be the limits of *all* possible systems of temporal objects. The general truths of formal logic are nonetheless "integral" to the particular truths of physics, or of any special science, because the bodies to which the particular truths refer must exist and interact on terms provided by the reality that generates the truths of formal logic. More-

over, when the laws of a given science change, "it can only be in reference to something else which is constant in relation to them," namely,
the "invariant laws according to which the changes take place."[37]
Cohen further illustrated his two-level ontology with an analysis of
concepts. In contrast to the view that concepts are general images, or
sums of abstract characteristics, he held that concepts are "signs" pointing to "invariant relations," and those relations are either abstract, as in
formal logic, or intrinsic to some segment of temporal reality, as in the
special sciences. The relations denoted by concepts "remain identical
despite the variations of the material in which they are embodied";
hence they "enable us to arrange in order and hold together diverse
phenomena, because of some real unity of process or relation which
constitutes an element of identity between them." James and Bergson
did not know what they were talking about when they condemned
concepts as too "static and fixed" to grasp a changing and growing reality; the mathematical concepts of science denote "the pattern of
these changes and the invariant characteristics which make things keep
their identity throughout the change."[38]

Yet the definiteness of the invariant relations denoted by concepts
varies greatly, Cohen added, as he tried to account for the fact that so
much of experience seems to refute the logician's law of contradiction.
The word "logical" had become a term of opprobrium in some quarters
because, Cohen admitted, logic's apparent insistence that "A is A," etc.,
was taken to be oblivious to the experience of "twilight zones," in
which it cannot be said that a man is definitely dead or still alive, that a
thing is warm or cold, or that day has become night. These twilight
zones do not exist in the reality studied by formal logic, Cohen observed, but they are so real in the temporal world that our concepts
must refer to "different degrees of definiteness." Nature "obeys the
laws of logic" to the extent that it is "determined" by the operations
our logical concepts denote, but nature includes "indetermination" as
well.[39]

Cohen's discussion of "determination" and "indetermination," like so much of his attempt to work out an ontology, stopped exasperatingly short of the extended, systematic treatment that might have clarified, for example, the criteria by which one is to judge the degree to which an object in nature is "determinate." Although he borrowed here and there from Plato, Aristotle, Hegel, Kant, Russell, and Peirce, Cohen chose not to give a very detailed account of how his ontology followed or differed from that of previous philosophers who had believed, like him, that permanence and change, form and matter, logic and history, are both real and, in some sense or other, interdependent. In one paper, at least, Cohen went so far as to identify his own outlook with that of Spinoza, and in so doing he produced his least ambiguous account of invariance and contingency.

"Amor Dei Intellectualis" endorsed what Cohen characterized as Spinoza's "constant distinction between time or duration as a category of existence and eternity as a category of essence or meaning." "Eternity" had become Cohen's word for the logical order, and eternity was understood as "not subject to the processes of material change of which time is the measure." The constants of being are thus not simply "invariant," but eternal, and their function is unambiguously to provide *meaning*. The "distinctive error of modern metaphysics" is "the false elevation of time . . . into the sufficient condition of all meanings." Time, to be sure, is a "necessary condition or aspect of all existent things," but Spinoza rightly brought about the "subordination of time to eternity."

By taking mathematical method seriously Spinoza was able to maintain . . . that universals, meanings, or essences (laws, in ultramodern language) unite infinitely different existing terms, but do not form additional particulars, and are not, therefore, subject to the temporal changes of such terms. To see things "under the aspect of eternity"– *sub specie aeternitatis*–is to see their actual meaning. All existing terms are bodies subject to change and therefore located in the time series. But if the whole time order has any meaning at all, the order of meaning includes it and is not exhausted by it.[40]

There could be no doubt now that Cohen's rationalism was "classical," that he did believe the world could be divided into halves of logical meaning and temporal flux, that however much he acknowledged the reality of the temporal, he was a worshiper of logic and a defender of its metaphysical priority over the temporal. The "eternal," he pointedly remarked, is not to be confused with the "everlasting," which for him denoted any elements *within* space and time that happen to endure.[41] Cohen saw no contradiction between this vision and the new physics because he did not consider eternality to be a *spatial* property. Cohen understood that, according to contemporary physics, the identity of a thing in space-time was a "continuity of motion," in the words of Milič Čapek, a "trajectory" that is "continuous in its relation to other phenomena." Cohen's geometric metaphors made it seem that he had introduced a de facto absolute space into his vision of nature, but he, unlike those who saw a spatial implication in all discourse about "being" as opposed to "becoming," believed his "eternity" was an order that both included and transcended the entire space-time continuum.[42]

His "general enterprise of rehabilitating the eternal," as Lovejoy referred in 1924 to Cohen's ongoing metaphysical endeavors,[43] was almost as dramatically counter to contemporary trends as he himself implied it was. While Bergson no longer got much attention from philosophers, or from the educated public, James remained popular, and the "Chicago pragmatism" of Dewey and his followers had become extremely influential in the 1920s. Dewey popularized the view that meanings are never functions of a "timeless spiritual ghost," nor of a "pale logical substance," but are products of a temporal "situation." Whatever in a situation could not be clearly designated as physical or psychical was defined by instrumentalism as social. Logic, said Harold Chapman Brown, "has its inception in social conditions and its justification in the fulfillment of social needs." As for the view that continuities in experience reveal something about the structure of being, George Herbert Mead spoke for a generation unwilling to let meanings escape their existential conditions: universals "derive their significance" from "social acts," and "really amount to" nothing beyond "more or less identical" ways of acting "in an indefinite number of particular situations."[44] The relentlessness with which Dewey and his associates grounded meanings in contingent physical, psychic, or social conditions went beyond what was then being said by philosophers in the realist and idealist traditions, but the gradual temporalizing of these two movements was in fact a major development in American metaphysics between the mid-1910s and 1930. The new realists dissolved, partly because the appeal of temporalism lured Ralph Barton Perry and E. B. Holt toward the claim that meanings were grounded not in relations, but in behavior. Later realists, notably those in the much-discussed "critical realist" movement, moved more explicitly toward the view expressed for them by A. K. Rogers: the first principle of a sound metaphysics is that "man is a being who lives in time . . . whose experience is incurably and fundamentally a temporal one."[45] Cohen's old sparring partner, Lovejoy, became adamantly all-temporal in the 1920s; he took specific and persistent issue with Cohen's position as stated in "Amor Dei Intellectualis," and outlined a metaphysics of his own in which objects with a great degree of sameness—for example, two newly minted coins—were painstakingly shown to be too different from one another to support the reality of universals.[46] The idealists, meanwhile, having long been concerned to contain change within the whole, moved toward the localization and particularization of "the whole" in time and space. While it had once been fashionable to exalt the Absolute for its ability to put the temporal in its place, it finally became necessary to defend the Absolute on the basis of its compatibility with the temporal.[47] Much of the official metaphysics remained the same, with meanings grounded in cosmic structure, but cosmic structure came to be described as a series of temporal functions. "Nature," announced a leading idealist in 1930, "is what it does."[48]

Just as this wave of temporalism crested in the United States, Cohen threw up his most massive and well-buttressed containing wall. *Reason and Nature*, appearing in 1931, endorsed the "medieval and Chinese" preference for "order" over "expansion," and expressed an impatience with the "dynamic," the "evolutionary," and the "progressive."[49] Almost simultaneously, Cohen was provided with four important forums for outlining his denunciation of the age. He preached "invariance" and "balance" in his presidential address to the Eastern Division of the American Philosophical Association, in his contribution to the *Nation*'s "What I Believe" series, in his critique of "Life, Experience, and Reality" for the *New Republic*, and in *Contemporary American Philosophy*, an important anthology in which leading philosophers outlined their world views.[50] These widely circulated papers made no new technical contributions, but they helped bring Cohen's reputation to its peak, and they functioned as advertisements for the long-awaited *Reason and Nature*.

Considered as formal metaphysics, however, *Reason and Nature* did not offer much beyond what its author had said before. Many of Cohen's previous papers were reprinted here,[51] and the book's "new" sections were of scant help in determining exactly how Cohen believed his ontology and his theory of meaning could be justified. At least Cohen acknowledged the closeness of his views to those of the greatest of the absolute idealists, F. H. Bradley. Once he had rejected unequivocally Bradley's mentalism, Cohen could critically employ Bradley's concept of "the Absolute" to express his own vision of the natural order. The presupposition of a "completed rational system" is necessary to science, and "coincides in part with the Bradleyan Absolute" insofar as the latter is taken as an "ideal limit" on what can happen in space and time. By contrast, the more distinctly Bradleyan view that an "absolutely total universe" *causes* its constituent parts to have this or that character must be rejected, for the causes of things are much more complicated than that, and there is no way consistent with science for us to ascribe to the universe as a whole a character definite enough to provide for the *determination* of all the things that we know, in fact, to be constituent parts of the universe.[52] As for what *is* the nature of things, as for exactly how the eternal order goes beyond its function as an "ideal limit" to interact on a more substantive basis with the contingent order, Cohen now enunciated and integrated three principles that had, in fact, informed his writings about nature since before 1914: the principle of sufficient reason, the principle of invariance, and the principle of polarity.

"Everything is connected in definite ways with definite other things, so that its full nature is not revealed except by its position and relations within a system." This is the "principle of sufficient reason," one of the points Cohen had sought to defend against Lovejoy in the early 1910s, but this time around he avoided the quicksands of technical discourse: he said nothing about what distinguished a "thing" from a "relation" or a "quality." Nor did he clarify what he meant by "system." Instead, he contented himself with the assertion that the principle of causality is merely "a special instance or application to temporal events" of the principle of sufficient reason, and with an attempted demonstration that causality and sufficient reason were compatible with temporal contingency and discontinuity. The latter demonstration consisted chiefly of the observation that even the most "mechanical forces" cannot be expected to operate "except on some given distribution of material particles," whose contingency is "as ultimate as the existence of the laws" that explain their operation.[53]

The "nature" of anything, Cohen went on, *is* the "group of invariant characters" that maintain the identity of an object "in the stream of change." These invariants are the "actual universals" that give form to matter, that constitute the "intelligible substance of things." For clarification and defense of his principle of invariance, he relied primarily on a condemnation of the "banal shibboleth" that "everything is pure change and nothing else." On the contrary, "Changes cannot have any definite character without repetition of identical pattern in different material." Now as always, Cohen thought the most formidable threat to his principle of invariance arose not from its own metaphysical ambiguity, but from the epistemological subjectivism of his enemies. He therefore resorted once more to his traditional affirmation of the "reality" of abstractions and universals.[54]

Cohen hoped that any remaining lacunae in his account of the relation between logic (form, meaning, law, invariance, eternity, etc.) and history (flux, temporality, contingency, matter, indetermination, etc.) would be disposed of with the "principle of polarity." This principle, which was to become the most-discussed of his ideas about nature, was spelled out in *Reason and Nature* as follows:

Opposites such as immediacy and mediation, unity and plurality, the fixed and the flux, substance and function, ideal and real, actual and possible, etc., like the north (positive) and the south (negative) poles of a magnet, all involve each other when applied to any significant entity.[55]

This principle represented what was "sound in the Hegelian dialectic without the indecent confusion at which we arrive if we violate the principle of contradiction and try to wipe out the distinctions of understanding." Polarity allows us to see that "being and nonbeing . . . are always opposed and never identical, though all determination involves both affirmation and negation." Polarity enables us to transcend apparent contradictions by making distinctions between the sphere in which, for example, one can eat one's cake, and that in which one can "yet have it too." Many alleged antinomies dissolve if we find "the proper distinction," such as that between crossing a river by swimming and crossing by boat: "the invention of boats enabled us to eliminate a former impossibility—namely, how to cross a river without getting wet."[56]

Cohen's favorite illustrations of the principle of polarity, both before and after it was so named, were the two blades of a pair of scissors and the two poles of a magnet (or of the earth itself). These metaphors embodied a sense of harmonious interaction and interdependence; it was, of course, the figure of the magnet that medieval men conventionally employed to express their faith in the harmony of cosmic forces. But if the solution's metaphor was the magnet, the problem's metaphor was the coachman: Cohen's first formal statement of the "principle of polarity" explicitly invoked "the necessity of applying a brake when going downhill."[57] Inertia and stampede, invariance and flux—these basic tensions were to be contained and controlled by the principle of polarity, the marrow of Cohen's entire vision of nature. Any thinker's work entails, obviously, an interaction between his psychological disposition and the forms of thought available to him, but rarely in a metaphysician is this process so open to view as in Cohen's case. The formal setting of argument and counterargument obviously put Cohen in a position where the idea of polarity could be of use to him, but this idea—and, indeed, the problem of logic and history to which it was an attempted answer— served psychological needs as well. Cohen, who at the age of eighteen had yearned for "a magnetic opposite," now tried as a mature philosopher to make certain that no significant entity in the universe would be left to drift about, unrestrained and unfulfilled.[58]

Although Cohen credited Felix Adler and Wilmon Sheldon with teaching him that "the nature of things depends upon the equilibrium of opposing forces," and that one should therefore "reason from opposing considerations,"[59] Cohen's decision to denote this view with the term "polarity" was probably prompted by Emerson, with whose *Essays* Cohen was quite familiar.[60] In "Compensation," Emerson insists that "POLARITY" resides in "every part of nature":

Superinduce magnetism at one end of a needle; the opposite magnetism takes place at the other end. If the South attracts, the North repels. . . . An inevitable dualism bisects nature, so that each thing is a half, and suggests another thing to make it whole: as spirit, matter; man, woman; odd, even; subjective, objective; in, out; upper, under; motion, rest; yea, nay.[61]

Cohen's eventual formalization of and reliance upon "the principle of polarity" in *Reason and Nature* bespeaks dramatically his difficulties in clarifying and justifying his metaphysical claims. He would simply depict form's relation to matter as "involvement": each side of a polarity was real, yet dependent upon its opposite. Cohen hoped that, however thin his principle might appear in the abstract, it would gain substance in the context of specific problems.[62] With this in mind, he offered most of *Reason and Nature* as a set of demonstrations, in one field after another, that neither absolute fixity nor absolute change characterizes the reality studied by physicists, biologists, psychologists, and social scientists, or the reality dealt with by jurists and political agents.

Reason and Nature's chapter on physics is a slightly revised version of "Mechanism and Causality in Physics," written first in 1911 and published in 1918. This paper and the new contributions on biology and psychology all follow the same pattern: an all-inclusive mechanistic position is contrasted to an extreme emphasis on contingency and novelty, each position is accused of narrow-minded reductionism, and the truth is alleged to include the insights of each. Law and contingency are both real aspects of physical, biological, and psychic nature, and the fact that intelligibility in each is a function of invariant relations in no way eliminates contingency from the field. But since "in the sane life" things must be "related to each other," we ought to concentrate on continuity; hence the errors of the party of law and mechanism in each discipline are less reprehensible than the errors of the party of flux.[63]

The publication of *Reason and Nature* occasioned widespread discussion of Cohen's views; finally, the hated "temporalists" had a book of his to review. Having waited for the volume since Cohen's 1918 announcement that it would be along presently,[64] and having had to content themselves with more or less private attacks on him at the annual meetings of the American Philosophical Association, Cohen's long-suffering victims among professional metaphysicians were at last to have their day. John Dewey himself, whose work at least one other reviewer took to be the "obvious" target of *Reason and Nature*,[65] discussed Cohen's magnum opus cautiously in the *New Republic*, mixing praise of Cohen's learning with the complaint that he won easy victories by setting up straw men. Predictably, Dewey doubted that Cohen really cared about the "interplay" of law and contingency: his sense that the "nature" of a thing was its logical aspect sidestepped the "crucial issue" of whether the logical forms we find in nature are "conditioned by" temporal existence. It was too bad, Dewey observed, that Cohen offered no arguments in support of his beliefs.[66]

A more extended critique along Dewey's lines was provided for the *Journal of Philosophy* by Cohen's admirer and former student Sidney Hook, who declared, somewhat incredulously, that Cohen "seems to introduce an ontological separation between change and eternity, history and logic." His "systematic disregard of the pervasive temporal character of existence" amounts to the denial of "genuine novelty or time," complained Hook, who linked Cohen with the ancient idealist dream of the world as "one systematic interrelated whole." Explicitly defending the temporalism Cohen had attacked, Hook insisted that his old mentor, the self-styled opponent of reductionism, had scandalously reduced the temporalist position to an absurdity: "He tries to make it appear that they reject all the categories of order and invariance. . . . He does not see that they try to *redefine* invariance in terms of change, tradition out of experiment, social stability out of revolution." Cohen failed to see that the principle of polarity was constantly applied by the temporalists, that the interaction of law and contingency was what modern thought was all about.[67]

The more general question philosophers asked about *Reason and Nature* was whether it had anything to do with metaphysics. One laughed at the vacuity of the principle of polarity, reminding Cohen that the matter of concern was exactly *when* a thing is in balance and when not, and just how we are to be assured that truth is midway between extremes.[68] Another found "nothing very original or very exciting," but recommended the book to social scientists, who, as a group, were badly in need of the ideal of "discriminating rationality" espoused so adamantly by Cohen.[69] The *Philosophical Review* noted that intelligibility and contingency may be real, but regretted that Cohen offered no "systematic inquiry into the conditions of either, or any frank facing . . . of the facts which point toward a more complex interpretation." Nowhere did Cohen attempt the necessary task of "pointing out under what conditions" reason characterizes nature, and under what conditions something else is dominant. "And what have we in this staunch refusal to face nature's chaos, this grim insistence that her nature is order, but wishful thinking reminiscent of the hated idealists with their comforting doctrines of a universe ultimately responsive to human needs?"[70] Hence it was put to Cohen that he was not only a mediocre metaphysician, but that he, who had so fiercely rejected the hospitality of the idealists, was in their tradition after all.

Yet even those who found fault with Cohen's technical metaphysics could see that beneath his philosophical failure there remained a large quantity of good sense. Even the anonymous reviewer for the British analytical journal *Mind* compared reading Cohen to having an enlightening "conversation" with "a very able, clear-minded, and well-informed man."[71] The problem, it seemed, was that Cohen had aimed at the wrong constituency, or, to put it more precisely, that he spoke less successfully to metaphysicians than to nonphilosophers who wanted to think some—but not too much—about metaphysics. The ostensibly technical sections of *Reason and Nature* turned out to be wise metaphysics for nonmetaphysicians.[72] Like so much of what Cohen wrote, *Reason and Nature* was less a contribution *to* philosophy than a contribution *from* it to the general cultural life of educated Americans.

The lawyer and legal scholar Jerome Frank, for example, pronounced *Reason and Nature* "the most important event of our times" in the intellectual realm; to Walter Lippmann it was "a superb book," one that kept his interest throughout the summer following its publication.[73] H. L. Mencken was greatly impressed, and reviewers for the *New York Times* and the *Nation* depicted *Reason and Nature* as a monumental episode in the history of philosophy.[74]

But Cohen was, for better or for worse, trying to justify his vision of nature in the formal court of metaphysics, and his efforts toward this end continued sporadically during the 1930s. Generally, Cohen went

over old ground[75] and scarcely deigned to respond to logical positivism, the movement that had suddenly defined the terms of most philosophical discourse in the United States. The climate of opinion changed
swiftly and decisively with the arrival—literally, since its leaders were
emigrés from Europe—of the "Vienna Circle." Broadly speaking, the
"logical positivists" were in the tradition of Mach and Pearson, whose
"nominalism" and "subjectivism" Cohen had routinely vilified during
the previous twenty years.[76] Logical positivism was a complicated
movement, but during the 1930s its complexities were less at issue than
the "verifiability theory of meaning" associated with Rudolph Carnap,
Moritz Schlick, and the movement's redoubtable propagandist, Herbert
Feigl.

The propositions of metaphysics, declared an early positivist manifesto, "are, strictly speaking, meaningless." Propositions can have
"meaning" only when they can be empirically verified, and neither the
verified "facts" nor the methods by which verification is achieved mean
anything beyond themselves: facts and methods do not manifest the
actual character of being because the latter is simply beyond our knowledge.[77] The exuberant iconoclasm of this movement's intellectual retrenchment later became a source of amusement, even for the few, such
as Feigl, who continued as late as the 1960s to identify themselves with
the tradition of logical positivism.[78] The rush with which analytical
philosophers of the 1950s and 1960s sought to disassociate themselves
from the movement's original world view ought not to conceal the extraordinary powers of intimidation that logical positivism developed in
the 1930s and 1940s, partly as a result of its then-unsurpassed mathematical rigor.[79]

Cohen saw the implicit nominalism of the logical positivists as "truly
nihilistic,"[80] but he was not, as his previous career would lead one to
expect, in the forefront of the discussion.[81] Increasingly preoccupied
with Jewish affairs after 1933, yet trying to keep in touch with a number of fields, Cohen did not master the highly technical literature of the
new movement as he had so impressively done in the 1910s with the

most current philosophical and scientific writings of that era. He generally gave short shrift to the movement, regarding it—not altogether wrongly—as a passing fashion of young men. Yet he was forced to confront it directly at the University of Chicago in the late 1930s, when he shared an office with Carnap and taught graduate students very much under Carnap's influence.[82] Cohen's basic aloofness toward the movement could not be modified even by Ernest Nagel, Cohen's former student and collaborator on a logic textbook, who became one of logical positivism's most careful and sympathetic interpreters among American-educated philosophers.[83]

Cohen satisfied himself with but one sustained assault on the verifiability theory of meaning, which he translated into just one more species of the denial of ontological status to logic. The issue between himself and Carnap, as Cohen defined it in "Meaning and Implication," a paper first drafted in 1936, was whether logic was *merely* part of language, or was also *the* structure of intelligibility within being itself.[84] Cohen took off from Carnap's claim that "From *Pirots karulize elatically* and *A is a Pirot*, we can infer that *A karulizes elatically*, without knowing the three words or the sense of the three sentences." Carnap had sought to show the independence of logical inference from "meaning." To this Cohen responded that since Pirots are members of a class, and anything that karulizes elatically is a member of another class, the *meaning* of the inference is that "a member of the first class is necessarily a member of the second class," for logical inference is a relation that has meaning for "all possible objects irrespective of any of their specific or differential traits." Carnap found it sufficient to say that the symbols used in logic, however useful, represent only themselves; Cohen replied that "the various letters and other marks" which enter logical discourse function "not in their status as specific physical objects, but rather as representatives of all possible entities."[85]

"The fundamental error of the positivists," declared their aging enemy, is their rigid categorization of the world into "determinate existence and nonexistence." They lose sight of the twilight zones "in which

most of our statements are made"; by marking off so strictly the realm
of coherence, they rob normal discourse of the intelligibility it obviously has, whatever the positivists may abstractly say to the contrary.
Meanings come into being when people share a sense that a particular
symbol denotes the same object, and verification is something that can
be performed only when meaningful propositions are before us:

> The realm of meaning is wider than the realm of verification. Questions
> and postulates, for example, are significant or meaningful even before
> we have means of verifying them. . . . It may well be contended, of
> course, that we do not have the full meaning of any proposition . . .
> until all the consequences can be determined, but that does not justify
> the contention that before such determination is made the proposition
> remains altogether meaningless. That would be equivalent to the proc-
> ess of climbing up a ladder and then denying its existence.[86]

With this reassertion of his faith that utility implies ontological status,
Cohen refused to trifle with the metaphysician's persistent question,
"In what *sense* does this ladder exist?"

When the influence of logical positivism was at its height in the late
1930s, Cohen's dogged loyalty to "the reality of universals" made him
appear increasingly archaic to many of the younger philosophers. At a
conference at the New School for Social Research, recalls one witness,
"Nagel turned on Cohen with great vehemence" for believing that the
"external world" had a logical structure; such beliefs, asserted Nagel,
were "meaningless." Cohen replied soberly that he did, indeed, hold
such beliefs. Cohen "became very pale" as the exchange went on, while
"the audience sat tense," watching Cohen's repudiation by one of his
most brilliant former students.[87]

In 1945 another young philosopher affectionately compared Cohen
to Don Quixote. *A Preface to Logic* had just appeared, with attacks on
the likes of Mach, Pearson, James, and Bergson that struck Henry David
Aiken as tilts against "nineteenth-century windmills."[88] More than
Quixote, it now seems that Cohen resembled Ludvico Settembrini, the
defender of humanistic rationalism in Thomas Mann's *The Magic Mountain.* Many aspects of Cohen's career, especially near its end, call forth

the image of this wise but tediously zealous and sometimes dogmatic pedagogue. Nowhere is the image more compelling than in the context of metaphysics. Settembrini was disturbingly ineffectual in his noble efforts to save the Castorp brothers from the diseases of their environment, especially the illogic and amorality embodied so attractively in the vital personality of Meyer Pepperkorn. Cohen, too, was felt to be largely correct about many fundamentals, and Cohen's constituency was also slow to share an appropriate sense of crisis. Settembrini condemned Pepperkorn and the fanatical religionist Leo Naphta from so great a distance that his arguments never seemed to meet the challenge directly. Similarly, Cohen's pronouncements persuaded all too few of his auditors that he knew what it felt like to believe what his enemies believed. It was almost as though Cohen, upon meeting someone moved by Proust, produced a copy of *In Memoriam* with some of the stanzas about the Deity penciled out. For some, a sturdy dose of Tennyson was just the thing, but others looked for more.

Cohen professed to be a "naturalist," and he was sufficiently accepted as one to have the movement's collective volume of 1944 dedicated to him.[89] Cohen certainly sought to achieve through "naturalistic" means some of the ends that distinguished idealists from "naturalists." His metaphysics had especially great affinities with the objective idealists of Cornell, who rejected mentalism in order to insist that "intelligibility and unintelligibility are of the object's making, not of our own."[90] But the term "naturalism" is probably the least expressive of the labels employed to distinguish twentieth-century philosophers from one another. The ends that distinguished naturalistic metaphysics were persistently difficult to define: a philosopher could get away with calling himself a "naturalist" so long as he rejected "disembodied spirits" and exhibited a modicum of interest in science. In fact, the label denoted a subculture more than a philosophical outlook: by the early 1940s being a "naturalist" was virtually synonymous with doing philosophy on Morningside and St. Nicholas Heights.[91]

The vision of nature Cohen tried so hard to clarify and defend in metaphysics permeated his writings in other fields. The statements he made about "legal science," politics, philosophy of history, and scientific method were not answers to metaphysical questions, formally considered, yet these statements so successfully embodied, implied, and reinforced (as opposed to *justified*, strictly speaking) his vision of nature as to make that vision more formidable as a referent point in the collective mind of his generation. And Cohen's work in these other areas was far from a postscript to his metaphysics; indeed, the latter is interesting chiefly for the clarity with which it stated the philosophical underpinnings of his contributions as a critic of contemporary ideas about scientific method, law, politics, and history. The same formulations that begged questions in metaphysics could appear to be stunningly lucid and complete when they found their way into contexts of discussion in which careful philosophical analysis was rare.

NOTES

1. MRC, "The Rivals and Substitutes for Reason," *JP* XXII (1925), 189 (*RN*, 44); *MHH*, 86. Cf. *RN*, 144.

2. MRC, "New Realism," *JP* X (1913), 214 (*SPS*, 132).

3. *The Education of Henry Adams* (Boston, 1918), 451.

4. Pierre Duhem, *The Aim and Structure of Physical Theory*, trans. Philip P. Wiener (Princeton, 1954), 73. Cohen read the French edition of 1905. The ideas of Poincaré, whose notoriety followed chiefly from his having termed the laws of nature mere "conventions," were disseminated in the United States by George Bruce Halstead's translation of *Science and Hypothesis* (New York, 1905). Pearson's *Grammar of Science* (1892) was already in its third London edition in 1911.

5. Charles Coulston Gillispie, *The Edge of Objectivity* (Princeton, 1960), 505, 518.

6. John Passmore, *A Hundred Years of Philosophy* (2nd ed., London, 1966), 327-328.

7. [W. M. Daniels,] "Scientific Speculations," *Nation* LXXXIX (1909), 154-155. Cf. Louis T. More, "Poincaré and the Philosophy of Science," *Nation* XCV (1912), 242-244.

8. James's "Does Consciousness Exist?," *JP* I (1904), 477-491, is usually credited with instigating the "new realism" as a movement; Moore's "Refutation of Idealism" first appeared in *Mind* in 1903.

9. Henri Bergson, *Introduction to Metaphysics*, trans. T. E. Hulme (New York, 1912), 65-68; Henri Bergson, *Creative Evolution*, trans. Arthur Mitchell (New York, 1911), 46, 163-165.

10. MRC, "The New Philosopher's Stone," *NR* III (1915), 338 (*FL*, 403); Edwin E. Slosson, "Twelve Major Prophets of Today—II: Henri Bergson," *Independent* LXX (1911), 1247-1261; Henry F. May, *The End of American Innocence* (New York, 1959), 227-229.

11. Walter Lippmann, "The Most Dangerous Man in the World," *Everybody's Magazine* XXVII (1912), 100-101; cf. Lippmann's eulogy to James, "An Open Mind: William James," *Everybody's Magazine* XXIII (1910), 800-801.

12. George Santayana, *Winds of Doctrine* (New York, 1913), esp. 13.

13. E.g., Nann Clark Barr, "The Dualism of Bergson," *PR* XXII (1913), 639-652; Lewis Ellsworth Ackeley, "Bergson and Science," *PR* XXIV (1915), 270-287.

14. E. B. Holt et al., *The New Realism* (New York, 1912).

15. Passmore, *Hundred Years*, 261; cf. May Brodbeck, "American Philosophy, 1900-1950," in Brodbeck et al. *American Non-Fiction, 1900-1950* (Chicago, 1952), 57-67.

16. MRC, "New Realism," esp. 197-199, 202, 204-205, 211 (*SPS*, 109-115, 118-119, 128). Cf. MRC, "The New Realism and the Philosophy of Royce," *PR* XXV (1916), 378-382 (*SPS*, 138).

17. Arthur O. Lovejoy, review of Ralph Barton Perry, *Present Philosophical Tendencies*, in *JP* IX (1912), 675.

18. MRC, "Letter," *JP* X (1913), 27-28.

19. Arthur O. Lovejoy, "Secondary Qualities and Subjectivity," *JP* X (1913), 214-218.

20. MRC, "The Supposed Contradiction in the Diversity of Secondary Qualities—A Reply," *JP* X (1913), 510-512.

21. William P. Montague, "Unreal Subsistence and Consciousness," *PR* XXXIII (1914), 56.

22. Arthur O. Lovejoy, "Relativity, Reality, and Contradiction," *JP* XI (1914), 421-430, esp. 430.

23. MRC, "Qualities, Relations, Things," *JP* XI (1914), 617-627, esp. 621-622.

24. MRC, "Address," in *Tribute*, 70; *DJ* 169. Cf. MRC, "The Faith of a Logician," in George P. Adams and William P. Montague, eds., *Contemporary American Philosophy* (New York, 1930), I, 225 (*SPS*, 7).

25. Bertrand Russell, *Principles of Mathematics* (London, 1903).

26. D. F. Pears, *Bertrand Russell and the British Tradition in Philosophy* (New York, 1967), 13. Cf. Passmore, *Hundred Years*, 216-228.

27. Bertrand Russell, *Introduction to Mathematical Philosophy* (London, 1919), as quoted in Passmore, *Hundred Years*, 227.

28. *DJ*, 170.

29. Pears, *Russell*.

30. "Mechanism and Causality in Physics" was published several years later: *JP* XV (1918), 365-386. Eventually it found its way into *Reason and Nature*, slightly revised (*RN*, 206-230).

31. MRC, "Mechanism and Causality," 378, 381.

32. MRC, "Mechanism and Causality," 382-386.

33. Review of eight books on Einstein and relativity, *NR* XXVII (1921), 172-174 (*SPS*, 237).

34. Ronald C. Tobey, *The American Ideology of National Science, 1919-1930* (Pittsburgh, 1971), 96-132, esp. 98.

35. MRC, "Einstein's Theory of Relativity," *NR* XXI (1920), 228-231 (*SPS*, 222, 230-231); MRC, review of eight books, 172-174 (*SPS*, 237). Cf. *RN*, 230-239. The metaphysical implications of postrelativistic physics were, and continue to be, a matter of disagreement. Cohen understood the new physics more thoroughly than most philosophers of the 1920s. His interpretations of the Einstein theory were taken seriously by the physicists who knew his work, according to his contemporary, the philosopher-physicist Victor Lenzen (conversation with author, Berkeley, California, November 18, 1968). Cf. Cohen's correspondence with Einstein in *Portrait*, 369-379.

36. MRC, "History vs. Value," *JP* XI (1914), 716 (*RN*, 385). The ambiguity in the "involvement" of the logical order with the temporal was not mitigated by the passages of Royce and Woodbridge that Cohen cited as ostensibly relevant: see MRC, "The Present Situation in the Philosophy of Mathematics," *JP* VIII (1911), 545; MRC, "New Realism and Royce," 378 (*SPS*, 136). The contributions of Woodbridge and

Royce to the *Congress of Arts and Science* both located logic at the center of things, but Woodbridge's emphasis was vaguely upon the power of things to control the nature of logic (*Congress*, I, 316), while Royce greatly compromised the "objectivity" of mathematics by speaking of the "peculiarly intimate relation" the eternal verities of mathematics had to the "purposes of [the mathematician's] own constructive will" (*Congress*, I, 153).

37. MRC, "The Subject Matter of Formal Logic," *JP* XV (1918), 675-676, 678, 688 (*PL*, 17-18, 21, 35). Cf. MRC, Introduction to Charles Peirce, *Chance, Love, Logic* (New York, 1923), xxxi.

38. MRC, "Concepts and Twilight Zones," *JP* XXIV (1927), 673-677 (*PL*, 81-85). Cf. MRC, "The Logic of Fiction," *JP* XX (1923), 477-488 (*PL*, 94-112).

39. MRC, "Concepts and Twilight Zones," 677-679 (*PL*, 86-87).

40. MRC, "Amor Dei Intellectualis," *Chronicon Spinozanum* III (1923), 4, 8-9 (*FL*, 308, 311-312).

41. MRC, "Amor Dei Intellectualis," 8 (*FL*, 312). Cf. MRC, "Einstein's Theory," 228-231 (*SPS*, 230).

42. Milič Čapek, *The Philosophical Impact of Contemporary Physics* (New York, 1961), esp. 391.

43. Arthur O. Lovejoy to MRC, February 19, 1924, Cohen MSS.

44. John Dewey, *Experience and Nature*, (2nd ed., New York, 1929), 138-170, esp. 158-162; John Dewey, "Experience and Meaning," *JP* XXV (1928), 348; John Dewey, *The Quest for Certainty* (New York, 1929), 162-163; Harold Chapman Brown, "The Definition of Logic," *JP* XVI (1919), 541; George Herbert Mead, *Mind, Self, Society*, ed. Charles W. Morris (Chicago, 1934), 90. Cf. the excellent characterization of the temporal cast of the pragmatic movement in H. S. Thayer, *Meaning and Action: A Critical History of Pragmatism* (Indianapolis, 1968), esp. 453. Cf. also Darnell Rucker, *The Chicago Pragmatists* (Minneapolis, 1970), 28-56.

45. E.g., Ralph Barton Perry, *Present Philosophical Tendencies* (New York, 1912), 298-303; E. B. Holt, *The Concept of Consciousness* (New York, 1914), 45; and A. K. Rogers, "Empiricism," in *Contemporary American Philosophy*, II, 232. On the break-up of the realist movements see Passmore, *Hundred Years*, 264.

46. Arthur O. Lovejoy to MRC, February 19, 1924; Lovejoy, "A Tem-

poralistic Realism," in *Contemporary American Philosophy*, II, 89, 93-94; Lovejoy, *The Revolt Against Dualism* (New York, 1930), 137-140.

47. E.g., Joseph Alexander Leighton, "The Principle of Individuality and Value," in Clifford Barrett, ed., *Contemporary Idealism in America* (New York, 1932), 149. Cf. Herbert W. Schneider, *A History of American Philosophy* (2nd ed., New York, 1963), 427.

48. John Elof Boodin, "Nature and Reason," in *Contemporary American Philosophy*, I, 143.

49. *RN*, xii.

50. MRC, "Vision and Technique in Philosophy," *PR* XXXIX (1930), 127-152 (*FL*, 365-391); MRC, "What I Believe," *Nation* CXXXI (1931), 128-131 (*FL*, 3-10); MRC, "In Dispraise of Life, Experience, and Reality," *NR* LXVI (1931), 124-126 (*RN*, 450-457); MRC, "Faith of a Logician."

51. Nearly half of *Reason and Nature* had appeared in print before 1927, chiefly in the *Journal of Philosophy*, including several papers from 1911 and 1914.

52. *RN*, 152-153, 158, 163.

53. *RN*, 156-159. Cf. MRC, "Faith of a Logician," 229 (*SPS*, 12). So thin, indeed, is Cohen's discussion of these problems in *RN* that his most friendly commentators have gone back to his 1912-1914 exchange with Lovejoy to discover what Cohen meant to claim and argue; see, as examples, Arthur Francis Smullyan, "The Philosophical Method of Morris R. Cohen," in Salo W. Baron et al., eds., *Freedom and Reason: Studies in Philosophy and Jewish Culture in Memory of Morris Raphael Cohen* (Glencoe, Ill., 1951), 59-67, and Cornelius Delaney, *Mind and Nature* (Notre Dame, 1969), 76.

54. *RN*, 156-164, Cf. *RN*, 143-145.

55. *RN*, 165.

56. *RN*, 165-167.

57. MRC, "Concepts and Twilight Zones," 678-679 (*PL*, 88). Although the 1927 publication of "Concepts and Twilight Zones" marks Cohen's first statement of polarity in print, this statement was included in a draft of the same paper read before the New York Philosophical Club in 1920; see Philosophical Club Collection, Columbia University Special Collections. Cf. MRC to Oliver Wendell Holmes, Jr., February 14, 1921, in *Portrait*, 335.

58. MRC, undated note of 1898, in *Portrait*, 23.

59. *DJ*, 170.

60. Andrew J. Reck goes too far in claiming that Cohen "derived" the principle of polarity from Sheldon; see Reck, *The New American Philosophers* (New York, 1969), 314. It is true, however, that Sheldon and Cohen discussed polarity and "duality" throughout the 1910s (e.g., Sheldon to MRC, July 29, 1919, Cohen MSS, in which Sheldon stresses the affinity of their metaphysical outlooks). Cf. Cohen's anomalously cordial review of Sheldon's *The Strife of Systems and Productive Duality* (Cambridge, Mass., 1921), in *NR* XXXII (1922), Special Supplement, 10-12.

61. Ralph Waldo Emerson, *Essays* (Boston, 1865), first series, 81-82; cf. 83-104. It is also possible that the term polarity was suggested to Cohen by the works of William Whewell; see, e.g., Robert E. Butts, ed., *William Whewell's Theory of Scientific Method* (Pittsburgh, 1968), 112, 180-183, 283.

62. *RN*, 165, 168.

63. *RN*, 206-330, esp. 330.

64. MRC, "Mechanism and Causality," 365.

65. E. A. Burtt, review of *RN*, in *PR* XLII (1932), 610.

66. John Dewey, review of *RN*, in *NR* LXVI (1931), 306-307. Cf. Cohen's petulant response, *NR* LXVII (1931), 127. Dewey seems to have been asked to review the book at Cohen's prompting: see the letters of *NR*'s literary editor, Malcolm Cowley, to Cohen, February 10 and March 6, 1931, Cohen MSS.

67. Sidney Hook, review of *RN*, in *JP* XXIX (1932), 9, 11-12, 14. When Hook was asked to do the review, he wrote to Cohen in embarrassment, wishing that a more distinguished philosopher had been given the honor; Cohen apparently encouraged Hook to proceed (Sidney Hook to MRC, April 13 and July 9, 1931, Cohen MSS).

68. Victor S. Yarros, "Reason in Science and Philosophy," *Open Court* XLVI (1932), 109, 115-116.

69. Arthur E. Murphey, review of *RN*, in *Ethics* XLIII (1932), 70.

70. Burtt, review of *RN*, 618. Cf. Santayana's letter to Cohen, which, after expressing agreement with Cohen's outlook, complained that such basic points as the "reality of universals" were not persuasively argued (Santayana to MRC, May 11, 1931, in *Portrait*, 380-381).

71. M.S.A., review of *RN*, in *Mind* XL (1931), 523. Cf. Paul Weiss, review of *RN*, in *City College Alumnus* XXVII (1931), 61-63.

72. There are, to be sure, a handful of references to Cohen in metaphysical discussions in the *Monist* and *JP* in the 1930s, but the infrequency with which his formulations played a role in technical metaphysical discourse is not to be contested. Dewey generally ignored Cohen, and one must go to his correspondence with Arthur F. Bentley to find him employing Cohen's ideas even as a referent point (Sidney Ratner and Jules Altman, eds., *A Philosophical Correspondence, 1932-1951* [New Brunswick, N.J., 1964], esp. 443). An associate of Dewey did try, in 1917, to use some of Cohen's formulations in working out a theory of meaning: Harold Chapman Brown, "Intelligence and Mathematics," in John Dewey, ed., *Creative Intelligence* (New York, 1917), 154-162. More significantly, Cohen was ignored by C. I. Lewis, who, of the leading metaphysicians of Cohen's generation, pursued most successfully the problem of logic's relation to the universe as a whole; whatever may be said for *RN*'s scope, its wisdom, or the cogency of its critiques of other thinkers, it is dwarfed as metaphysics by Lewis's *Mind and the World Order* (New York, 1929). It is also instructive that Cohen's name appears but once in a recently published, comprehensive volume on Lewis's thought and its context, and this is in the autobiographical sketch, where Lewis recalls how, in his undergraduate days at Harvard, he was excited by the dinner-table discourse of a graduate student named Morris Cohen (C. I. Lewis, "Autobiography," in Paul A. Schilpp, ed., *The Philosophy of C. I. Lewis* [La Salle, Ill., 1968], 65). Santayana and Russell, both of whom Cohen admired extravagantly, took no significant account of his work. Among the very few attempts made during the 1950s and 1960s to build from Cohen's metaphysical formulations are Louis W. Norris, *Polarity: A Philosophy of Tensions Among Values* (Chicago, 1956), esp. 1-12, and Charles Hartshorne, *Reality as a Social Process* (New York, 1960), 86.

73. Jerome Frank to MRC, April 2, 1931, Frank Papers, Yale University Library; Walter Lippmann to MRC, September 16, 1931, Cohen MSS. Cf. Frank to Harry Hansen (editor of the *New York World-Telegram*), April 22, 1931, Cohen MSS. Cf. also the many letters Cohen received from admirers of *RN*, e.g., the eminent physician Israel S. Wechsler (letter to MRC, June 3, 1931, Cohen MSS) and the young literary critic Kenneth Burke (letter to MRC, October 31, 1934, Cohen MSS).

74. H. L. Mencken, "In the Grove of Athene," *American Mercury* XXIV (1931), 123-124; Henry Hazlitt, review of *RN*, in *Nation* CXXXII (1931), 411-412; Harold Ward, "Adventures of a Mind in Quest of Truth," *New York Times Book Review* (April 12, 1931). Im-

mediately upon publication, 500 copies of *RN* were purchased by the Julius Rosenwald Foundation; see Alfred Harcourt (MRC's publisher) to MRC, June 11, 1931, Cohen MSS.

75. In "The Statistical View of Nature" (*PL*, 140-167), Cohen assured the American Statistical Association that the quantum revolution in physics and the Heisenberg uncertainty principle did not affect the philosophical views he had long believed to be sound: Heisenberg's world is not "lawless," but one in which a "law" denotes the *distribution* (as opposed to the behavior) of particles (see esp. 156). Cf. the essay "On Probability," *PL*, 113-139. Cohen's other papers bearing the most directly upon metaphysics were "Hegel's Rationalism," *PR* XLII (1932), 283-301 (*SPS*, 176-198) and "Some Difficulties in Dewey's Anthropocentric Naturalism," *PR* XLIX (1940), 196-228 (*SPS*, 139-175). Cohen's metaphysical views informed some parts of the textbook he coauthored with Ernest Nagel, *Introduction to Logic and Scientific Method* (New York, 1934); the volume's constant distinction between formal and material truth drew predictable fire from Dewey (*Nation* CXXXVIII [1934], 513). Cohen claimed in 1939 to be well along on a systematic book on metaphysics, but the "trunkful of notes" he had rendered into typescript that summer has not survived, nor has the typescript; see MRC to Ernest Nagel, July 11 and August 18, 1939, in *Portrait*, 406-407.

76. This tradition did have a handful of American adherents, e.g., the redoubtable Berkeleyan Mary Whiton Calkins. See her *The Persistent Problems of Philosophy* (4th ed., New York, 1917), esp. 405-406, and "The Philosophic *Credo* of an Absolutistic Personalist," in *Contemporary American Philosophy*, I, 208-209. Cf. the entire "personalist" wing of idealism, including Warner Fite, and the less influential but numerous Methodist philosophers at Boston University and the University of Southern California (e.g., Edgar Sheffield Brightman, Ralph Tyler Flewelling, and A. C. Knudson).

77. Alfred E. Blumberg and Herbert Feigl, "Logical Positivism," *JP* XXVII (1931), 282.

78. See Feigl's memoir of his experiences as a positivist and an emigré, "The Wiener Kreis in America," *Perspectives in American History* II (1968), 630-673.

79. Peter Achtinstein and Stephen Barber, eds., *The Legacy of Logical Positivism* (Baltimore, 1971).

80. MRC, "Meaning and Implication," *PL*, 53.

81. A number of American philosophers less adamantly antinominalist than Cohen took on the logical positivists, e.g., William Henry Werkmeister, "Seven Theses of Logical Positivism Critically Examined," *PR* XLVI (1937), 276-297, 357-376; C. I. Lewis, "Experience and Meaning," *PR* XLIII (1934), 124-146; C. J. Ducasse, "Verification, Verifiability, and Meaningfulness," *JP* XXXIII (1936), 230-236.

82. Cohen's clashes with Carnap's students have been described by Roderick Chisholm (quoted in *Portrait*, 89), Charles Hartshorne (conversation with author, Berkeley, California, July 1970), and Paul Goodman (conversation with author).

83. Ernest Nagel, "Analytical Philosophy in Europe," *JP* (1936), 5-24, 29-53; Nagel to MRC, September 14, 1934, and June 4, 1935, in *Portrait*, 394-395, 399-401. Cf. the friendly overtures to Cohen made by leaders of the positivist movement: Otto Neurath to MRC, February 7, 1935, and Charles W. Morris to MRC, August 16, 1935, Cohen MSS.

84. MRC, "Meaning and Implication," 53. In the 1944 text Cohen cites Carnap's *The Logical Syntax of Language* (London, 1937), esp. 1-8, although he used the original German edition of 1934 in the preparation of the paper for presentation at the 1936 meeting of the Eastern Division of the American Philosophical Association.

85. MRC, "Meaning and Implication," 54-55.

86. MRC, "Meaning and Implication," 69, 71, 78.

87. Lewis Feuer, letter to author, April 9, 1974. Nagel, in a brief intellectual autobiography written in 1956, has described both his debt to Cohen and his efforts to resolve the conflict between the empiricism of the 1930s and the "Aristotelian realism" he had earlier absorbed from Cohen; see Nagel, *Logic Without Metaphysics* (Glencoe, Ill., 1956), Introduction, esp. xii-xiii.

88. Henry David Aiken, review of *PL*, in *NR* CXII (1945), 307.

89. Yervant H. Krikorian, ed., *Naturalism and the Human Spirit* (New York, 1944).

90. G. Watts Cunningham, *The Idealist Argument in Recent British and American Philosophy* (New York, 1933), 517. On objective idealism generally, see Schneider, *American Philosophy*, 403-406, 515. Passmore has noticed Cohen's kinship with the movement (*Hundred Years*, 292). Cohen himself used the phrase at least once as a synonym for logical realism: *RN*, 237.

91. Krikorian, *Naturalism*, included fifteen essays, four by members of the Columbia University Department of Philosophy (John Dewey, Ernest Nagel, John Herman Randall, Jr., and Herbert Schneider), two by City College philosophers (Krikorian and Abraham Edel), and many by persons who had taken degrees at one of these institutions (e.g., Sidney Hook, who studied with Cohen at City College and with Dewey at Columbia). The only essay devoted to the philosophy of an individual was Harry Todd Costello's study of J. F. E. Woodbridge, the venerable Columbia naturalist who died in 1940. The task of figuring out just what the contributors agreed upon was taken up stoically by Randall, "Epilogue: The Nature of Naturalism," 354-382. Cf. Manley Thompson, "Metaphysics," in Roderick M. Chisholm et al., *Philosophy* (Englewood Cliffs, N.J., 1963), 183. It is interesting that the leading American "naturalist" (excluding Santayana) not connected with the New York group—Roy Wood Sellars—was in fact an out-and-out "nominalist," one of the few in Cohen's generation to apply this label to himself voluntarily. For representative attempts to classify Cohen as a "naturalist" on the grounds of his ideas, rather than his social associations, see Joseph Blau, *Men and Movements in American Philosophy* (Englewood Cliffs, N.J., 1952), 334-343; Krikorian, "Cohen's Rationalistic Naturalism," *Philosophy and Phenomenological Research* XXIX (1968), 264-273; and Delaney, *Mind and Nature*. Delaney's work is distinguished by its attempt to find affinities between Cohen and, of all people, Sellars.

What the searchlight makes visible will depend upon its position, upon our way of directing it, and upon its intensity, colour, etc.; although it will, of course, also depend very largely upon the things illuminated by it. Similarly, a scientific description will depend, largely, upon our point of view, our interests, which are as a rule connected with the theory or hypothesis we wish to test; although it will also depend upon the facts described. Indeed, the theory or hypothesis could be described as the crystallization of a point of view. For if we attempt to formulate our point of view, then this formulation will, as a rule, be what one sometimes calls a working hypothesis; that is to say, a provisional assumption whose function is to help us to select, and to order, the facts. But we should be clear that there cannot be any theory or hypothesis which is not, in this sense, a working hypothesis, and does not remain one. For no theory is final, and every theory helps us to select and order facts.

K. R. Popper

When the learned combat between Ludvico Settembrini and the Jesuit Leo Naphta reached its most intense stage, the exhausted gladiators touched the gravamen of their hostilities. Naphta shrieked, "The Passion!" and Settembrini, "the Reason!"[1] The rivalry between the modes of passion and reason seemed to Morris Cohen, too, the issue of the age, but he, unlike Thomas Mann, had no difficulty choosing sides. The field of modernity, as Cohen envisioned it, had at its center the fortress of "civilization," which had been constructed out of classical humanistic values during centuries of "rational labor"; against this bastion marched the armies of will and intuition, led by Bergson, Nietzsche, James, and Spengler, whose goal was to replace wisdom with "Dionysian frenzy."[2]

What Cohen called the "insurgence against reason"[3] was the methodological counterpart of some of the ideas about nature that his metaphysics was designed to contain and refute. Bergson's object of knowledge, for example, was often defined as a "feeling" beyond the reach of the logic of identity and of all categories of the scientific intellect; it was to be apprehended through "intuition" and "creative imagination." Vitalist metaphysics and intuitionist epistemology were so mutually reinforcing that the latter "method" was almost as intrinsic to Bergson's message as the élan vital itself. So it often is with methods and metaphysics, and so Cohen clearly perceived the setting of his own work. Cohen's conception of nature as the home of logical invariants was indissolubly bound up, from the very beginning, with methodological rationalism; he wanted a metaphysics that would help justify scientific method, rationalistically defined, and he wanted a methodology that would help justify his metaphysical faith that "the laws of logic and mathematics do hold of nature." Cohen's analysis of "scientific method" was ultimately addressed, therefore, to the problem of "logic" and "history."

Unlike metaphysics, which presented itself to Cohen as a set of precisely formulated problems around which a sophisticated and technical discourse had developed, "methodology" was scarcely a discipline at all in 1910, or even in 1930. Scientists, social scientists, legal scholars, journalists, and philosophers exchanged ideas about how to do science, some of which derived from such classical theorists of science as Bacon, Descartes, and Mill. Simultaneously, many American intellectuals were involved in an even less formal, almost "literary" discourse about the relative merits of scientific reason and its challengers. Both of these methodological discussions, although they had obvious epistemological components, were distinct from the discipline of epistemology. Epistemology itself was concerned with how, as a behavioral and logical fact of life, humans obtain knowledge of things. The nondiscipline of methodology was driven instead by a practical interest in resolving genuine *choices* between rival means of seeking knowledge, insight, or control over things. Arguments about "methods," in this sense, took place when D. H. Lawrence's "blood Knowledge," for example, was offered as an alternative to scientific reason, or when adherents of scientific method debated the value of "observation," "experimentation," "deduction," and other activities associated with the doing of science. Debates of this second sort—which by the mid-1930s had helped to spawn philosophy of science as a discipline—paid little attention to "methods" like "blood Knowledge" and "will," which were generally felt to be too antagonistic to science to merit consideration by its partisans.

Of these partisans, Cohen was unusual for his sense of what was at issue. He believed that the more general controversy between reason and passion, far from having been resolved within the ranks of science, was being fought out there in muted form. In the eagerness of empiricists to rely on the "facts" of particular, immediate sense experiences, Cohen detected an affinity with the out-and-out irrationalist's scorn for logic. Empiricism to Cohen was but a softer version of the "romantic effort to enthrone Dionysus."[4] There were, in fact, two different levels of methodological discourse, but Cohen made no distinctions; he treated adherents and skeptics of scientific method the way an evangelist might comport himself toward a single congregation embracing both converted and unconverted souls. The preacher must persuade the unconverted to reject the temptations of Bergson and Nietzsche, and instead to adopt rational science as their approach to experience. He must also exhort those within the fold to keep their scientific faith untainted by the worldly compromise of empiricism.

Although Cohen expended an impressive store of polemical energy attacking the blatant "irrationalism" that lay behind mere empiricism, the methods of "passion" were so foreign to him that he regularly assumed they could be disposed of simply by pointing to their lack of rationality. James's doctrine of the "will to believe" is "childish foolishness," said Cohen, because what is actually the case shall always remain unaffected by belief: we cannot make God "come into existence" through this method. Renan's insistence that no one ever "got inspiration" from "accurate knowledge" struck him as "one of the most perverse sentences ever penned"; Cohen replied that "sustained flights of imagination are always helped by vivid and accurate perception, memory, and much studied judgment as to what is and what is not fitting or coherent." As for the claim that instinctual and unconscious drives, and material conditions, control our lives more than rationalism has been willing to admit, he observed that "though the flowers of life may be rooted in dark soil, their energy comes from the sun." Since "old-fashioned rationalism" had helped abolish "slavery, serfdom, and persecution for witchcraft," the eclipse of that rationalism might well "bring these abuses back into full force." The tactic Cohen relied on most, however, was to charge the proponents of passion with an inability to distinguish between sanity and insanity; repeatedly, he associated their outlook with primitive mankind's "awe for the ravings of the frenzied or insane."[5]

Cohen matched these salvos against "the barbarians outside the gates," as the *Journal of Philosophy* characterized them,[6] with a critique of the popular empiricism he found within the fold of science. When channeled into his commentaries on scientific method, the rage Cohen felt against the enemies of reason took more coherent form and elicited a larger body of written work. Cohen's defense of the method of reason was carried out in the general context of what historians have

invariably seen as the early twentieth century's fascination with the
passionate emotions, the subconscious mind, and the "primitive" instincts,[7] but the specific context of his enterprise was popular attitudes
toward science.

How men get their knowledge of nature, or how they ought to, has
been discussed since Aristotle, at least, but the concept of "scientific
method" has had only a very brief history as a major referent point in
learned and popular discourse. It did not appear until the 1830s, when
John Herschel and William Whewell introduced a new genre of writing
about nature and knowledge, the attempt to spell out in detail the steps
taken by scientists in making discoveries and the criteria by which validity is determined.[8] This new type of treatise was stimulated by intellectual and social conditions that need not concern us here, but interest in
such work was undoubtedly sustained for the next century by a widespread belief that the methods employed by physicists and biologists
could be transferred to objects of many other kinds; the demand for
accounts of scientific method was partially a function of the desire to
apply this method to human affairs. Somewhat chastened, this desire
continues to find expression in some quarters, but its demands are now
met more by journalists than by philosophers. The latter almost never
speak of "scientific method": the author of the essay on this topic in
the 1967 *Encyclopedia of Philosophy* was transparently embarrassed by
the assignment, and the new *International Encyclopedia of the Social
Sciences* eschews such talk altogether, preferring to speak successively
of the history, philosophy, and sociology of science, and of "Scientists"
and "Scientific Communication." Yet as late as the 1930s the structural
core of the *Encyclopedia of the Social Sciences* was Morris Cohen's
article, "Method, Scientific."[9] In the decades dividing the new social-
science encyclopedia from the old, the academic intelligentsia rejected
what one philosopher now refers to as the "full natural-history-cum-
logical-account of scientific method."[10] Now philosophers seek instead
to analyze the logical structure of the concepts, explanations, and argu-

ments found in science. Even those philosophers who go beyond logical structure to study the historical progression of the sciences avoid the term "scientific method," for the methodological unity of the sciences has come very much into doubt.

These changes in the aims of philosophy of science have diverse causes, the two most obvious being ones that involved Cohen, albeit indirectly. The breakdown of the simple concept of "scientific method" followed partially from the diversity of the procedures discovered once the systematic study of the sciences was organized on a large scale, an academic innovation greatly promoted by Cohen. The emphasis on the *logical* analysis of concepts at the expense of a synthetic account of "scientific method" as an integrated, prescribable temporal-and-logical process fulfilled with ironic vengeance Cohen's oft-repeated plea for a more distinctly logical account of science to replace a sometimes crudely antirational empiricism.

Cohen's generation as a whole was heir to the assumption that "science," beyond a body of knowledge, consisted of a discrete set of principles and procedures that could be abstracted and prescribed. This assumption was ultimately at odds with another salient fact about American attitudes toward science in Cohen's time: the ambiguity of what was meant by "scientific," the indeterminate *content*, in other words, of what everyone referred to as the "methods of science."

The ambiguities in "scientific method" were not limited to its divergent use by the idealist philosophers and their critics to support, alternately, the unity of knowledge and the autonomy of specialized inquiries into particular aspects of immediate experience. This tension in the scientific ideal was of course a controlling condition of Cohen's search for a philosophical métier, but there were, in various quarters, a number of other senses of what it meant to be "scientific." Frequently, the word was used to refer to a vision of nature rather than to a methodological postulate; to think "scientifically" was to see nature "Red, Tooth and Claw," to depict it in materialistic or evolutionary terms, or to think of it as a set of "processes" or "functions," as in the case of

Albion W. Small, America's leading sociologist in 1916:

> Everyone who ranks as a scholar today assumes, in one lobe of his
> brain, that the reality which it is the common task of social scientists to
> interpret is an incessant working of impulses as causes, transformed in
> and through their workings into effects, and reappearing in the changed
> form, or in repetition of the original form, or both, as modified causes,
> reproduced in modified effects, in series to which our knowledge can
> assign no limits.[11]

One's sense of "what's there" to be studied always has methodological
implications, but it is one thing to imply that an account of something
is "scientific" by virtue of the functionalist (or vitalist, or mechanistic)
terms in which it is cast, and it is quite another to require of a scientific
inquiry that it proceed according to certain principles and canons of
evidence that can distinguish one functionalist account from another.

In a more strictly methodological idiom, it was often said that to be
scientific was to imitate the physical and biological sciences, and this
was taken to mean, at the very least, observation, experimentation,
classification, exactness, objectivity, ethical neutrality, and fidelity to
evidence, and was sometimes taken to mean, in addition, prediction,
control, and efficiency. What these terms meant, in turn, was so obvious to some as to obviate the necessity for further clarification. But to
others the meaning was less obvious; discourse about "scientific method" was carried on in the interests of those who wanted to apply it in
previously nonscientific contexts. Many social scientists, legal scholars,
administrators, and "pragmatic" philosophers sought to codify the
methods of science in order more confidently to practice them in fields
other than those in which they had been generated. The attempt of the
social-science community during the 1920s to spell out "scientific
method" encapsulated this discourse neatly; it revealed how indeterminate such terms as "observation" and "objectivity" were, yet it made
articulate the crude "Baconianism" that endowed the theory of social
research with what few philosophical underpinnings it then had.

Hoping to improve their disciplines and to settle more firmly the old question of their "scientific" status, the political scientists and sociologists of the 1920s made their most determined effort yet at what the Social Science Research Council called a rigorous reassessment of existing research procedures in the light of "scientific method."[12] The campaign paid almost no attention to the metaphysical reflections of Mach, Duhem, and other philosophers of physics. Novel as the average social scientist may have found their testimony, he was generally concerned less with the epistemology and metaphysics of science than with whether his own procedures were authentically scientific. The social scientists produced a plethora of handbooks, compendia, and symposia that can be well represented by a widely used textbook, Howard W. Odum and Katherin Jocher's *An Introduction to Social Research.*[13] This was a wildly eclectic book, consisting mainly of brief quotations from men of letters, philosophers, and scientists of all persuasions. The contribution of Odum and Jocher was little more than to organize the quotations around nineteen "types" of approaches and methods; the implication was that almost every friendly statement ever made about science had an equal claim to truth, and that every method ever employed by a self-styled scientist partook of the "universal scientific method," which, unfortunately, Odum and Jocher found difficult to define. A method was scientific, they concluded, so long as it provided "a comprehensive plan, delimitation of the field, technique for gathering data, classification and analysis, and procedure for interpretation and presentation of the results." Readers interested in more detail were asked to wait for the upcoming case book on scientific method, sponsored by the Social Science Research Council itself.[14]

When the long-awaited compendium, *Methods in the Social Sciences: A Case Book*, finally arrived in 1931, it was marked by the same conflict in motivation that had prevented Odum and Jocher's volume from making useful distinctions. Eager to establish the "scientific" status of social-science methods, yet unwilling to adopt a standard that might disqualify methods known to be in use, these editors could do little more than summarize, in methodological language, what their colleagues were doing and then declare that this was what being "scientific" consisted in. The editor of the *Case Book*, Stuart Rice, began his work in the spirit of Odum and Jocher, with "an inductive examination of the uses given to the word [scientific method] in the literature of the social sciences," but he, at least, understood that this would serve only to exposit, not to clarify, so he moved toward a definition of scientific method in logical terms. Unfortunately, this raised for him the possibility that the methodologist would be "replaced by the logician." This prospect was so distressing that he gave up altogether on logic, and announced that scientific method was "a term of variable meaning." Still, Rice retained his a priori confidence in the methodological unity of science; upon the concept of scientific method, he admitted, "depended the purpose and organization of the entire work." As for the text itself, the reader was left to induct an account of scientific method from the fifty-two particularistic analyses of various methods employed by various social scientists.[15]

Rice and his colleagues got relatively little help from the philosopher most closely identified with social science, John Dewey. This was because what Dewey said about scientific method was designed chiefly to show that it was a form of social action. He endorsed the Baconian ideal of active experimentation in order to control nature, but the closest he came to an account of what scientists actually did was his analysis of how this activity arises from and serves social needs. As formulated during the 1910s and 1920s, instrumentalism remained a theory of science's role in culture, not an analysis of how one knows when this or that proposition about nature satisfies the needs that gave rise to inquiry.[16] Whatever influence Dewey had in making social science respectable, his role was not to provide the sorts of distinctions the Social Science Research Council felt more or less obliged to discover and take account of.

Beyond the instrumentalist tradition there were a handful of philosophers working on problems potentially relevant to Rice's task. Cornelius Benjamin, R. D. Carmichael, and several philosophically inclined physicists sought to update classical empiricism's account of "induction" by discussing it in terms of the modern logical theory deriving from Frege, Russell, and Whitehead,[17] but their efforts remained obscure to nonphilosophers, and attracted very little attention even among philosophers. Actually, it was not absurd for Rice to steer clear of the logicians, for he and they shared the empiricist conviction that logic applies to "proof," but not to "discovery," which Rice singled out as his major concern.[18] According to this distinction, the process of observing nature and finding particular data does not have a logical structure, but is, rather, prior to logic. The social scientists picked up such empiricist ideas partially through osmosis, and partially from popularizations of Mill, especially those of F. W. Westaway and Abraham Wolf.[19] It was the empiricist tradition as filtered through these popular manuals of "scientific method" that provided most educated Americans with their sense of logic's role in science.

Scientific method, in this general view, was chiefly a matter of "observation" and "inference." The starting point of science was "observed sense data," the "particulars" of experience, whether that experience derived from passive observation or active, experimental observation. After observation came inference, which was of two kinds, "inductive" and "deductive." Induction was the making of generalizations based on the particulars of observation. An "inductive inference," then, was an interpretation of the "facts" of sense observation. Inductive inference entailed the comparison of identifiable entities with one another (in Mill's classic terms, the canons of "agreement" and "difference"), a process ultimately "logical" because it employed the principles of identity, contradiction, and excluded middle, taken since Aristotle as the sine qua non of ratiocination. Yet the "logic of induction" was not to be confused with "deductive logic," the syllogistic pattern of thought with which the term "logic" was generally associated. Deduction began with general propositions, not particulars, and exposed the various particular truths necessarily implied by these propositions. Deduction's role in scientific method was to check the internal consistency of the body of knowledge and to deduce particulars that had not, for one reason or another, been "observed." Deduction, therefore, had its uses so long as it was not allowed to become a substitute for observation and induction. And "observation" was not a logical process at all; it existed prior to even the "logic" of induction.

Mill himself had taken "inference" very seriously, as had Bacon before him, but the sophisticated and qualified empiricism of these thinkers was transmogrified by the widespread tradition of popular empiricism into a denigration of logic in general and of deduction in particular. The names of Bacon and Mill were continually invoked in connection with views they themselves had warned against. Although Cohen sometimes sought to criticize Mill and Bacon, his commentaries on scientific method were aimed chiefly at the popular empiricism that claimed the great empiricists. He was only slightly hyperbolic when he attributed to the scientism of his age the motto, "Don't reason, find out."[20] Odum and Jocher could not allude to the utility of deductive inference without warning against its attendant dangers, "wishful thinking," "rationalization," and "subjectivity." Even contributors to Stuart Rice's cautious *Case Book* could be found distinguishing sharply between the unreliable "logical method" and the more scientific collecting together of the facts of "observation"; indeed, the volume opened with a paean to August Comte for his having put aside "metaphysics" in order to look upon "observed realities."

When the great European social scientist Karl Mannheim was asked for his opinion of the *Case Book*, he had to deny the Americans their coveted recognition as methodologists: an excessive fear of theories, he said, had led the book and its contributors to sterility. It is an interesting index of the depth of popular empiricism that as late as 1931, when Cohen had become recognized as one of the nation's leading, if idiosyncratic, authorities on scientific method, only one contributor to the *Case Book*, W. Y. Elliott, cited him. And Elliott's critique of political science for its inability to achieve a complete deductive system was so anomalous that Rice took the exceptional step of providing for its rebuttal in an appendix.[21]

The differences between the context of discussion in metaphysics and that in "methodology" make it possible to take up Cohen's critique of popular empiricism as a whole, rather in the bits and pieces of its chronological development. Cohen's analysis of science did not, in contrast to his work in metaphysics, entail an epical struggle to make his ideas clear. When he wrote on the nature of science, he was responding to the general climate represented by Stuart Rice's *Case Book*; he did not have to worry about a highly developed philosophical apparatus in the minds of his auditors, according to which someone could always say, "Ah, but you are begging the question unless you deal with this," and so on. It was one thing to explain to professional metaphysicians exactly how nonmental logical invariants could be both intrinsic to nature and compatible with the radical contingency of the physical world. It was quite another thing to defend, in a less professionally rigorous setting, the simple proposition that logical reasoning is essential to the scientific process. This contrast between the two environments in which Cohen put forth his metaphysics and his protophilosophy of science would not hold today, of course; if Cohen's most detailed and systematic work[22] were published afresh in the 1960s or 1970s, it would be evaluated according to the success with which it spoke to questions currently of interest to philosophers of science, who have now created for themselves a discourse every bit as demanding as that of metaphysics. This increase in sophistication began while Cohen was still around, in the mid-1930s, but well after his own views had received their complete articulation. Cohen's role in the discourse of the later period can therefore be taken up separately, as an epilogue to his response to the prevailing atmosphere of the 1910s and 1920s.

Central to Cohen's critique of popular empiricism was his insistence that scientific method begins with and is sustained by "theories." Against the view that the scientist must banish all preconceived ideas before he proceeds to observe, collect, and generalize, he argued that "wisdom does not come to those who gape at nature with an empty head." Only with a "well-reasoned anticipation" of "what we expect to find" can we even identify "what is relevant to our search." Inquiry originates with primitive judgments about what is the case—prototheories, as it were, that inform even "prescientific" observations of nature.

The empiricists err in thinking that science begins outside of myth, superstition, and ancient metaphysical ideas, for without the judgments these modes contain, science would have no "base from which to start," nor any "certain direction in which to proceed." Prescientific senses of reality possess "the seeds of truth as well as the noxious weeds of error and illusion"; the history of science is marked by the gradual refinement and testing of these judgments through trial and error.[23]

Science proceeds according to the relentless doubting of what appears to be true, but this systematic doubt does not enable one to dispense with logic, nor does it require the a priori rejection of the truth claims embodied in what is doubted. Doubt itself is a profoundly logical process whereby our rational powers construct alternatives to what we have been inclined to believe: "effective doubt of any proposition means that we consider that some other proposition may be true." The "true method of science" is to control speculation "not by a return to pure experience devoid of assumptions, but by multiplying through pure logic" the alternative possibilities to old theories and assumptions. The great effort of science is not to get oneself to face fact, but to get oneself to theorize actively. Only then can one hope to expand knowledge beyond what it happens to be at a given point in time. The greater his store of alternative testable theories, the more prepared is the scientist to discover new truths. While the proliferation of theories is thus crucial to the advance of science, it by no means follows that we must jump to one of the new theories whenever difficulties are encountered by an old one. Choices between theories are not choices between those that explain and those that do not, but rather between theories that explain to a greater or lesser degree; this is the case even in the most "advanced" stages of scientific development. Therefore, one does not "throw out" an old theory because of a few instances of disconfirmation. On the contrary, "if we did not hold onto old ideas tenaciously . . . we could never develop any strong ideas and our science would have no continuity of development."[24]

By "continuity of development" Cohen referred to his view that the truth of science is never contained in any one-to-one relationship between a "fact" and a "theory." The "one essential trait of developed science is *system*," he insisted, and all "other traits are incidental to it." The very search for accurate knowledge of nature is an "attempt," ultimately, to "organize and systematize human judgments." When scientists seek to evaluate the explanatory power of rival theories, they do so in the framework of the existing body of knowledge: if a given set of experiments, for example, seems explicable within the terms of rival theories, the choice between the theories will be resolved tentatively according to which is the most clear, coherent, and consistent with the system of knowledge as a whole. The ultimate scientific ideal is to connect elements according to a deductive system on the model of geometry. In science, of course, we explain whatever aspects of contingent reality we have been able to observe and experiment upon (as observation and experimentation are guided by our assumptions), but the ideal of system remains implicit. Individual propositions "need the support of other propositions (through evidence and proof) to find a position of stability within the system," but the system as a whole "needs no support." In this the system of knowledge is rather like the earth: its stability does not come from "resting on something else," as the ancient astronomers thought, but from properties intrinsic to itself. The stability of knowledge, like the stability of the earth, is more easily explained if we regard it as being in motion. Apart from the invariant relations of all being, there is no hard-and-fast reality outside the structure of knowledge on the basis of which one might be able to show "that the whole body of scientific or demonstrative knowledge is false."[25]

Science can be challenged only by some other system which is factually more inclusive, and, through the demand for proof, logically more coherent. But such a system would simply be science improved. Science must always be ready to abandon any one of its conclusions, but when such overthrow is based on evidence, the logical consistency of the whole system is only strengthened. Progress in science is possible because no single proposition in it is so certain that it can block the search for one better founded.[26]

Finally, the actual process of "reasoning" that enables us to improve the system of knowledge is in no way clarified by the conventional distinction between induction and deduction. Normally, deduction is taken to be reasoning from generals to particulars, and induction the reverse. We should, on the contrary, see induction and deduction as variations on the syllogism, distinct from one another only according to the certainty of the premises from which we reason. The "particulars" and "generals" from which the two kinds of reasoning are held to begin are actually premises: what the empiricists call "particulars" are poorly grounded premises from which to reason, while the "generals" possess the only possible kind of solidity: solidity within the system of science. In inductive reasoning, then, we begin with a small number of instances, which we assume to be members of a class of instances about which we are trying to obtain certain conclusions. However, our knowledge is insufficiently complete to assure us that these instances are, in fact, members of that class; hence, the conclusions we reach do not have a level of certainty higher than that of the original premises. The difference between induction and deduction is thus, ultimately, one of degree. We proceed from one level to the other as a given branch of inquiry builds up a system sufficient to endow what the empiricists would call the "particulars" of its experience with a certain enough identity to enable us to reason from the behavior of these "particulars" to a potentially valid conclusion.[27]

Cohen's critique of popular empiricism thus embodied his own version of the scientific ideal, according to which the method of reason achieves continuity and balance by clinging "tenaciously" to old ideas while seeking new ones that will integrate the bits and pieces of experience yet more tightly into a mathematical system. This "tantalizingly slow method" manifests the great "virility" of science, which consists in "fearlessly facing the abysmal darkness that envelops us and in persistently applying logic to experience."[28] The method of reason, like the metaphysics of polarity, overcomes inertia but contains stampede; through its "measured straining in opposite directions," it preserves invariance, system, and sanity amid a world of sensual, material contingency. The most obvious philosophical sources of Cohen's account of the role of logic in science are the Kantian sense of knowledge as an internally consistent system, and the Cartesian belief that certainty is a mathematical condition. He in effect recast the Cartesian ideal of certainty in terms of probability, in order to take account of the modern, statistical view of "law" that would have been anathema to Descartes's absolutism. While Cohen achieved a strikingly cogent popularization of the insights of the rationalist tradition, he was less a contributor to the growth and development of rationalism than a propagandist for a consensus about logic and experience to which most of the great methodologists, including Bacon, were party. Historically, rationalists have had no monopoly on reason; some of Cohen's denunciations of "pure experience" are matched in the prose of Bacon himself, for whom an autonomous sense datum was "nothing but a loose fagot."[29] The antilogical cast of the "Baconianism" of Cohen's time enabled him to function not simply as a popularizer of rationalism, but as an ambassador of classical methodology to the courts of social science, "legal science," popular scientific thought, and even to some of contemporary philosophy.

Suspect as Cohen's rationalism was, he was recognized throughout the 1920s as an authority on scientific method. The *New York Times* treated one of his denigrations of Bacon as a news event. Walter Lippmann tried to enlist him as the *New York World*'s regular commentator on scientific affairs. The methodologists of social science found themselves taking more and more account of him; his views on the all-important question of social science's relation to natural science were solicited by William F. Ogburn and Abraham Goldenweiser for the 1927 compendium *The Social Sciences*, and he was assigned a host of topics for the *Encyclopedia of the Social Sciences*, including the notorious source of frustration for the Social Science Research Council, "Method, Scientific."[30]

No individual can be singled out as the founder of philosophy of science as a discipline in the United States, but no one was more instrumental than Cohen in creating the social and intellectual climate in which *Philosophy of Science* began to be published in 1934, and in which a number of colleges and universities added the subject to their curricula. The immediate occasion for these developments, however, was the sudden arrival of the polemically "scientistic" logical positivists in the early 1930s. The new discipline emerged out of the fusion of the interests of the Vienna Circle with those of two home-grown groups: the logicians Stuart Rice had tried to avoid, and the diverse participants in the more strictly "methodological" discourse of which Cohen had become the leader.[31]

Paradoxically, the influence of Cohen the archrationalist was reduced by the success of Cohen the ambassador of sophisticated methodology in general. The discipline he helped found soon left him behind, chiefly because of the success with which the logical positivists forced other discussants to accept their distinction between the "context of justification" and the "context of discovery." In this view, there are two kinds of questions about scientific method. Those in the "context of justification" have to do with "what sorts of evidence, and what general objective rules and standards govern the testing, the confirmation or disconfirmation, and the acceptance or rejection of knowledge-claims in science." Those in the "context of discovery" deal with the following sorts of problems: How does science proceed as a matter of behavioral fact? What is the "psychology and sociology of scientific discovery"? How does the procedure of science interact with the structure of knowledge and myth that exists in a given time and place?[32] The distinction greatly sharpened empiricism's traditional dichotomy between "discovery" and "proof."

The continental philosophers did two things with this distinction that profoundly affected philosophy of science. First, they insisted that the business of the discipline was to consider problems only within the "context of justification," and that other disciplines were free to take up problems of discovery. Second, they took it for granted that questions in the "context of justification" were ultimately questions in logic. Rudolph Carnap, Hans Reichenbach, Herbert Feigl, and their colleagues appeared on the American scene with so much prestige, flourish, and polemical skill that the discipline took form by responding to *their* formulations, not Cohen's.[33]

For more than twenty years Cohen had been trying to get people to admit that logic was the essence of scientific method. This claim was distinct enough in American discourse as late as 1930 that scholars would sometimes cite him when they had occasion to refer to this concept.[34] Among Cohen's ploys had been the argument that induction was ultimately as "logical" as deduction; for him, it was a point scored to show that induction was merely deduction without well-confirmed premises. But now the discipline discussed only the various senses in which this truism was to be taken; Carnap and Reichenbach took the whole problem to be one of defining what was meant by "the degree of confirmation."[35] The logical positivists, moreover, were not ones to doubt that "theories" were essential to the progress of science. Cohen built a bridge from crude Baconianism to a mathematically sophisticated philosophy of science, but few cared to linger on the bridge when there was so much action beyond. Although there is thus a sense in which philosophy of science developed within the terms Cohen advocated, the logical positivists were emphatically not rationalists of his sort. The positivists dealt with the particulars of sense experience, not with any "nonmental logical invariants"; the metaphysical and epistemological context of their philosophy of science was radically distinct from that of Cohen's. Moreover, they were hard-core empiricists in their assumption that however "logical" the process of "proof" or justification may be, the order of "observation" or discovery is not a logical process.

If the logical orientation of the positivists made half of Cohen's critique of empiricism seem clichéd, their aloofness from questions about "discovery" made the remaining half seem irrelevant. The positivists were resolutely ahistorical, while Cohen based his account of scientific method on interpretations of episodes in the history of science. The positivists wanted to mark off rigidly a sphere of verified, factual knowledge from the remaining world of "nonsense"; in contrast, Cohen emphasized the continuity between science and prescientific judgments. For him, myths and superstitions performed some of the same functions, albeit imperfectly, that a developed system of scientific knowledge could perform. Cohen's entire account of the role of logic in science was in fact embedded in a view of how science functions *as a part of culture*; his description of the growth of knowledge out of primitive judgments could hence be dismissed on the grounds that it was not about "justification," but sought to answer questions in the "context of discovery." He had always tried to get people to distinguish between history and logic, yet to retain a sense of their interdependence; now a more uncompromising formulation of this dualism was turned against Cohen himself. He was not a strong enough polemicist to force the relevance of his critique of empiricism on the logical positivists; not until thirty years later would American philosophers of science seriously consider the possibilities that discovery itself has a logical structure and that the distinction between justification and discovery had been overdrawn.[36] By that time Cohen's work was all but unread.

   The decision of the logical positivists to omit discovery from the logic of science was conducive to the growth of what Cohen considered an "irrationalist" view of the parts of science the new philosophers ignored. For years he had defended disinterested reason against the implication of Marxists and instrumentalists that scientific knowledge was a function of social conditions, and had fought for the view that the growth of science could be attributed to rationalistic motives.[37] Now Cohen's position was undercut by the positivist doctrine that the motives and interests that gave rise to and sustained inquiry were outside the scope of logical analysis. So long as the logic and history of science were combined in a single account of scientific activity, so long, that is, as the rules of justification could be interpreted as controlling influences on the flesh-and-blood scientists who sought to perfect the system of knowledge, one could make the case for science as the operation of disinterested reason. Once a radical distinction was made between logic and history, however, it became more difficult to refute the claim that the motives and interests behind inquiry were to be defined in economic, sociological, ideological, and psychological terms. Although "sociology of knowledge" was not yet much of a discipline, the steps taken toward its establishment by Karl Mannheim in Europe, and Talcott Parsons and Robert K. Merton in America, were more readily received in a learned world where logical positivists were responsible for philosophy of science. Hence the beginnings of sophisticated studies of science as an aspect of human culture tended to repudiate, rather than fulfill, Cohen's faith that the method of reason was *simultaneously and indissolubly* a logical form *and* a historical force.[38]

The emergence of philosophy of science and the more halting beginnings of "sociology of science" siphoned off to more technical pursuits some of the energies that had gone into the attempt to codify "scientific method" and to determine the relative import of "logic" and "experience" within that method, but discussion on this now-secondary level of academic discourse did continue, and Cohen was at its center. It was here that his views, especially as outlined in the *Encyclopedia of Social Sciences,*[39] were "authoritative." In the year 1939 alone, Cohen was the authority on scientific method in two ambitious symposia, one on "Science and Democracy," sponsored by the United States Department of Agriculture, and another on "Generalization in the Social Sciences," under the auspices of the University of Chicago Committee on Social Science Research. At both of these gatherings, Cohen characteristically promoted logical analysis and the use of "theories" in the company of many who thought it a mark of true science to observe nature without any "preconceived notions."[40] Here his defense of the method of reason continued to function as an incisive and provocative treatment of live issues.

It was in this sphere beyond formal philosophy of science that the

Introduction to Logic and Scientific Method achieved its greatest stature. This textbook of 1934, while it was cited occasionally by philosophers of science (especially for its dissents from Mill), was designed primarily for undergraduates and for others outside the philosophers' guild, who could turn to it for the sorts of guidance Wolf and Westaway had provided to the social scientists of the 1920s. Hence its "rationalistic" as opposed to "empiricist" bent was less important, again, than its cogent and forthright presentation of basic ideas about logic and science that were relatively uncontroversial among philosophers. However, the book belongs as much to the intellectual biography of coauthor Ernest Nagel as to that of Cohen, for the text itself, while its formulations expressed in greater precision and detail a point of view Cohen had long espoused, was predominantly Nagel's work.[41]

As the social scientists and scientific journalists of the 1940s and 1950s achieved a more theoretical orientation, they sometimes aligned themselves explicitly with positions Cohen had taken against their more anti-intellectual forebears.[42] Even here, however, Cohen's "influence" was in his capacity as the ambassador of sophisticated methodology in general, not as a classical rationalist.[43] Cohen's long-term impact on scientific journalism, the methodology of social research, and the history of science,[44] as with philosophy of science proper, was basic and general, but almost never specific. His rout of popular empiricism did not produce a succession of neo-Cartesians. Rather, it was Cohen's achievement to help persuade an ambitiously scientific generation that the nature of science could not be taken for granted.

NOTES

1. Thomas Mann, *The Magic Mountain*, trans. H. T. Lowe-Porter (New York, 1927), 466.

2. MRC, "Insurgence Against Reason," *JP* XXII (1925), 113, 117 (*RN*, 3, 9).

3. MRC, "Insurgence," 113 (*RN*, 3).

4. MRC, "Insurgence," 117 (*RN*, 9).

5. MRC, "Insurgence," 116-117 (*RN*, 8-9, 21); *RN*, 67, 69; MRC, remarks quoted in John Herman Randall, Jr., "The Twenty-Fifth Annual Meeting of the Eastern Division of the American Philosophical Association," *JP* XXIII (1926), 45; MRC, review of Leon Brunschvicg, *Les Étapes de la Philosophie Mathématique*, in *PR* XXIV (1915), 94 (*SPS*, 258).

6. Randall, "Twenty-Fifth Annual Meeting," 38; MRC, "The Rivals and Substitutes for Reason," *JP* XXII (1925), 141-150, 180-189 (*RN*, 23-75).

7. E.g., H. Stuart Hughes, *Consciousness and Society: European Social Thought, 1890-1930* (New York, 1958); Willson Coates and Hayden V. White, *The Ordeal of Liberal Humanism* (New York, 1970), 253-291; Henry F. May, *The End of American Innocence* (New York, 1959).

8. Laurens Laudan, "Theories of Scientific Method from Plato to Mach: A Bibliographical Review," *History of Science* VII (1968), 1-63, esp. 29; Edward H. Madden, ed., *Theories of Scientific Method: The Renaissance through the Nineteenth Century* (Seattle, 1960), esp. 152; Peter Caws, "Scientific Method," in Paul Edwards, ed., *Encyclopedia of Philosophy* (New York, 1967), VII, 339.

9. Caws, "Scientific Method," 339; Thomas S. Kuhn et al., "Science," in D. E. Sills, ed., *International Encyclopedia of the Social Sciences* (New York, 1968), XIV, 74-111; MRC, "Method, Scientific," in Edwin R. Seligman, ed., *Encyclopedia of the Social Sciences* (New York, 1937), X, 389-396. Cf. the philosophical analysis of the concept "method," without any expressly "scientific" associations, pursued in recent years by Justus Buchler, *The Concept of Method* (New York, 1961). Buchler, incidentally, begins with a commentary on Cohen's use of the concept (see pp. 1-8).

10. P. H. Nidditch, ed., *The Philosophy of Science* (New York, 1968), 4.

11. Albion W. Small, "Fifty Years of Sociology in the United States," *American Journal of Sociology* XXI (1916), 797. Cf. Small, "General Sociology," *American Journal of Sociology* XVIII (1912), 209; A. Lawrence Lowell, "The Physiology of Politics," *American Political Science Review* IV (1910), 1-15; and esp. Arthur F. Bentley's critique of the German philosopher Rudolph Jehring, in *The Process of Government*, ed. Peter Odegard (Cambridge, Mass., 1960), 80-91 (originally published 1908).

12. Charles E. Merriam, "Report of the Social Science Research Council

for 1926," quoted in Stuart A. Rice, ed., *Methods in Social Science: A Case Book* (New York, 1931), 732.

13. Howard W. Odum and Katherin Jocher, *An Introduction to Social Research* (New York, 1929). Cf. Walter Earl Spahr and Rinehart John Swenson, *Methods and Status of Social Research: With Particular Application to the Social Sciences* (New York, 1930) and W. F. G. Swann et al., *Essays on Research in the Social Sciences* (Washington, 1931).

14. Odum and Jocher, *Introduction*, esp. 21-26, 58, 318, 320.

15. Rice, *Case Book*, esp. 4-7.

16. E.g., John Dewey, *Reconstruction in Philosophy* (New York, 1920), esp. 132-160; John Dewey, *The Quest for Certainty* (New York, 1929), esp. 223-253.

17. E.g., R. D. Carmichael, "Concerning the Postulational Treatment of Truth," *Monist* XXXIII (1923), 513-555; A. Cornelius Benjamin, "To Exist or Not To Exist," *Monist* XXXVI (1926), 326-339; A. Cornelius Benjamin, "Science–Existential and Non-Existential," *PR* XXXVI (1927), 346-356; H. R. Smart, "The Problem of Induction," *JP* XXV (1928), 18-20.

18. Rice, *Case Book*, 7.

19. F. W. Westaway, *Scientific Method: Its Philosophy and Practice* (London, 1910; later editions in 1919, 1924); A. Wolf, *Essentials of Scientific Method* (New York, 1925). Cf. the widely cited text of "scientistic" history, Ch. V. Langlois and Ch. Seignobos, *Introduction to the Study of History*, trans. G. G. Berry (London, 1898).

20. *RN*, 76.

21. Odum and Jocher, 318, 320; Rice, *Case Book*, 29, 32, 70-72, 93-94, 111, 381; Karl Mannheim, review of *Case Book*, in *American Journal of Sociology* XXXVIII (1932), 277-278.

22. *RN*, 76-146.

23. MRC, "The Role of Logic in the Law," *Harvard Law Review* XXIX (1916), 626 (*LSO*, 169); MRC, "Insurgence," 180 (*RN*, 17); MRC, "Rivals and Substitutes," 184-185 (*RN*, 39); MRC, "Mechanism and Causality in Physics," *JP* XV (1918), 374; MRC, "The Myth about Bacon and the Inductive Method," *City College Alumnus* XXII (1926), 307 (*SPS*, 104); MRC, "Law and Scientific Method," *American Law School Review* VI (1928), 234-238 (*LSO*, 190, 193, 195); *RN*, 76-79.

24. MRC, "Logic in the Law," 626 (*LSO*, 129); MRC, "Rivals and Sub-

stitutes," 184-185 (*RN*, 39); MRC, "Law and Scientific Method," 238 (*LSO*, 195); *RN*, 81, 84-86.

25. MRC, "Jus Naturale Redivivum," *PR* XXV (1916), 774-777; MRC, "Logic in the Law," 626 (*LSO*, 169); MRC, "The Process of Judicial Legislation," *American Law Review* XLVIII (1914), 192 (*LSO*, 144); *RN*, 87, 102, 106-109.

26. *RN*, 87.

27. *RN*, 115-119.

28. MRC, review of F. H. Bradley, *Principles of Logic*, in *NR* XLIV (1925), 149 (*PL*, 206).

29. Francis Bacon, *Novum Organum*, Book I, aphorism 82, quoted in Madden, *Theories*, 80.

30. *New York Times* (October 10, 1926), 20; Walter Lippmann to MRC, July 28 and October 9, 1925, Cohen MSS; William F. Ogburn and Abraham Goldenweiser, *The Social Sciences* (Boston, 1927), 437-466; Alvin Johnson to MRC, December 20, 1927, Cohen MSS. Cohen engaged in frequent discourse with several prominent social scientists at Columbia during the 1910s and 1920s, especially at meetings of the "Karl Pearson Circle," described briefly in Robert Lowie, "Reflections," *American Anthropologist* LVIII (1956), 1012.

31. The history of philosophy of science in the United States (and elsewhere, for that matter) is yet to be written. My sense of it is based partially on information contained in the very ahistorical account of Herbert Feigl, "Philosophy of Science," in Roderick M. Chisholm et al., *Philosophy* (Englewood Cliffs, N.J., 1963), 467-539. Cf. Victor F. Lenzen, "Philosophy of Science in America," in Marvin Farber, ed., *Philosophical Thought in France and the United States* (Buffalo, 1950), 505-524. A contemporary bibliographical essay remains the most helpful starting point for work in this area: Charles W. Morris, "Some Aspects of Recent Scientific Philosophy," *Erkenntnis* V (1934), 142-149, 195-199. Cohen himself was a founding member of the editorial board of *Philosophy of Science*, and was recognized by the emigrés as the most important American theorist of scientific method since the time of Peirce (see esp. Feigl, "The Wiener Kreis in America," *Perspectives in American History* II [1968], 660).

32. Feigl, "Philosophy of Science," 473; Ernest Nagel, "Probability in the Theory of Knowledge," *Philosophy of Science* VI (1939), 226.

33. To be sure, there were occasional references to Cohen's work in

Philosophy of Science, e.g., I (1934), 231, 341; II (1935), 467, 489, 497; III (1936), 152; V (1938), 193, 487. Cf. the references to Cohen in two textbooks: A. Cornelius Benjamin, *An Introduction to the Philosophy of Science* (New York, 1937), 37-38, 112, 126; W. H. Werkmeister, *A Philosophy of Science* (New York, 1940), 23, 26, 28, 197.

34. E.g., Alexander William Stern, "The Role of Mathematics in Modern Physical Theory," *Monist* XXXIX (1929), 267.

35. Feigl, "Philosophy of Science," 485-486.

36. E.g., Thomas S. Kuhn, *The Structure of Scientific Revolutions* (Chicago, 1962); Peter Caws, "The Structure of Discovery," *Science* CLXVI (1969), 1375-1380; Imre Lakatos, "The Logic of Scientific Research Programmes," in Lakatos and Alan Musgrave, *Criticism and the Growth of Knowledge* (Cambridge, Eng., 1970), 91-195; and the scattered writings of Paul Feyerabend, of whose ideas a strikingly cogent overview can be found in the introduction to Robert E. Butts and John W. Davis, eds., *The Methodological Heritage of Newton* (Oxford, 1970), 10-12.

37. E.g., MRC, "Insurgence," 113-117 (*RN*, 3-7).

38. Karl Mannheim, *Ideology and Utopia*, trans. Louis Wirth and Edward Shils (New York, 1946; originally published 1929); Robert K. Merton, "Science, Technology and Society in Seventeenth Century England," *Osiris* IV (1938), 360-632.

39. MRC, "Method, Scientific."

40. United States Department of Agriculture, Graduate School, *Ten Lectures on Science: Its History, Philosophy, and Relation to Democracy* (Washington, 1929), 77-110 (*SPS*, 48-89); Louis Wirth, ed., *Eleven Twenty-Six: A Decade of Social Science Research* (Chicago, 1940), 227-273.

41. I have discussed the nature of this collaboration with Nagel (New York City, December 31, 1968), and I have compared *ILSM* with the handwritten draft Nagel originally presented to Cohen. The two went over Nagel's draft line by line, with the following results: Chapters I and XIX were substantially revised, Chapters II and III were published without several pages of Nagel's draft, and Chapter XX was expanded by a four-page (399-403) conclusion. In addition, *ILSM* includes an essay on "Logic and Critical Evaluation" (Chapter XVIII) written exclusively by Cohen (for a discussion of Cohen's "ethical science" see below, Chapter 7, "The Science of Justice"). The remainder of the published text, including all of Chapters II and III, and most of Chap-

ters I, XIX, and XX, was taken from Nagel's draft, word for word, with only infrequent and minor changes.

42. E.g., William J. Goode and Paul K. Hatt, *Methods in Social Research* (New York, 1952); William P. McEwen, *The Problem of Social Scientific Knowledge* (Totowa, N.J., 1963). Cohen was cited with more obvious enthusiasm, however, by theorists of the social sciences who remained critical of even the chastened "scientism" of the 1940s and 1950s: e.g., F. A. Hayek, *The Counter-Revolution in Science* (Glencoe, Ill., 1955), esp. 207, 212, 214, 221; Vernon Van Dyke, *Political Science: A Philosophical Analysis* (Stanford, 1960), esp. 60, 196, 212, 228; Barrington Moore, *Political Power and Social Theory* (Cambridge, Mass., 1958), 106-110.

43. For example, Stuart Chase, in *Guides to Straight Thinking* (New York, 1956), cited Cohen along with Victorian empiricist John Tyndall in support of the general insight that only confusion can result from ignoring logical principles (xii, 3).

44. *SBGS*, prepared in collaboration with I. E. Drabkin, became a standard reference work for historians and classicists.

And thus, as I have shown, Socrates, injustice, when on a sufficient scale, has more strength and freedom and mastery than justice; and, as I said at first, justice is the interest of the stronger, whereas injustice is a man's own profit and interest.

Thrasymachus, when he had thus spoken, having, like a bath-man deluged our ears with his words, had a mind to go away. But the company would not let him; they insisted that he should remain and defend his position; and I myself added my own humble request that he would not leave us. Thrasymachus, I said to him, excellent man, how suggestive are your remarks! And are you going to run away before you have fairly taught or learned whether they are true or not?

Plato

Like so many nineteenth- and early-twentieth-century advocates of "scientific method," Morris Cohen was not always certain about its scope. It was obviously "a method," but of doing what? Sometimes Cohen even challenged the distinction between science and art by implying that specific "scientific" enterprises such as the doing of physics or the dispensation of justice were "rational arts." Even if defined as a method of inquiry, as a means of obtaining knowledge about things, how wide was the scope of knowledge? The entire scientistic movement from Comte and Mill through Dewey and Cohen had believed that this method could be "applied" to a diversity of tasks, some of which were hard to characterize in terms of *cognitive* control over experience. Was the more rational administration of human affairs, for example, an advancement of knowledge? It was convenient to distinguish between "pure" and "applied" science, but there always remained within the realm of "pure" science the problem of identifying the kinds of questions that could be resolved scientifically. Cohen, like most promoters of the extension of science into social and moral realms, preferred to dodge the question through the "pragmatic" claim that only after having tried to do something scientifically could one judge the applicability of science to that endeavor. On the basis of his sense of reason's precariousness, it seemed unwise to labor over the limitations of science when one's time could be so much better spent getting people to respect and understand science's positive possibilities. Cohen did not believe that scientific reason, by itself, was a sufficient mode of living, but he never let his respect for resignation and undisciplined contemplation get in the way of his scientific evangelism. The limits of science were to be acknowledged in the abstract, but not defined in the concrete.

Yet it was impossible for Cohen to avoid argument with many of those who shared his interest in social science and "ethical science." The unavoidable issue was the moral and anthropological implications of scientific method: Does the application of scientific method to human affairs entail the elimination from view of the very properties that distinguish human beings from the rest of nature? Since the methods of science have been refined in the process of dealing with objects apparently devoid of "purposes," "values," and "ideals," does it follow that the application of such methods to the study of humans must either leave purposes, values, and ideals out of account or treat them as mere rationalizations for behavior that can, in fact, be explained by the operation of forces functionally identical to those on which explanations are based in the physical sciences? Beyond the "factual" questions asked by social science, must the pursuit of "ethical science" be limited to the discovery of what given human beings have in fact believed to be good and right? Or, if ethical science is recognized as an attempt to determine what we ourselves shall regard as good and right, does the scientific status of the enterprise depend on the rigor with which we redefine purposes, values, and ideals in terms of psychophysical "interests"? Is ethical science predicated on the translation of imperatives into indicatives?

When Cohen confronted the problem of science's ultimate scope, therefore, he did so in the context of his defense of the authenticity of purposes, values, and ideals. He believed that nihilism, in the form of "might makes right," was lurking unrecognized just beneath the surface of his generation's "scientific" social, moral, and legal philosophy; he therefore aimed to detach from "the scientific way of thinking" the implication that justice is the will of the stronger, that ethical obligations are ultimately functions of power relationships, and that human affairs are inevitably governed by brute force. This mission, in turn, Cohen pursued in the setting of jurisprudence.

Unless the insights of relativism and absolutism were carefully balanced, Cohen warned his generation of jurists and lawyers, the ship of law would be "wrecked on either the Scylla of totalitarianism or the Charybdis of anarchy."[1] American jurisprudence spent the first half of the twentieth century trying to work out the implications of the recognition that law is a distinctly human product, that the justice dispensed by courts is in fact made by judges. Cohen wanted the legal profession to control carefully its revulsion at the archaic, "prescientific" formalism of traditional jurisprudence, according to which law had been depicted as a system of deductive derivations from principles embedded in statutes, in common law, and in the structure of the universe. Balance might easily be lost in the process of taking hold of the new and valid insight that law is a living, changing, relative aspect of social experience; perhaps some would rush to the foolish conclusion that law could therefore have no stability, no certainty, no logic, and no claim to justice.

Maintenance of the proper balance between the new relativism and the old absolutism required, above all, a sound understanding of science, for the very notion of "judge-made law," as presented so compellingly by Oliver Wendell Holmes, Jr., derived from an attempt to make the law an object of empirical, anthropological scrutiny.[2] What properties were attributed to, and what denied to, "the law" when so viewed? If, for example, the object being scrutinized turned out, because of a prior assumption about the nature of science, to be a social process, did it follow that the search for *justice* was not, in itself, a "scientific" study of "the law"? If the indicative aspect of law could be studied scientifically, what remained to be said about its imperative aspect? Further, did there attend upon the scientific study of the "legal process" (if this, indeed, was what "law" reduced to under the eye of science) certain senses of the role played by rationality and ethical ideals in any social process? In these ways the problems of jurisprudence were indissolubly bound up with questions about the nature of science; thus Cohen's arguments with his contemporaries over what counted as a "balanced" jurisprudence were inevitably part of a more general struggle for possession of the scientific ideal.

The prospect that the law might become devoid of logical consistency and too far removed from ethical ideals seemed remote in April of 1913, when the first Conference on Legal and Social Philosophy brought to Morningside and St. Nicholas Heights many of the lawyers, social scientists, and philosophers excited by what Cohen himself called

"The Process of Judicial Legislation."[3] In a paper so entitled, Cohen attacked the "phonograph theory of law," according to which the judicial function was simply to play the right record at the right time.[4] This paper, and the entire conference, aimed chiefly to affirm the truth of the Holmesian view of law and to outline its positive possibilities. The conference, organized by Cohen himself and chaired by John Dewey, was opened by Roscoe Pound, the great advocate of "sociological jurisprudence." Pound sought to exploit the opportunities of "judge-made law": let the law be made on the basis of scientific social knowledge, he urged; let judges improve society by putting the appropriate social ideals into effect.[5] This was a theme of Cohen's address, too: judges were to calculate the social consequences of all alternatives open in a given case and make a decision according to a clearly articulated set of social priorities.[6]

For Holmes himself, the recognition that judges make law implied the necessity of judicial restraint: judges were not to mistake their own views for "natural law," but were to acknowledge these views as their own appropriate contributions to fill lacunae left by statutes. Holmes was not at all eager to have courts turn themselves into conscious agents of social reform. But the scholars Cohen brought to City College and Columbia were more explicitly connected with "progressive" politics than was Holmes, and they were more willing than he to outline a program for what the courts could do to advance the progressive cause. To this group the very plausibility of "judge-made law" had become clear in a political context. They had watched the behavior of the conservative jurists who, while protesting their inability to countermand the intentions of the authors of the laws, defended the most reactionary social policies of the age through the application of the due process clause of the Fourteenth Amendment to situations for which it could not possibly have been designed. Surely progressives had everything to gain by making the courts more directly responsive to contemporary social needs. It was not a time for worrying about how one might justify the priorities according to which a "scientifically trained"[7] jurist would find that J. P. Morgan's sense of "contemporary social needs" was less accurate than that of the American Federation of Labor.

Caught up as Cohen was in this confident insurgency, it was he, of course, who expressed the most reservations; it was he who sketched out even then the frightening things that might happen if the revolt against the old jurisprudence were to lose its balance, if the "frenzied" ravings of the insane were to replace logical reasoning as the model for judicial action.[8] But the format of Cohen's attack on anti-intellectualism and nihilism was an index of his solidarity with Holmes, Pound, and their great ally, John Chipman Gray.[9] Cohen exempted them from the charge of having made the impending dangers to jurisprudence more real; he placed these three thinkers in the middle of the road, with himself. The spectrum of opinion, as Cohen sketched it, had at one extreme the nineteenth century's "mechanical jurisprudence," and at the other several "positivists" whose ideas were anything but standard referent points in American discourse. In "The Place of Logic in the Law," for example, he castigated Hans Wustendorfer, Ernst Fuchs, Arthur F. Bentley, and Brooks Adams for their denial of "all value to logic and general principles."[10] The idiosyncratic Adams has always been of interest to literary historians, and Bentley was to become significant for political scientists of later decades, but Cohen was one of very few legal theorists of the 1910s to pay attention to either. By talking about them, and about obscure Europeans, Cohen could condemn anti-intellectualism while wrapping himself in the robes of Holmes, whom, from Cohen's characterization, one would never recognize as the author of that notorious aphorism, "the life of the law has not been logic, it has been experience." Cohen's "The Place of Logic in the Law" appeared in an issue of the *Harvard Law Review* (1916) dedicated to Holmes, whom Cohen depicted as the exemplar of balance between logic and experience, between extreme intellectualism and extreme anti-intellectualism. It was in the context of this defense of what he took to be Holmesian balance that Cohen first used his metaphor of the coachman: "We urge our horse down the hill and yet put the brake on the wheel—clearly a contradictory process to a logic too proud to learn from experience."[11]

Although his general sense of what Holmes intended to claim about how judges function was not necessarily mistaken, Cohen's "The Place of Logic in the Law" was an unusually transparent example of what was soon to become a standard ploy in American jurisprudence: the attempt to dignify one's own views by attributing them to Holmes. It would not be an overstatement to say that American legal philosophers worked out the meaning of "judge-made law" by quoting Holmes against each other. This was a result not simply of Holmes's genuine heuristic brilliance, nor even of his prestige. He was, in fact, ambiguous about the relation of law to modern science, a relation that his successors, too, found difficult to clarify.

Holmes had sought to distinguish between "law" and "ethics,"[12] but from Cohen's viewpoint the distinction had to be handled very carefully to prevent its being used to deny that there could be a "scientific" determination of right and wrong. The distinction between "is" and "ought" must not be taken to limit scientific reason solely to the discovery of actually existing, concrete, historical, and in this case *social*, "facts" of the indicative order; imperatives, too, must be subject to rational, scientific justification. Otherwise, law becomes merely "the will of the sovereign," the manifestation of a power relationship. Cohen's philosophy of law was an attempt, first, to outline a view of "legal science" that did not limit it to a factual description of the legal process and, second, to defend as "scientific" an account of the legal process itself in which logical reasoning, general principles, and ethical ideals were historically and materially active. He rarely distinguished these two levels of his work from each other, but preferred to think of them as a single set of statements about the nature of "law," which for him could be only a system of rationally justified imperatives.

Cohen's actual career as a philosopher of law falls into two distinct phases, both qualitatively and chronologically. Between 1913 and 1916 he published nine substantial papers in which he worked out the position he was to defend for the rest of his life, but most vehemently in the succession of papers published in the early 1930s in dialogue with the "legal realists." In the earlier period Cohen's stance was primarily prophetic; he could point to few active participants in American legal discourse who jumped off what was, to him, the deep end. But some of the realists seemed to do exactly this, so Cohen's work in the second phase participated in give-and-take polemics with his enemies. The distinctness of these two periods makes it possible to consider first the substance of his philosophy of law, as put forth in the 1910s, and then the controversies of the later periods.

When Cohen discussed the legal process itself, viewed as an aspect of historical existence, he characteristically denounced two extreme positions. On the one hand was the traditional, comforting but naive "idealism" that "saw nothing in the common law but justice and the accumulated reason of mankind." On the other was the "modern" and ostensibly "scientific" realism that could see in law nothing but "force, the will of the sovereign, or the interest of the stronger or dominant class."[13] Both views contained elements of truth but erred by denying the insights vouchsafed to the other. The excesses of idealism were readily recognized by an age that understood law to be "a province in the life we call civilization,"[14] but the excesses of realism lurked in the wrongheaded assumption that the "civilization" of which law was part lacked rational and altruistic motives. Cohen saw nothing unscientific in the traditional practice of explaining human conduct in terms of reasons and ideals. It was "absurd," he said, to deny the "fact" that "ethical ideals have been powerful factors in making the law":

It would seem that religion has moulded the greatest part of the law under which mankind lives. Religious conceptions, for instance, have had more to do with making our marriage laws than has anything else. . . . Whether we take the pretorian law, English equity, or the influence of seventeenth- and eighteenth-century natural law on international law, constitutional law, and criminal law, we everywhere find ethical ideals exercising profound influence, apart from, and often contrary to, the interest of the class that the jurists represent.[15]

The issue, of course, was the precise status of what are conventionally called "religious conceptions" and "ethical ideals," and Cohen simply refused to trifle with attempts to translate them into "interests." He took his stand on the autonomy of ethics and logic, and he was inclined neither to "explain" the development of "religious" ideas about marriage in terms of the physiological, psychological, social, and economic conditions of human life in a given society, nor to conclude therefrom that the "laws" justified in the name of religion were best understood as functions of such prior conditions. Hence Cohen cautioned his colleagues against overreacting to outmoded idealism and intellectualism; they must retain in their accounts of the legal process a description of exactly how respected legal principles not only justify judicial decisions after the fact, but also control the decision itself. This caution passed as good sense until challenged by the overt behaviorism and psychosocial determinism of the legal realists.

Meanwhile, Cohen was devoting most of his attention to the defense and clarification of the more important, more overtly "normative," mission of legal science. He viewed the court's act of judgment as an emblem for what the judge's supporting cast of legal and social thinkers were supposed to be doing; scholars, too, were in the business of seeking justice. They were not to betray this mission by seeking solely to predict judicial behavior, nor were they to confuse an inquiry into right and wrong with the discovery of what specific ideas of right and wrong happened to have prevailed in a given society, including American society. Cohen warned explicitly that the sciences of ethics and law might be seduced by the appeal of "the genetic fallacy."[16] Here he was arguing against a moral philosophy, historicism, but his ultimate target was the same nihilism he had sensed in "realistic" descriptions of the legal process: historicism claimed to recognize the reality of values and norms, yet abdicated the truly evaluative role to history itself. What passed for scientific, historically oriented "legal science" was too often a species of covert historicism, Cohen charged; it implied that whatever institutions, practices, and norms survived in history were somehow more "right" than those that perished along the way. The dominant social values of the United States in 1915 might not, after all, be the best of all possible standards for public policy.

Historicism was not altogether a straw man. Indeed, the frequency with which American thinkers of the period were guilty of "the genetic fallacy" was to cause a recurrent lament in subsequent social criticism.[17] Cohen had no trouble finding texts to cite: ethics should be "an objective study of what has happened, not in the least of what ought to happen," one philosopher had claimed.[18] John Dewey himself did not go as far as this, but Cohen correctly saw in Dewey's anthropological approach a drift toward covert historicism. *Ethics*, the influential textbook Dewey coauthored with James H. Tufts in 1908, defined its subject as "the science that deals with conduct, in so far as this *is considered* as right or wrong, good or bad."[19] Cohen's fears that such attitudes led down the road to nihilism were of course rejected, and almost laughed at by their spokesmen, but Cohen was led to persist by the example of nineteenth-century German jurisprudence, which proved to him at least that historicism could drain the science of justice of its capacity to do more than endorse the status quo.[20]

Cohen's answer to genetic evaluation was his doctrine of natural law. It was a rather bold strategy, for, as he himself noted, the status of natural law among the cognoscenti was barely that of witchcraft.[21] Certainly the very insight of "judge-made law" seemed antithetical to natural law. And natural law had been notoriously interpreted from a historicist point of view as a force that controlled, and thereby vindicated, existing social and economic conditions in the United States and elsewhere. Moreover, natural law was presumably the citadel of the old superintellectualistic formalism according to which more or less permanent and transcendent principles were available as premises from which the law's content could be deduced. Cohen's claim, on the contrary, was that the idea of natural law was intrinsically connected to neither the historicist nor the transcendentalist interpretation.

The essence of all doctrines of natural law, said Cohen, is the "appeal

from positive law to justice, from the law that is to the law that ought
to be." Unless we reject the very concept of "a law that ought to be,"
the "roots of natural law remain untouched." Cohen's strategy was to
identify natural law with justice itself, to make the two concepts inter-
changeable, and thereby to establish natural law as the standard by
which the positive law was to be evaluated. As he defined the issue, to
reject natural law was to embrace absolute relativism. The existence of
natural law was implied by the possibility of evaluation; only by denying the latter could the former be doubted.[22]

   This was a most difficult doctrine to uphold, for natural-law philosophies had traditionally been distinguished from other moral philosophies by their characterization of the source and the firmness of imperatives, not by their simple affirmation of the reality of imperatives.[23]
Cohen's maneuver was inspired by Rudolph Stammler, a German legal
philosopher admitted only grudgingly into the ranks of natural-law
theorists by keepers of that tradition. Cohen's needs were well served
by Stammler's view that the mere possibility of establishing a formal
criterion for evaluating laws implied the existence of natural law;[24] this
view enabled Cohen to disown unwanted associations yet retain the
feeling of natural law. The phrase "natural law" connoted that the
realm of the "ought" was somehow or other (an ambiguity never fully
resolved by Cohen) an authentic and substantial part of the nature of
things.

   There were actually two sorts of questions Cohen's normative jurisprudence, his "systematic science of justice or natural law," was designed to answer. First, what means are to be adopted in a particular
situation if one wants to fulfill a given moral end, or principle? Questions of this type have always been relatively easy for would-be "ethical
scientists" to bring within the scope of science, for the unambiguously
moral element is taken for granted. The determination of moral ends is
prior to science, which retains only an instrumental role. As Cohen put
it, the judge's effort to render justice is methodologically akin to the
engineer's attempt to build a bridge: the engineer's responsibility is to

get the bridge built by whatever methods he thinks are right, but it is not part of his job to decide whether or not a bridge shall be built.[25] The premises of such an "ethical science" would be imperatives to begin with, so the endeavor could not be refuted with the old saw, "but you can't derive imperatives from indicatives." Indeed, one can insist that the scientific pursuit of any given means-to-end question is exclusively an *inquiry into facts*, and that the act of *evaluation* is strictly independent from it. In any case, much of "sociological jurisprudence" could be defended within a moral philosophy that sought to use science in this strictly instrumental fashion. Cardozo, for example, had no doubt that the law must accept "as the pattern of its justice the morality of the community whose conduct it assumes to regulate." When component groups in that community disagree about moral values, Cardozo added, the law must follow "the principle and practice" of those whom "the social mind would rank as intelligent and virtuous."[26]

Sometimes Cohen spoke as though the instrumental questions were the only sort he intended his science of justice to resolve. "Reason has to do with judgments (determining the appropriateness of means to end) and cannot determine the ultimate ends that are a matter of ultimate choice," he once declared, adding that Hobbes was therefore right "in putting will above reason in the law." Cohen was quick to qualify this with the observation that reason, as a means, can indirectly influence the choice made by the will, simply because possession of an instrument enables one to think of new things to do: "Give a boy a hatchet and he will want to do things for which he had no desire before."[27] Yet Cohen's flirtations with untrammeled will are important primarily for the ambivalence and uncertainty they reveal in his moral philosophy; on other occasions during the same period, and later, he committed the science of natural law to the more difficult task of justifying its own premises; he thereby took up the second, more difficult and more authentically ethical question of moral ends.

It was in keeping with Cohen's view of scientific method that reason was to "organize," "systematize," and refine primitive judgments (and *not* only judgments of the appropriateness of means to ends); he did, after all, hold that the more developed a science becomes, the more reliable are its premises. And it is in his outline of a science of natural law that may be found the most detailed general account of scientific method that Cohen produced in any context during the 1910s. He approached principles of natural law explicitly "from the point of view of the requirements of a scientific theory." Candidates for basic principles in the new science were to be assessed in the same way one would assess a proposition in the physical sciences: the assertion that "all men have a right to live," for example, must be treated like the "Copernican hypothesis in astronomy." The reliability of either of these depends on whether "they yield a body or system of propositions which is preferable to that which can possibly be established on the basis of their denial." Whether or not a system of propositions is "preferable" to others depends on its clarity, consistency, and coherence, and on its integration with other ideas taken to be right and true. The content of "the rules of justice" are thus "dependent upon social science" because only the latter can allow us to achieve clarity, consistency, and coherence in our basic moral values.[28] Those values, contrary to popular misconception, are not matters of mere opinion, variable as the winds from one society and subsociety to another, Cohen insisted; he believed science would reveal a moral consensus in the collective will of the human race. Thus "will" may be prior to "reason," but the choice made by the will fits into a pattern: the principles of natural law are hence discoverable, by reason, in the uniformity of human ethical instincts.[29]

Cohen's case for the science of natural law was thus predicated on a denial of ethical relativism. The "variability" of ethical judgments had "as a matter of fact been greatly exaggerated," he claimed: soon we shall "soberly" examine the reports of anthropologists and see in them the "fundamental resemblances of all human races and modes of life." Cohen tried to support this faith by quoting Franz Boas and James Harvey Robinson, two thinkers of the period identified conspicuously

with the drift toward ethical relativism, but the ironic tactic did not
quite come off: the most he could get out of Boas was the observation
that "variations of moral opinion are explicable by the variation of
social conditions," which, of course, begged the entire question.[30] Ultimately, Cohen's argument against the indeterminacy of ethical judgments took the form of the principle of polarity. There had to be moral
permanence because experience shows us nothing in flux "except by
reference to something constant."

We may generalize change as much as we like, saying that even the most
general laws of nature that we know, such as the laws of mechanics, are
slowly changing, but this change can be established and have meaning
only by means of or in reference to some logical constant. The belief
that the world consists of all change and no constancy is no better than
the belief that all vessels have insides and no outsides.[31]

On this basis Cohen could make "natural law with a changing content" the slogan of his jurisprudence.[32] The moral as well as the physical order had invariant relations, which, in turn, were not *so* invariant as
to prevent them from changing slightly now and then. He is elliptical
here, but he seems to imply that the objects of ethical science, like the
objects of physical science, exist only within contexts of intersecting
relations; what is "right" may be contingent, just as "truth" in physics
may be contingent, but the search for the right is a search for "natural
law" in the same sense that the search for truth is an endeavor to discover the "laws" of physics. The invariants of value are thus analogous
to the invariants of logic. "Values, like mathematical relations, may
involve characteristics independent of the time order," but justice is to
be found in the interaction of ethical invariants with contingent social
experience, in the same sense, broadly speaking, that the nature of
physical objects is found in the interaction of logical invariants with the
contingency of the physical world.[33]
    Dependent as his moral philosophy was on this analogy between logic
and ethics, Cohen did not push it very far. The invariants of logic were,
after all, readily identifiable, but what "characteristics" of values could

he actually point to that were "independent of the time order"? Further, was not the method by which the "science of natural law" would eventually discover such invariants dangerously close to historicism? If the ground of imperatives was the moral consensus of the race, would not one be resolving "ought" questions by collecting historical facts? Do not normative questions therefore become resolved by the moral status quo? Cohen did not take up this problem directly, but he seems to have believed that the moral experience of humanity as a whole, ancient and modern, primitive and civilized, constituted an object of knowledge so vast that it was transformed, by its sheer generality, into a source of imperatives. When he condemned the reduction of "ought" to "is," he referred to the abdication of a critical perspective on the status quo in specific local situations; that critical perspective was itself to be grounded in a cosmopolitan understanding of the moral potentialities and limitations of human beings in general. The very universality of these potentialities and limitations endowed them with ontological status, just as the fact that "logic holds of nature" justified Cohen's belief in the metaphysical distinctness of logical invariants.

The philosophy of law Cohen set forth in the 1910s was thus decidedly more formalistic than the outlook that has come to be associated with the "new" jurisprudence. Yet he was readily accepted as an ally by Pound, Holmes, Benjamin Cardozo, and their party. The quick and extensive rapport the latter group felt with Cohen is an index of how restrained the "revolt against formalism" of the 1910s was in contrast with what Morton White correctly calls the "reign of terror" that was to follow.[34] Cohen's attack on historicism was cited with approval in 1915 by Holmes himself.[35] The agreement Holmes and Cohen claimed may have been exaggerated by the personal pleasure Holmes took in encouraging his young disciple, and by the latter's expressed joy at having his "intellectual output appreciated" by the likes of Holmes.[36] Still, the justice persisted in his praise of Cohen, not only in letters to him, but to Einstein, Laski, and Frederick Pollock. Much has been made of Holmes's affinity with the philosophical outlook of John

Dewey, but the justice, at least during the last two decades of his life, identified himself with exactly those formalistic views of Cohen that were at odds with Dewey. Holmes seems not to have flinched even at Cohen's adherence to "natural law."[37] Pound, too, carried on a regular and congenial correspondence with Cohen,[38] whose acceptance into American law's intellectual establishment got formal recognition as early as 1914, when he was asked by the editors of the American Legal Philosophy Series to edit a volume on legal method.[39]

In the early 1920s, while Cohen's scattered legal writings were solidifying his position as a leading interpreter of the Holmesian tradition,[40] there appeared an adamant, organized movement to defend the pre-Holmesian view of law. Believing still that the law was applied rather than made, some of the bar's most distinguished members looked to a "restatement" of the law as the means of achieving greater uniformity in the decisions of courts. One judge would presumably be less likely to act in contradiction to another if both had at their disposal a clearer, more completely codified common law to guide them. Although jurists of various persuasions hoped for practical benefits from the "restatement" attempted by the American Law Institute, the institute became associated primarily with its conservative theoretical underpinnings.[41] The A.L.I. was, by the end of the 1920s, a favorite whipping boy for the law teachers who would soon be dubbed the "legal realists." To these young scholars, struggling to integrate the law curriculum with the social sciences, the contrasting efforts toward autonomy and certainty on the part of Elihu Root and other antediluvians at the A.L.I. were a pathetic joke at best, and at worst an obstacle to progress. While laughing at the A.L.I., this "left" flank of the Holmesian tradition became more and more outspoken in its skepticism toward the actual or possible utility of principles and precedents. Although they intended to deny not that regularities existed in the legal process, but rather that these regularities conformed to the doctrinal rules expressed in treaties, the legal realists often overstated their case. By 1930 the more-Holmesian-than-thou pronouncements of these younger scholars became so provocative that "realism" replaced "sterile formalism" as the starting point for jurisprudential discourse. The most discussed contributions to the law journals were either by or about Herman Oliphant, Underhill Moore, Walter Cook, Hessel Yntema, Jerome Frank, and Karl Llewellyn. Diverse as were the technical interests of the legal realists, they had more in common than they liked to admit. Although most sought to improve the law, they almost always agreed that "ought" questions could be put aside until "is" questions were more completely answered: the law needed to be accurately described before one could properly deal with its normative aspect. What counted as a "description," further, was generally determined by what the realists understood of contemporary psychology, anthropology, and sociology. Underhill Moore, for example, connected the insight of "judge-made law" to a distinctly up-to-date view of what judges, as human beings, actually were: the view of behaviorism as espoused by John D. Watson himself. Moore concluded that law was simply an aspect of behavior, and that legal institutions were "certain habits."[42] Jerome Frank's *Law and the Modern Mind*, the most well-known single work to come out of the movement, applied a simplistic and single-minded Freudianism to the judicial process.[43] The realists assumed, for the most part, that if law is a *human* product, it must be a series of particular, largely irrational responses to social and psychological conditions. Humans, the realists believed, respond to immediate, concrete conditions with a minimum of intervention by inherited culture in the form of "rules," "principles," or "precedents." Since judges are human in exactly this way, judicial behavior cannot be predicted on the basis of precedents.[44]

The realists were suddenly and decisively put on the defensive in the spring of 1931 when Pound and Cohen took the occasion of Holmes's ninetieth birthday to denounce, in the name of the master, the group Pound called "our younger teachers of law."[45] Cohen's "Justice Holmes and the Nature of Law" appeared in the *Columbia Law Review*

just as the *Harvard Law Review* published Pound's "The Call for a Realistic Jurisprudence"; soon each review printed a rejoinder from an embattled realist, and the most celebrated controversy in twentieth-century American jurisprudence was under way.[46] Pound and Cohen were
later joined by John L. Dickinson, Lon L. Fuller, and Herman Kantorowicz in the pro-Holmes but antirealist camp; these five critics had no
distinguishing "label," but their writings so frequently cited and reinforced each other that they became an identifiable group.[47] By the
1930s a third party, the Catholic defenders of natural law, had joined
the attack on the relativism and behaviorism of the entire Holmesian
tradition, but the Catholic contribution was a marginal episode in what
was essentially a controversy between moderate and radical followers of
Holmes.[48] Nowhere was the nature of the argument more clear than in
the dialogue between the realists and Cohen himself; Cohen pushed his
foes to the very limits of their philosophical ideas, and the realists, in
turn, drew out of him a critique of realism with which most legal scholars of later decades were inclined to agree.

   "Justice Holmes and the Nature of the Law" aimed first to refute the
view that law is "synonymous with what people actually do, i.e., with
social behavior." Cohen quoted Holmes occasionally, but his assertion
that behaviorism was alien to Holmes was supported primarily by the
demonstration that legal realism was alien to Cohen. Whatever Holmes
actually intended to claim, Cohen was explicit in distinguishing between two things denoted by the term "legal rules": the "uniformities"
that can be discovered in human conduct, and the "norms according to
which justiciable issues should be decided." The study of uniformities,
of custom, belongs to "descriptive sociology," while "juristic science"
is "concerned with norms that regulate." Both inquiries are essential,
said Cohen, and neither can be allowed to obscure the other; it is one
thing to ask, "what are people doing," and quite another to ask whether such behavior "should or should not receive legal protection." The
distinctness of the second question is in no way threatened by the fact
that "legal norms are the historical outcome of social behavior"; the

regulative aspect of norms is dependent upon, but not reducible to, uniformities in "habits of obedience" and in other behavior.[49] The realists ignored the "obvious and rudimentary" distinctions between uniformities and norms, between behavior and regulations because, Cohen insisted, they had a naive view of scientific method. Believing that science consists in the observing of physical facts and the extracting of "laws and uniformities," the realists failed to distinguish between the properties of physical laws and those of legal rules:

The laws that natural science seeks to discover . . . are uniformities which if valid at all cannot be violated. . . . We cannot go counter to the law of gravitation. . . . But it is of the very essence of legal rules that they are violable and that penalties or sanctions are provided for their various violations. They do not state what is, but attempt to decide what ought to be.

Therefore, even to call a judicial decision "behavior" is to "confuse physically organic with social-teleologic categories." A judge's organism "functions" and "behaves" when he speaks or writes, but "the legal effect of a judicial decision is altogether different from the physical effects" of his behavior. Behavior exists in the physical world of time and space, but "a legal decision relates situations remote in time and space through a purely logical connection"; it is "nontemporal."[50]

Failure to make this metaphysical distinction, and to recognize the "reality of universals" within the nontemporal realm, was behind the absurd attempt of the realists to deny that principles play an active and regulative role in judicial decisions. It was the implicit "nominalism" in Herman Oliphant, for example, that led him to view the "facts" of a case as a stimulus and the decision as a "response." On the contrary, Cohen declared, it is "not at all certain that a similar state of facts in two cases will always produce a similar decision," for there can be differences in "what the judge thinks are the facts and what law he thinks applicable." And "what the judge thinks" includes everything he brings to the case, including his knowledge of the entire legal system; the categories in the judge's mind, not the "facts" alone, determine the judge's "response." Even if, as Oliphant claimed, judicial language is made up of "pious platitudes," those platitudes influence what the judge actually does. Only a nominalist could fail to see the inevitable dependence of the judicial process on general principles. The relation of a decision to a rule is analogous to the relation between a point and the line that relates that point to other points: "No single point, nor, in strict accuracy, any finite number of points can by themselves completely determine the nature of the line or curve that passes through them," for "every curve is the locus of an infinite number of points that conform to its rule or formula."[51]

Worst of all, to Cohen, the realists, through their emphasis on descriptive sociology, seemed to deny to legal science any standard by which existing law could be criticized. To view the law "exclusively as uniformities of existing behavior," he alleged, leads to the "conservative" dependence of "norms" on "habit and inertia."[52]

The realists were stung and bewildered by Cohen's attack. Hessell Yntema of the Johns Hopkins Institute of Law drew the assignment of answering Cohen, who, Yntema observed, was a most "unexpected" opponent. "No one has given a more inspired interpretation of modern physical science nor such a vindication of its freedom" as Morris R. Cohen; "no one has more vigorously attacked the sanctification of 'the Past's blood-rusted key' by conventional legalism," no one has so fully "appreciated the needs of actual justice."[53] Had Yntema and his colleagues paid closer attention to Cohen's previous legal writings, they would not have been so shocked, but Cohen had been so completely assimilated into the progressive legal tradition that its inheritors were taken aback by his straightforward extension of doctrines he had held publicly for nearly twenty years.

Yntema protested that he and his comrades were passionately committed to attaining more perfect justice. Cohen's attempt to saddle them with an antireformist bias was in itself "illiberal," and was a function of Cohen's unaccountable failure to abide by Holmes's sound distinction between law and morality. Worse, Cohen had hopelessly confused scientific jurisprudence by bringing in metaphysics. It was a fallacy to judge a scientific movement "according to its metaphysics," as proven by the fact that "nominalism" and "the reality of universals" had nothing whatever to do with legal science, nor with the claims made by individual legal realists. Should legal science shackle itself to a given metaphysical doctrine—Cohen's—or should it proceed on its own? Must science be stopped until philosophers agree on a "correct" metaphysics? Yntema sidestepped Cohen's case for "principles" by characterizing his argument as "metaphysics" and by observing that realists did not deny explicitly that "universals" exist.[54]

Cohen's case for "normative" legal science was "illucid," Yntema added. If "norms" are to be "the subject matter of legal science, we intensely desire to be informed how they are to be formulated, how proved, and how utilized." Yntema had searched Cohen's writings for an account of how moral ends are justified; he found that Cohen's views were expressed elliptically. He challenged Cohen to provide an account of the scientific determination of moral ends. Pending this, Yntema insisted, one must hold to a distinction between "objective description" and its "professional use." In this view, "judges decide and science asks why"; legal science must confine itself to "detailed descriptive study," while the actions of the judge remain outside the scope of science even if he employs scientific knowledge in making his decision.[55]

Cohen's reply to Yntema, "Philosophy and Legal Science," argued that there is simply no escaping metaphysics. There were metaphysical ideas even in Jerome Frank's book: when Frank said that "rules are merely words," he was, explained Cohen, stating a metaphysical dogma. The problem, then, is not whether to be metaphysical but how to avoid bad metaphysics. Frank and other realists would do well to look more carefully at the general idea that "for every case there is a legal principle." This postulate, so loudly scorned by the realists, is easily detachable from the excessive formalism of outmoded nineteenth-century jurisprudence which the realists properly seek to avoid. The "juristic postulate" is analogous to the physical scientist's postulate that "for every physical event there is a cause." Neither claim has been "logically proved by experience," but we continue to accept them because they lead to the extension of knowledge and to the perfection of the law. The "juristic postulate" does not insist that "the rule of every case is known and understood before the case arises," but rather that no decision can come into being unless it can be made consistent with principles implied by other decisions. The fact that legal rules expand and change does not make them any less real, or any less essential to the process whereby judicial behavior becomes transformed into lawmaking. The law, like science itself, is a self-correcting system of principles.[56]

Such a sound metaphysics ought to inform legal science in two ways, Cohen insisted. Certainly the "descriptive" work Yntema and his colleagues wanted to undertake must proceed with the knowledge that what a court does is partially determined by the legal system itself. Further, the "normative jurisprudence" of which Yntema is so skeptical can clarify and expand legal rules in the same way that science seeks to clarify and expand its understanding of nature: the organization of judgments into a "rational and coherent system."[57]

Yntema waved the flag of peace: Cohen's article was "illuminating," and its agreements with the realists were more important than its disagreements. Cohen had, after all, conceded that there was such a thing as the "descriptive" study of the legal process; why not get on with it, and leave aside troublesome disagreements over the question of defining the "normative" aspects of jurisprudence? Whether or not the "professional use" of science was in itself a scientific act, at least we can all agree, observed Yntema, that the sorts of empirical studies being undertaken by the realists are of potential use in improving the law.[58]

The realists were not sufficiently interested in moral philosophy to push Cohen any harder, but Yntema had been right to complain of ambiguities in Cohen's "normative jurisprudence." He had even read[59] Cohen's most frontal assault on the topic, an essay published that very year of 1931 in *Reason and Nature.* "The Possibility of Ethical Science" was, without doubt, one of Cohen's most elliptical and indirect essays. It picked up most of the threads of moral philosophy he had left lying about in 1916, but it did remarkably little with them. The crucial question was still how, if at all, science could determine ethical ends if, as Cohen now repeated, the choice of such ends "is a matter of will." His first answer this time around was that science can "directly" enlighten us *only* as to means necessary to attain a given end. This was the strictly "instrumental" view he had sometimes taken before, as when he had compared the role of a judge with that of an engineer building a bridge on someone else's orders. Yet he turned about, once more, to assert that not all ethical assumptions are "equally true or equally false." Then he made more explicit than he had in the 1910s that the science of justice can determine this truth or falsity, and that it does so not by a superior intuition, but by rules that science generalizes out of *all* moral intuitions. An individual moral intuition can be shown to be wrong only when we can show its "inconsistency with other moral perceptions." In this respect, ethics operates like any science or "rational art"; it takes judgments and "organizes" them into a "rational system," which is continuously self-corrective.[60] The degree of certainty that can be attained in ethical science can be expected to remain less than that in physical science, however, simply because the basic moral values of human beings are so diverse and contingent; the task of ethical science is therefore to reject extreme claims that values are either absolutely fixed or absolutely relative and proceed, instead, to say: "Taking the most important factors into account, these rules seem to fit most cases best." Hence the principle of polarity enables the ethical scientist to take cognizance of the indeterminacy of natural law, yet to seek it scientifically.[61]

Cohen's reluctance to take on more directly the question of science's role in the determination of moral ends is especially striking because he, of all the major American theorists of law of his generation, was the only trained philosopher. Moreover, his "naturalistic" world view as a whole depended, for its integration, upon the analogy between logical and ethical invariants, and upon the location of each within the structure of nature. This indisposition to work out in more detail his sense of morality's position in nature was more than a function of his critical, as opposed to systematic, philosophical style; he had tried, after all, to do formal metaphysics and philosophy of science. In the field of ethics he never reviewed, nor did he deign to mention, the two most formidable works of the 1920s: Ralph Barton Perry's *General Theory of Value* (1926), the summa of behaviorist ethics, and the tenth chapter of John Dewey's *Quest for Certainty* (1929), the most lucid formulation of pragmatic ethical theory.[62] Further, Cohen did not take direct issue with the aggressive "emotivism" that appeared in the late 1930s.[63] This movement denied all rationality to ethical judgments, and thereby challenged even the basic faith in "ethical science" that united Cohen with Perry and Dewey. It is difficult to avoid the conclusion that Cohen was either so confident of his basic vision that he did not recognize challenges to it, or so aware of his inability to justify that vision that he chose to avoid formal discourse in moral philosophy. In any case, his own sketchy formulations, in turn, played almost no role in the technical discussion of ethics on the part of professional philosophers.[64]

Important as these facts are for marking the limits of Cohen's own ethical thinking, the legal profession itself was rarely troubled by what philosophers would regard as lacunae in his moral philosophy. Critics of the realists found his statements about "nominalism" and about "is" and "ought" eminently quotable and fully satisfactory as the philosophical foundation for an attack on realism;[65] the realists themselves cared so little about the classical problems of moral philosophy that they were quite willing to let Cohen score his points, so long as he did not discredit their own endeavors too forcefully. The only important realist to do any systematic work in conventional moral philosophy was Cohen's own son, Felix, who had earned a Harvard Ph.D. in philosophy before deciding to make his career in law.[66]

Felix Cohen's *Ethical Systems and Legal Ideals* was actually a more substantial contribution to ethics than anything his father ever wrote. Felix sought to employ Bentham's hedonistic utilitarianism to give philosophical content to Morris Cohen's ideal of "natural law."[67] The elder Cohen never gave his unqualified assent to Felix's moral philosophy,[68] but the simple fact that Felix attempted to do "normative jurisprudence" as well as descriptive studies of legal "functions" made the younger Cohen less vulnerable to his father's repeated attacks on the incipient nihilism of the realist movement.

The distinctive and decisive impact of Morris Cohen's views of justice on the thinking of his age thus followed from his decision to ignore the technicalities of formal philosophical discussion and to concentrate, instead, on what jurists and lawyers were saying. He was supremely qualified to argue philosophical points with the most brilliant and accomplished leaders of the realist movement, whose philosophical ideas were invariably general and, from a philosopher's point of view, imprecise. Even Cohen's "principle of polarity," which generated such scant interest among metaphysicians, became a standard referent point in legal discourse, and was taken up with especially great enthusiasm by Pound and Fuller.[69]

When Cohen pulled together most of his legal papers for *Law and the Social Order* in 1933, reviewers could not say enough good things about the book. The *Columbia Law Review* called it the most important recent work in all European and American jurisprudence; the *Harvard Law Review* found it comparable only with Holmes's almost sacred *Collected Legal Papers*; the *California Law Review* observed that even the oldest essays in the book read like fresh contributions to contemporary debate.[70] Herman Kantorowicz acclaimed Cohen as "America's most universal thinker" and praised him for so skillfully steering "a sound middle course between the Scylla of ignored social implications . . . and the Charybdis of those modern 'realists,' who . . . ought to have heeded Goethe's advice to attend first *collegium logicum.*"[71]

Law and the Social Order included "Justice Holmes and the Nature of the Law" and Cohen's subsequent rejoinder to Yntema, but it also contained a piece that was perhaps as influential as any of his essays in making him a respected and remembered critic of legal realism: his review of Frank's *Law and the Modern Mind*. This review did not convey the substance of Cohen's disagreement with the realists as completely as did his exchange with Yntema, but it did join direct and sustained issue with the most celebrated—and vulnerable—book to come out of the realist movement.[72] What distinguished *Law and the Modern Mind* was the lengths to which it went to deny certainty, stability, and continuity in the legal system. Frank insisted that each case was too unique to be properly subsumed under conventional legal categories, and that judges, instead of applying "rules," acted on the basis of a range of extralegal, especially emotional, considerations.[73] Frank's book, flippant and iconoclastic, probably did more than any of Cohen's writings to force Americans to take account of the human character of law. But Cohen was put off by the extreme position of his would-be ally. Frank's campaign against the myth of certainty was so uncompromising, his interpretation of the judicial process so adamantly irrationalist, and his use of psychoanalysis so crude, that Cohen was able to attack him for being off balance. This time Cohen's "balance and moderation" argument was no truistic, Olympian attack on the barbarians beyond the gate, but a direct discussion of the most talked-about work in a proudly up-to-date discipline. Certainty is no all-or-nothing proposition, Cohen said; both uncertainty and certainty are in the law, and it is worthwhile to try to define the relationship and to extend the range of certainty as far as possible. The quest for certainty, which Frank ridiculed as a "childish" attempt to find a surrogate father, is, Cohen counseled, a necessary part of civilized life. Frank denied that judges are controlled by rules, but what then is left to control judicial discretion?[74]

Cohen's perennial complaint that the realists betrayed justice to the whims of prevailing opinion was pressed even further in critiques of Thurman Arnold and Edward Stevens Robinson. The insistence of Robinson, in *Law and Lawyers*, that ethical ideas are ultimately psychological data infuriated Cohen;[75] but no work could have been more calculated to call forth his wrath than Arnold's *The Symbols of Government.* Arnold identified "rational thinking" and "principles" as obstacles to progress, and he was cavalierly oblivious to the classical problems of political ethics.[76] The brilliance with which Arnold satirized the conservative principles of his enemies was undermined, Cohen argued, by Arnold's own lack of a standard for "what is good and what is harmful." Arnold's belief that our problems will diminish if we stop theorizing and start collecting more scientific information missed the whole point: "a study of biologic facts," Cohen explained, "may enable us to determine whether a diet of buttermilk will prolong life in a case of Bright's disease, but it cannot settle for any of us the question of whether we should wish to live on such a diet or prefer Bright's disease."[77]

Arnold and Frank, of the realists with whom Cohen argued, were especially given to the recklessness of formulation that made the realists so vulnerable to attack from a critic of Cohen's philosophical predilections and skills. When the realists urged attention to "actual behavior," they were often thinking of the operation of commercial law and the law of contracts, fields in which it has always been understood that a major part of law's task is to formalize and objectify the conduct of the marketplace. Yet an indisposition on the part of the realists to particularize their points enabled such critics as Cohen to interpret their statements as claims about "the nature of law," which was true to only a limited extent. The realists did become excited by the prospect of transforming their various technical contributions into a new jurisprudence, and this led them to endorse, directly or implicitly, a series of abstract, highly general claims about "law" that they were not, in intellectual fact, prepared to defend. Hence Cohen was able to come into the argument at the most abstract possible level and score simple but telling points against them. It was, after all, Frank's determination to connect a highly specific point in courtroom practice with a general philosophical proposition about the relation of logic to psychology that ensnared him in the acrimonious personal correspondence with Cohen discussed in Chapter 4.[78]

By the end of the 1930s the realists began to take more seriously the strictures Cohen and his allies had offered. The "identification of law with the actions of government," observes the most recent historian of the breakup of realism, "gave even the most offensive Nazi edict the sanction of true law."[79] The realists spent more and more of their time assuring themselves, and everyone else, that the divorce of "is" from "ought" had been a *temporary* expedient, that law was, obviously, normative, and that right and wrong were "real." By 1945 Frank himself made friendly noises about "natural law," even of the Catholic variety.[80] Some of the realists, especially those at Yale, began to speak of their work in the normative language of "policy studies":[81] the determination of ultimate moral ends was still left outside the scope of legal science, but understanding behavior seemed less important now than controlling it in the public interest.

The shift in emphasis in how American legal scholars of the 1940s dealt with the stability of law can scarcely be attributed to Cohen's influence, but he helped to create what was eventually to become the consensus of opinion concerning what was defective in the realist movement. By the 1960s the never-ending succession of postmortems on legal realism had made conventional, if not banal, the very point of view that Cohen had espoused thirty years before. "Law," as one representative commentator explained,

has rules, some vague and some precise, but as occasion demands, it modifies its rules and creates new ones to fit unforeseen contingencies. Once our generation overcomes the compulsions generated by the Realist dogma that there are no rules in Law we may be able to sit down and describe the bounds and character of the logic of the law.[82]

The "greatest challenge" of contemporary jurisprudence, said even a self-styled *defender* of the realist tradition in 1965, is normative and theoretical: a philosophy is needed for "evaluating and accepting or rejecting governmental actions."[83]

NOTES

1. MRC, "Should Legal Thought Abandon Clear Distinctions?" *Illinois*

Law Review XXXVI (1941), 243 (*RL*, 178).

2. See esp. Holmes's "The Path of the Law," in *Collected Legal Papers* (New York, 1920), 167-202.

3. William Ernest Hocking, "Conference on the Relation of Law to Social Ends," *JP* X (1913), 512-528. This report contains abstracts of the thirteen papers given at the conference and discusses Cohen's role in the affair. Cohen's "The Process of Judicial Legislation" appeared in *American Law Review* XLVIII (1914), 161-198. The essay is reprinted, with a number of changes, in *LSO*, 112-147.

4. MRC, "Judicial Legislation," 164.

5. For the most famous manifestos see Roscoe Pound, "Mechanical Jurisprudence," *Columbia Law Review* VIII (1908), 607-608, and "The Scope of Sociological Jurisprudence," *Harvard Law Review* XXV (1912), 489-516.

6. MRC, "Judicial Legislation," esp. 181, 197.

7. MRC, "Judicial Legislation," 192-197.

8. MRC, "The Place of Logic in the Law," *Harvard Law Review* XXIX (1916), 638 (*LSO*, 182).

9. John Chipman Gray, *The Nature and Sources of the Law* (New York, 1909).

10. MRC, "Logic in the Law," 623 (*LSO*, 166, 381).

11. MRC, "Logic in the Law," 639 (*LSO*, 183).

12. For a lucid discussion of Holmes's treatment of this distinction see Morton G. White, *Social Thought in America* (New York, 1949), 59-75, 208-212.

13. MRC, "Real and Ideal Forces in the Civil Law," *Ethics* XXVI (1916), 347-348 (*LSO*, 248-249).

14. MRC, "Logic in the Law," 622 (*LSO*, 165).

15. MRC, "Forces in Civil Law," 354-355 (*LSO*, 255).

16. MRC, "History vs. Value," *JP* XI (1914), 710 (*RN*, 379).

17. The locus classicus is, of course, White, *Social Thought*.

18. George Clark Cox, "The Case Method in the Study and Teaching of Ethics," *JP* X (1913), 346.

19. John Dewey and James H. Tufts, *Ethics* (New York, 1908), 1 (emphasis added).

20. Although the politically conservative dimensions of nineteenth-century German historicism are proverbial to American scholars today, few legal writers of the 1910s read in, or cared about, that tradition. Pound and Cohen were even criticized for introducing irrelevant European literature into American discourse: see, e.g., Robert L. Fowler, "The New Philosophies of Law," *Harvard Law Review* XXVII (1914), 718.

21. MRC, "Jus Naturale Redivivum," *PR* XXV (1916), 761.

22. MRC, "Jus Naturale," 769.

23. What does and does not count as a doctrine of "natural law" is a matter of disagreement among philosophers; see the very helpful discussion of this problem by Richard Wollheim, "Natural Law," in Paul Edwards, ed., *Encyclopedia of Philosophy* (New York, 1967), V, 450-451. Cf. John R. Carnes, "Whether There Is a Natural Law," *Ethics* LXXVII (1967), 122-129, and the ongoing debates in *Natural Law Forum*. For a definition wide enough to include Cohen see William K. Frankena, "Ethics," in Roderick M. Chisholm et al., *Philosophy* (Englewood Cliffs, N.J., 1963), 368.

24. Rudolph Stammler, *The Theory of Justice*, trans. Isaac Husik (New York, 1925; originally published 1889). On Stammler's position in the natural-law tradition see Husik's introduction, esp. xxxviii. On the orthodox Kantian framework out of which Stammler's doctrine emerged, see Morris Ginsberg, "Stammler's Philosophy of Law," in W. Ivor Jennings, ed., *Modern Theories of Law* (London, 1933), 38-51. Cohen was probably led to Stammler by Roscoe Pound, who first introduced Cohen to the literature of continental European jurisprudence; see the correspondence between Pound and Cohen in *Portrait*, 297-303; cf. *DJ*, 177.

25. MRC, "Forces in Civil Law," 355 (*LSO*, 255-256).

26. Benjamin Cardozo, *The Paradoxes of Legal Science* (New York, 1928), 37.

27. MRC, "Forces in Civil Law," 354-355 (*LSO*, 256); MRC, "Rule versus Discretion," *JP* XI (1914), 214 (*LSO*, 266).

28. MRC, "Jus Naturale," 774-777.

29. MRC, "Jus Naturale," 772-773. Cf. Cohen's private expression of yet greater hopes for "the science of ethics," MRC to Felix Frankfurter, June 5, 1916, in *Portrait*, 244-246.

30. MRC, "Jus Naturale," 773. On Boas's and Robinson's centrality in

the drift toward ethical relativism see Henry F. May, *The End of American Innocence* (New York, 1959), 165, 350.

31. MRC, "Jus Naturale," 773.

32. MRC, "Judicial Legislation," 192, and MRC, "Jus Naturale," 762, where Cohen acknowledges Stammler as the originator of the phrase.

33. MRC, "History vs. Value," 716 (*RN*, 385).

34. White, *Social Thought*, 241. For a representative and influential portrait of "the new jurisprudence" see Henry Steele Commager, *The American Mind* (New Haven, 1950), 374-390.

35. Oliver Wendell Holmes, Jr., "Ideas and Doubts," *Illinois Law Review* X (1915), 1-20, reprinted in Holmes, *Collected Legal Papers* (New York, 1920), 303; Holmes to MRC, March 9, 1916, in *Portrait*, 315. Cf. the enthusiastic response to Cohen's critique of historicism on the part of *NR* I (1915), 19.

36. MRC to Holmes, April 10, 1915, in *Portrait*, 313.

37. Holmes to MRC, September 3 and 28, 1918, in *Portrait*, 318-319. Cf. Holmes, "Natural Law," *Harvard Law Review* XXXII (1918), 40-44 (*Collected Legal Papers*, 310-316). Cf. also Holmes to Albert Einstein, April 1, 1928, in James Bishop Peabody, ed., *Holmes-Einstein Letters* (New York, 1964), 280, and Holmes to Frederick Pollock, October 19, 1923, and May 15, 1931, in Mark De Wolfe Howe, ed., *Holmes-Pollock Letters* (Cambridge, Mass., 1941), I, 122, 287.

38. See the correspondence in *Portrait*, 297-310.

39. Felix Frankfurter to MRC, July 23, 1914, in *Portrait*, 242. The volume referred to by Frankfurter appeared in 1922: Pierre de Tourtoulon, *Philosophy in the Development of Law*, trans. M. Read, Editorial Preface by Morris R. Cohen (New York, 1922), volume 15 of American Legal Philosophy Series.

40. MRC, review of Oliver Wendell Holmes, Jr., *Collected Legal Papers*, in *NR* XXV (1921), 294-295 (*LSO*, 363-369); MRC, review of Benjamin N. Cardozo, *The Nature of the Judicial Process*, John Chipman Gray, *The Nature and Sources of the Law* (2nd ed.), and Roscoe Pound, *An Introduction to the Philosophy of Law*, in *NR* XXXIII (1922), 4-6; MRC, review of Roscoe Pound, *The Spirit of the Common Law*, in *JP* XX (1923), 155-165; MRC, "Legalism and Clericalism," *NR* XLI (1924), 15-16 (*LSO*, 157-161); MRC, review of John Henry Wigmore, *Rational Basis of Legal Institutions*, in *Yale Law Journal* XXX

(1924), 892-894; MRC, review of Roscoe Pound, *Law and Morals*, in *Harvard Law Review* XXXVIII (1925), 1123-1126.

41. The American Law Institute has long since ceased to be associated with "conservative" jurisprudence. A sketch of its work can be found in Herbert F. Goodrich and Paul A. Wolkin, *The Story of the American Law Institute, 1923-1961* (St. Paul, Minn., 1961).

42. Underhill Moore, "Rational Basis of Legal Institutions," *Columbia Law Review* XXIII (1923), 609-617, esp. 610.

43. Jerome Frank, *Law and the Modern Mind* (New York, 1930).

44. Legal realism as a whole awaits a historian who can build from and integrate the contrasting virtues of Grant Gilmore, "Legal Realism: Its Cause and Cure," *Yale Law Journal* LXX (1961), 1037-1048, and Edward A. Purcell, Jr., "American Jurisprudence between the Wars: Legal Realism and the Crisis of Democratic Theory," *American Historical Review* LXXV (1969), 424-446. Purcell's major concern is to place the realist controversy in the context of American society's attempt to absorb ethical relativism into a system of democratic political values. Gilmore explains the rise and fall of the movement through an analysis of conditions peculiar to the American case-law system. Much of the preliminary work for a good history of the movement has been done by Wilfrid E. Rumble, Jr., whose well-researched *American Legal Realism* (Ithaca, 1968), is regrettably thin, conceptually. Cf. David H. Moskowitz, "The American Legal Realists and an Empirical Science of Law," *Villanova Law Review* XI (1966), 480-524, and David E. Ingersoll, "Karl Llewellyn, American Legal Realism, and Contemporary Legal Behaviorism," *Ethics* LXXVI (1966), 253-266.

45. Roscoe Pound, "The Call for a Realistic Jurisprudence," *Harvard Law Review* XLIV (1930), 697-711.

46. Pound was answered by Karl Llewellyn, "Some Realism about Realism—Responding to Dean Pound," *Harvard Law Review* XLIV (1931), 1222-1259. Cohen's "Justice Holmes and the Nature of the Law," *Columbia Law Review* XXXI (1931), 352-367 (*LSO*, 198-218), was answered by Hessell E. Yntema, "The Rational Basis of Legal Science," *Columbia Law Review* XXXI (1931), 925-955.

47. See esp. L. L. Fuller, "American Legal Realism," *Pennsylvania Law Review* LXXXII (1934), 429-461; Herman Kantorowicz, "Some Rationalism about Realism," *Yale Law Journal* XLIII (1934), 1240-1253; and John Dickinson, "Legal Rules: Their Function in the Process of Decision," *Pennsylvania Law Review* LXXIX (1931), 833-868. The

Aristotelian philosopher Mortimer J. Adler cited Cohen frequently and approvingly, but Adler's critique of the realists extended, explicitly in some respects, to Holmes, Pound, and Cardozo; see Adler's "Legal Certainty," *Columbia Law Review* XXXI (1931), 91-108, esp. 91, 100.

48. E.g., Walter B. Kennedy, "Psychologism in the Law," *Georgetown Law Journal* XXIX (1940), 139-164, and Francis J. Lucey, "Natural Law and American Legal Realism: Their Respective Contributions to a Theory of Law in a Democratic Society," *Georgetown Law Journal* XXX (1942), 493-533. The role of the Catholic thinkers has been given more emphasis by Purcell, "American Jurisprudence," 439-441, 444-446.

49. MRC, "Holmes and the Nature of the Law," 357-360 (*LSO*, 204-207).

50. MRC, "Holmes and the Nature of the Law," 358, 365 (*LSO*, 205, 216). Cf. Cohen's attempt to define the qualities in social life that made any "behaviorist" analysis of it incomplete: MRC, "The Social Sciences and the Natural Sciences," in William F. Ogburn and Alexander Goldenweiser, eds., *The Social Sciences* (New York, 1927), 437-466 (*RN*, 333-368), esp. 439-450 (*RN*, 335-343).

51. MRC, "Holmes and the Nature of the Law," 364-366 (*LSO*, 214-217).

52. MRC, "Holmes and the Nature of the Law," 360 (*LSO*, 208).

53. Yntema, "Rational Basis," 936-937.

54. Yntema, "Rational Basis," 937, 939, 943, 946.

55. Yntema, "Rational Basis," 943, 953.

56. MRC, "Philosophy and Legal Science," *Columbia Law Review* XXXII (1932), 1106, 1112-1114 (*LSO*, 223, 231-233).

57. MRC, "Philosophy and Legal Science," 1123-1124 (*LSO*, 242-244).

58. Hessell E. Yntema, "Legal Science and Reform," *Columbia Law Review* XXXIV (1934), 210-211. Cf. Yntema's recollections of the controversy, "American Legal Realism in Retrospect," *Vanderbilt Law Review* XIV (1960), 317-330, esp. 324.

59. Yntema, "Rational Basis," esp. 945.

60. *RN*, 427-449.

61. *RN*, 448. Compare Cohen's emphasis on the indeterminacy in the

objects of the science of justice (*RN*, 414) to the attitude expressed
fifteen years earlier in "Jus Naturale," 773. Cf. also, in the 1930s,
ILSM, 366, and *PL*, 190. The *PL* reference is to Cohen's final attempt
at moral philosophy, an essay written, probably, before 1940: "Values,
Norms, and Science." Although it grants that "basic and ultimate uniformity in human ethical perceptions" may not be discovered despite
our hopes, it endorses the scientific search for such uniformity as the
surest way to avoid both "vicious absolutism" and "vicious relativism."

62. Ralph Barton Perry, *The General Theory of Value* (New York,
1926); John Dewey, *The Quest for Certainty* (New York, 1929), 254-
286. For my understanding of American moral philosophy during the
1920s and 1930s I am greatly dependent upon Frankena, "Ethics."

63. See esp. the early work of C. L. Stevenson, as discussed helpfully in
J. O. Urmson, *The Emotive Theory of Ethics* (New York, 1968), 12-23.

64. When historians of philosophy have attempted to characterize and
classify Cohen's moral philosophy at all, they have most often interpreted him somewhat differently than I have. Frankena, for example,
depicts him as a "postulationist" and a "noncognitivist"("Ethics,"
398), which minimizes too greatly, I think, Cohen's belief that ethical
judgments, however generated, are justified in the same way that judgments in the physical sciences are justified. Frankena shares with Bernard E. Brown ("Morris Cohen's Search for Justice," *Journal of the History of Ideas* XIV [1953], 257-259) what I believe is a failure to put
Cohen's remarks about "will" and "moral intuitions" in the context of
his account of the science of justice (see esp. "Jus Naturale," 767-777;
RN, 413, 447; "Philosophy and Legal Science," 1121-1124 [*LSO*, 242-
244]; and *PL*, 182-191).

65. E.g., Zachariah Chafee, Jr., "Law," in Harold Stearns, ed., *America
Now* (New York, 1938), esp. 323-324; and the almost deferential attitude of even L. L. Fuller, "American Legal Realism," esp. 443. By the
end of the decade Fuller had extended his own critique of the realists
to points with which Cohen disagreed; see Fuller's *The Law in Quest of
Itself* (Chicago, 1940), and MRC, "Clear Distinctions," *passim*. Cf.
MRC to Hessell Yntema, November 7, 1941, in *Portrait*, 310-311.

66. Within the legal profession of his generation, Felix Cohen
(1907-1953) was a figure of legendary learning and intelligence. After
taking his Ph.D. at Harvard at the age of twenty-one, he attended
Columbia Law School and began a career of government service, including a tenure as Solicitor General for the United States Department of
the Interior. He made many contributions to legal scholarship, the most

important of which have been collected by his widow, Lucy Kramer Cohen: *The Legal Conscience* (New Haven, 1960). The distinctness of his philosophical interests among the realists has been noted by Rumble, *Legal Realism*, 186.

67. Felix Cohen, *Ethical Systems and Legal Ideals* (New York, 1933), esp. 291. Felix Cohen's distinctive commitments, coupled with his ability to speak in a philosopher's idiom and his considerable learning in the social sciences and the humanities, make him one of the most interesting and complicated contributors to the realist movement. See, for example, his attempt to define "functionalism" in terms consistent with his father's ostentatiously antifunctional metaphysics: Felix S. Cohen, "The Problems of a Functionalist Jurisprudence," *Modern Law Review* I (1937), 7. Cf. Felix S. Cohen, "Transcendental Nonsense and the Functional Approach," *Columbia Law Review* XXXV (1935), 849.

68. *AT*, 222-223; MRC to Roscoe Pound, July 9, 1938, in *Portrait*, 307.

69. Fuller, "American Legal Realism," 452; Roscoe Pound, "Fifty Years of Jurisprudence," *Harvard Law Review* LI (1937), 471. Cf. Roscoe Pound to MRC, August 25, 1931, in *Portrait*, 306.

70. Max Lerner, review of *LSO*, in *Harvard Law Review* XLVII (1933), 380; Herman Kantorowicz, review of *LSO*, in *Columbia Law Review* XXXIV (1934), 187-189; John A. Gorfinkel, review of *LSO*, in *California Law Review* XXIII (1934-1935), 454-456. Cf. Irving J. Levy, review of *LSO*, in *Cornell Law Quarterly Review*, XIX (1933-1934), 515-518. Cf. also the respectful review of *RN* by a leading realist, Walter Wheeler Cook, in *Columbia Law Review* XXXII (1932), 725-728.

71. Kantorowicz, review of *LSO*, 189.

72. MRC, review of Frank, *Law and the Modern Mind*, in *Nation* CXXXI (1931), 259-260 (*LSO*, 356-362).

73. Frank, *Law and the Modern Mind*. For a competent study of Frank see Julius Paul, *The Legal Realism of Jerome N. Frank: A Study of Fact-Skepticism and the Judicial Process* (The Hague, 1959).

74. MRC, review of *Law and the Modern Mind*, 259-260 (*LSO*, 357-362).

75. MRC, review of Robinson, *Law and Lawyers*, in *Cornell Law Quarterly Review* XXII (1936), 171-178 (*RL*, 185-194). Robinson had argued that Cohen's earlier legal writings were insufficiently empirical (*Law and Lawyers* [New York, 1935], 220-226).

76. Thurman Arnold, *The Symbols of Government* (New York, 1935). For an analysis of the actual effect on New Deal politics of Arnold's philosophical views, or, more properly, his lack of them, see Douglas Ayer, "In Quest of Efficiency: The Ideological Journey of Thurman Arnold in the Interwar Period," *Stanford Law Review* XXIII (1971), 1049-1086.

77. MRC, review of Arnold, *Symbols of Government,* in *Illinois Law Review* XXXI (1936), 411-418 (*FL*, 136-148).

78. See pp. 85-88.

79. Purcell, "American Jurisprudence," 441.

80. Jerome Frank, *Fate and Freedom: A Philosophy for Free Americans* (New York, 1945), 295. Cf. Karl N. Llewellyn, "On Reading and Using the Newer Jurisprudence," *Columbia Law Review* XL (1940), 593, 603. The retrenchment of the realists under the pressure of the war is discussed in Purcell, "American Jurisprudence," esp. 441-443.

81. See the pivotal essay by Myres S. McDougal, "Fuller v. the American Legal Realists: An Intervention," *Yale Law Journal* L (1940-1941), esp. 834-835. For an excellent account of the drift toward "policy science" (at Yale, especially) see William Twining, "Pericles and the Plumber," *Law Quarterly Review* LXXXIII (1967), 396-426, esp. 411-413.

82. Edward J. Bloustein, "Logic and Legal Realism: The Realist as Frustrated Idealist," *Cornell Law Quarterly Review* L (1964), 33.

83. Ralph J. Savarese, "American Legal Realism," *Houston Law Review* III (1965), 198. Cf. Bernie R. Burrus, "American Legal Realism," *Howard Law Journal* VIII (1962), 36-51; and Calvin Woodard, "The Limits of Legal Realism: An Historical Perspective," *Virginia Law Review* LIV (1968), 689-739.

Truth forever on the scaffold, Wrong
  forever on the throne—
Yet that scaffold sways the future, and,
  behind the dim unknown,
Standeth God within the shadow, keeping
  watch above his own.

James Russell Lowell

"There are times in world history," a communist reviewer of *Reason and Nature* explained in 1932 to Morris Cohen, when both truth and man are served only if we "abandon the side of the angels and follow the banner of Lucifer."[1] Sidney Hook's counsel was anathema to his one-time mentor, whose "angelic" politics were based on a very literal acceptance of the ancient axiom, "You shall know the truth, and the truth shall make you free." Cohen got his political start in the age of "progressive scholarship," when conferences like the one on legal and social philosophy that he led in 1913[2] were felt to have a distinctly political significance without being in any way "partisan." In all of his political activities, he was to remain a scholar, a philosopher, an intellectual; indeed, he saw himself as a "priest" ordained "to keep alive the sacred fires on the altar of impartial truth."[3] Even in the 1930s, when Hook and others importuned him to adopt a more "realistic" political outlook, he remained devoted to this truth-seeking and truth-telling mission.

This mission, as Cohen saw it, was fully consistent with a commitment to political liberalism. "Liberalism," he said, was "simply scientific method stubbornly at work on human problems."[4] The "truth" that intellectuals were to find and express was not, therefore, that of any particular cultural or religious tradition; it was instead the truth yielded by "free inquiry," and hence aloof, in Cohen's view, from conventional political ideologies of any sort. This nonideological pursuit of truth was taken by Cohen to be the essence of liberalism as a political philosophy, the bedrock upon which a liberal civilization could be built. He was concerned about the social and economic well-being of people, but his sense of liberalism was predominantly cerebral: "*all* our material comforts and present intellectual resources," he insisted, are "derived from the spirit of free inquiry" and from the cosmopolitan tolerance upon which free inquiry itself is socially dependent.[5] Tolerance and freedom of thought and expression were the root values in Cohen's entire social outlook. The free exercise of reason was his paradigm for good citizenship; the political agent as rational liberal sought, like the scientist, to consider all possible alternatives and to evaluate each one logically. The enemy of liberalism, and of science, was "fanaticism," which Cohen understood as the refusal to submit one's beliefs to rational scrutiny. He never tired of repeating that there was an "intimate connection between scientific method and liberal civilization."[6] The ease with which this "intimate connection" could be felt early in the twentieth century was one obvious source of liberalism's appeal to Cohen, who was simultaneously finding his philosophical home in a rationalistic formulation of the scientific ideal. But liberalism was more to Cohen than a political outlook compatible with his devotion to science; liberalism had a direct and primary appeal to many of the same dispositions that made science itself attractive to him. Liberalism was a classically middle-of-the-road style of politics, halfway between the more revolutionary Socialist Labor party, with which he had been affiliated in his youth, and the more conservative, self-help philosophy of Samuel Smiles, which had been his introduction to political economy. Liberalism in general stood midway between collectivism and individualism, totalitarianism and anarchy, communism and fascism; and American constitutional liberalism in particular manifested a system of "checks and balances" to which Cohen was especially sensitive.

The liberalism Cohen espoused was also well suited to his social circumstances as a Jewish immigrant. The liberal segment of the American intellectual community was the most ready to welcome the likes of Cohen, and, in turn, it was easier for him to adopt their political tradition than to take up the more blatantly nativist politics of the American conservatives of 1910. Further, liberalism was a strategy for dealing with the sheer fact of the Jew's differentness from the established majority culture; an argument for tolerance and pluralism was an argument for full participation in American life on the part of persons not born into the official, majority culture. The "universalism" Jews have characteristically adopted in the United States, according to Charles Liebman's "theory of Jewish liberalism," encases the interests of Jews within the interests of "mankind," as when the Jewish liberal "fights for the separation of church and state in the name of a secular ideal, not in the name of a Jewish ideal." The sense of estrangement that feeds the liberal impulse among Jews has reached its peak, Liebman concludes, "in the postemancipation period" when gentile society has ceased to be formally Christian, and when "secularization [has swept] the Jewish people," not only destroying a host of stabilizing values, but eliminating specifically the expectation that the estrangement of Jews will be ended by the coming of a Messiah.[7]

Cohen came to political maturity just when American progressivism was at the "crossroads of liberalism," as Charles Forcey has characterized the conditions under which Herbert Croly, Walter Lippmann, Walter Weyl, and others sought to turn liberals toward the conscious, cooperative use of governmental power for reform. Whatever the actual pattern of use of state power in the United States in the nineteenth century, that century did bequeath to the twentieth an almost official political economy according to which progress toward the greatest possible fulfillment of individual wants was to be achieved automatically through the freewheeling exercise of individual rights.[8] The intellectual revolt against this traditional, highly individualistic style of liberalism was of course well under way before the *New Republic* was founded in 1914, but it was at this undeniably pivotal point in the transition to a more "socialized" liberalism that Cohen appeared.

Although he was one of the *New Republic*'s most frequent contributors, especially during its first decade of existence, Cohen's most sustained efforts on behalf of the values he shared with the *New Republic* group were published elsewhere, in the professional journals of law and philosophy. As one of the most academically learned representatives of his political persuasion, Cohen sought to expand upon a set of more or less conventional *New Republic* insights in several specific legal contexts, and thereby to provide a more formal and complete justification for the abandonment of "conservative liberalism." His most extensive and influential hatchet jobs on the ideological obstacles to social democracy dealt with the "conservative" claims that private property was prior to governmental power and the appropriate beneficiary of it; that freedom of contract was endangered by public regulation of the relations between employer and employee; and that the Constitution was a fixed embodiment of eternal reason.

In 1927, for example, Cohen complained in the *Cornell Law Quarterly Review* of the widespread confusions about the nature of private property and of state sovereignty. These confusions, said Cohen, prevent the state from looking after "the general welfare." The private employer still had "the absolute right to threaten and discharge any employee who wants to join a trade union," and the right, equally absolute, "to pay a wage that is injurious to a basic social interest." Cohen offered a "dispassionate scientific study" of the concepts of property and sovereignty in which he argued that "dominion over things is also *imperium* over our fellow human beings." Democratic ideals with reference to "sovereignty" were prevented from operating in certain areas of social life because of the wrongheaded assumption that "property" is a thing apart, yet any close analysis of how our property laws actually "function in society" must show that these laws "do confer sovereign power on our captains of industry and . . . finance." Cohen gave numerous examples of how de facto "power" is exercised through property and then focused on the question he said most judges and property lawyers skirted: How can society protect freedom and yet restrict private enterprise "in the interests of the common good"? His purpose was not to answer this question, but to insist, first, that it be asked and, second, that its answers be based on the understanding that property owners are wielders of power with "positive duties in the public interest":

The owner of a tenement house in a modern city is in fact a public official and has all sorts of positive duties. He must keep the halls lighted, he must see that the roof does not leak, that there are fire-escape facilities. . . . Similar is the case of the factory owner. He must install all sorts of safety appliances, hygienic conveniences; see that workmen are provided with a certain amount of light, air, etc.

There is no reason, Cohen concluded, why the same sorts of restrictions ought not to be placed on the wages paid to employees; in any case, it did not make sense to oppose such restrictions with abstract arguments about "private property."[9]

A few years later Cohen presented a parallel analysis of the law of contracts in the *Harvard Law Review*. His specific target was resistance to the standardization of contracts, especially "wage contracts" between employers and employees. Against the view that state controls necessarily infringe upon the "freedom of contract" of both parties, Cohen held that such "freedom" for the poor man in need of work is fraudulent. He pointed to the need for an external force to balance the situation for the general good. "Regulations . . . involving some restrictions on the freedom to contract are as necessary to real liberty as traffic restrictions are necessary to assure real freedom in the general use of our highways." The question is, what sort of regulations are needed? And this question cannot be justly answered by saying that the courts should enforce all contracts made "freely"; the latter doctrine merely brings the power of the state into action on the side of the stronger party: "To put no restrictions on the freedom of contract would logically lead not to maximum of individual liberty but to contracts of slavery, into which, experience shows, men will 'voluntarily' enter under economic pressure."[10]

It was through such essays that Cohen practiced his liberalism: he was acting as a philosopher and scholar, yet managing to perform a highly practical, specific political task. His aim was not to perfect liberal philosophy, as a philosophy, but to apply it more widely. He was not, in these essays, pursuing any philosophical question on the order of "What political arrangements best serve the common good?" Rather, he was using his analytical and polemical skills to expose a discrepancy between liberal principles and the then predominant justification for a social arrangement of which he disapproved.

Another influential essay of this sort was Cohen's "Constitutional and Natural Rights in 1789 and Since," a contribution of 1938 to the *Na-*

tional Lawyers Guild Quarterly that sympathized with the New Deal's attempt to reorganize the courts. Here, too, Cohen took up time-honored themes; what mattered was not his theoretical originality, but his ability to marshal historical evidence to prove that courts had repeatedly interpreted the Constitution in ways the actual drafters could not have possibly had in mind. Cohen's attack on the "fiction that the courts only follow the words of the Constitution"[11] was greeted as a formidable contribution to the cause; Bruce Bliven reported—with some exaggeration, no doubt—that Cohen's piece was being regarded as "about the grandest thing ever written since the book of Genesis."[12]

By the 1930s the social democracy Cohen espoused was outflanked on the left, especially among New York intellectuals, by communism. This "extreme" outlook did not attract as much of Cohen's political attention as the established conservatism at the other pole, but his opposition to communism was widely disseminated through his essay, "Why I Am Not a Communist," written for V. F. Calverton's nonsectarian radical journal, *The Modern Monthly*, in 1934. Calverton asked Cohen, John Dewey, and Bertrand Russell to justify their liberalism, so that three of the most respected bourgeois ideologues could simultaneously be held to answer by commentator Sidney Hook.

Cohen, who was then a supporter of Norman Thomas's Socialist party,[13] explained to Calverton's readers that whenever told he "must choose between" a communist dictatorship and fascism, he felt the choice was between "being shot and being hanged." It would be "suicide" for liberals to "accept this as exhausting the field of human possibility." He objected specifically to the communists' reliance on armed uprising and their conviction that the working class, rather than a consensus of the interests of all classes, must constitute the foundation for the ideal state. The communist program "of civil war, dictatorship, and the illiberal or fanatically intolerant spirit which war psychology always engenders" may in fact make things worse than they are now; certainly there is not likely to be room for "freedom of discussion" and "freedom of thought," said Cohen. Class-based rebellions, especially, may be self-defeating:

When armed uprisings have been undertaken by single oppressed classes, as in the revolt of the gladiators in Rome, the various peasant revolts in England, Germany, and Russia, the French commune of 1871, or the Moscow uprisings of 1905, they have left a deplorably monotonous record of bloody massacres and oppressive reaction.

What is needed instead is "compromise," Cohen added, a notion now regarded as "hopelessly antiquated and bourgeois," but which has been the key to whatever social "improvements" history has recorded. Through "cooperation among different groups, each of which is wise enough to see the necessity of compromising" in the common interest, a better social order might be achieved. Cohen denied the communist claim that this liberal faith in reason, discussion, and accommodation is in itself "a peculiar excrudescence of capitalism." "The essence of liberalism—freedom of thought and inquiry, freedom of discussion and criticism—is . . . the mother of Greek and modern science."[14]

Cohen's definition of the liberalism communists would supplant, Hook replied, was loaded; it was as though one had referred to Cohen's opposition to radicalism and had then defined radicalism as "an attitude which [goes] to the root of the problems." Of course communists are for freedom of thought and discussion; the problem is that the present social order provides these and other freedoms only for a few. Furthermore, the

notion that all matters can be settled by free discussion today presupposes that it is possible for both sides to engage in it, that they are willing to do so, that they are pledged to abide by the consequences of the discussion, and that the fundamental class conflicts over the distribution of the social product and social power can be affected by such discussion.

Cohen fails to see, Hook continued, that the denial of liberties during the transitional period of the revolution is directed only against "the class enemy"; the restrictions will cease once this enemy has been destroyed. Cohen's blanket condemnation of armed class rebellion fails to consider the crucial question of whether a given war can "remove the sources and causes of future wars and, therefore, the evils which flow

from war including the denial of civil liberty." Hook disassociated his
own brand of Marxist communism from that of the Communist party
of the United States, of whose leadership he was critical, but he insisted
that "a mass revolutionary movement" was the best defense against
fascism, if only that movement could find "intelligent and militant
leadership."[15]

The Stalinists themselves denounced Cohen in their own organ, the
New Masses,[16] and Cohen was to wear the "anticommunist" tag for the
remainder of the 1930s. His "Why I Am Not a Communist" became
something of a classic of "independent liberalism" in the minds of its
friends as well as its enemies, and it eventually found its way into the
textbook for introductory philosophy produced by three of Cohen's
City College colleagues, Daniel Bronstein, Yervant Krikorian, and Philip
Wiener.[17] And the essay was, especially in its reaffirmation of reason,
discussion, and accommodation as political ideals, highly expressive of
the frame of mind Cohen brought to the most thoroughly political endeavor of his career, the effort to organize against anti-Semitism.

Shortly after the Nazi triumph in 1933, Cohen urged the establishment in the United States of "an effective intelligence service for the
Jewish people in their fight against the forces which would degrade
them and deprive them of their human rights."[18] He used his authority
as one of the most eminent Jewish-born members of America's secular
academic intelligentsia to issue the call that soon enlisted Albert Einstein, Felix Frankfurter, Harry Wolfson, Salo Baron, Edward Sapir, and
a number of others; the organization was designed to unite "professional people . . . who will not let their differences in regard to religious
orthodoxy, Zionism, socialism, or communism hinder them from co-
operating to prevent the permanent degradation of the Jews as human
beings."[19] The Conference on Jewish Relations was so much Cohen's
creature in its early years that his own home was its only office, and he,
as its chairman, was its chief administrator.[20] Through its publications
and meetings, the Conference sought especially to bring before "the
world's conscience the character and dimensions of the German assault

upon Jewish, and therefore upon human rights."[21] The Conference also tried to help refugee intellectuals find employment in the United States, but its contribution was chiefly and intentionally informational: it sponsored "a series of factual studies of the composition of the Jewish population and its place in the economy of the country, to serve as a basis of welfare programs, vocational guidance, and intelligent answers to the problems of discrimination." Efforts of this sort culminated in 1939 in the founding of the journal *Jewish Social Studies.*[22]

Although the Conference sometimes tried to answer charges made about Jews by anti-Semites, Cohen preferred other kinds of studies, on the grounds that "such answers add to the publicity" craved by anti-Semites, and hurt the "morale of the Jews, who are the principal readers of such attacks and replies." Moreover, Cohen reminded his fellow Jews that to some extent "anti-Semitism arises from the very fact that we suspect it where it does not exist, and our very suspiciousness makes us intolerant and disagreeable to our neighbors." Cohen, who had not forgotten the role of racial and religious discrimination in delaying his own career as a teacher of philosophy, was afraid that exaggerated claims about the extent of anti-Semitism in the United States would hurt the cause of the Jews in general, and would impair the credibility of the Conference in particular.[23]

Cohen insisted that the Conference was a "scientific" enterprise, and that to maintain its standing it must not flinch at the publication of information that might seem to be unfavorable to Jews. To a friend of the Conference who doubted the wisdom of a study of Jewish convicts, he replied that it was "silly . . . to pretend that there are no Jewish criminals. . . . What is important is to establish . . . that we are a normal people" and hence "no worse than the rest of the population" in regard to criminal behavior. Almost haunted by the fear that the Conference would be perceived as "another propaganda institute," Cohen could not declare often enough that the dissemination of even "unfavorable facts" was a surer method, in the long run, of combating unfavorable "misinformation," which was the real enemy.[24]

The Conference owed its existence and most of its character to Cohen's feeling that other organizations interested in defending the Jews lacked scholarly detachment. Nowhere in all the groups that were mobilizing in 1933, as Cohen recalled in his autobiography, did he see any that had mastered the Talmudic precept, "Teach thy tongue to say, 'I do not know.' " Zealous and well-meaning as these organizations may have been, they were afraid to confess frankly "the vast ignorance that is ours concerning the position of the Jew in the modern world." Too many would shun scientific inquiries on the grounds that they already knew that they were "right"; to them, Cohen replied that one could never be too cautious: "What . . . should we think of the captain of a boat who, with dangerous rocks ahead of him, shuts his eyes and steers blindly?"[25] In 1936 he said he had "no solution to offer to the Jewish problem except to preach caution."[26]

Cohen brought to the project his conspicuous aloofness from Zionism. As early as 1919 he had stated that this "nationalist philosophy" directly challenged "all those who still believe in liberalism." He took issue with the position Louis Brandeis and Horace Kallen, particularly, had affirmed, that Zionism and Americanism were compatible. This "profoundly mistaken" belief ignored the fact that "liberal America has traditionally stood for separation of church and state, for the free mixing of races," and for an "ideal of freedom" that Zionists actually feared. Zionism partook of "tribalism," a doctrine that may eventually triumph in history, but which is "none the less evil."[27] Kallen had disputed this hotly with Cohen in the pages of the *New Republic*, and the line of demarcation between Cohen and his Zionist friends was quite clear.[28] When some Zionists were persuaded to join with him in the work of the Conference after 1933, he was inclined to attribute their cooperation not so much to a common interest in Jewish survival, but to the consolidating power of the Conference's ideal of "objective truth."[29]

The Conference was an ideal vehicle for Cohen's desire, strongest after 1933, to defend Jews as a social group without identifying himself in any way with Judaism. He remained avowedly agnostic, although he began to attend the Passover Seder he had so pointedly avoided in earlier years.[30] He took offense when called a "post-Hitler Jew" by those who claimed to have maintained their Jewish identity more proudly during the years when his pronouncements on Jewish affairs were rare.[31] His post-1933 activities did not, however, entail any explicit repudiation of secular, cosmopolitan, or assimilationist ideals. What little Cohen had said about Jewish affairs before the advent of Hitler was to the effect that all minorities, including Jews, would be better off in a pluralistic, cosmopolitan setting than in an environment of self-sustained particularism. He seems to have accepted the "immigrant's gifts" ideal, according to which each ethnic group was to contribute its distinctive character and talents to a pluralistic, democratic culture. "The American tradition," he said, "is federalism, which allows for diversity instead of dull uniformity." His always sincere patriotism never included the sense that he and other immigrants "should wipe out their past and become simple imitations of the existing type," as he characterized the view he opposed.[32]

The prescriptions Cohen gave to American Jews after 1933 invariably linked their cause explicitly with assimilation into the pluralistic liberal democracy most completely fulfilled by the society and politics of the United States. "Let me put my finger on the main point," he said:

Assimilation was not the cause of the tragedy of the German or the Polish Jews. Assimilation is the fruit of that liberalism which opened the gates of the Ghetto and enabled the Jews to enjoy their days of prosperity and to make their great contributions to the world's art, science, and literature. What has happened recently was a frantic reaction against liberalism.[33]

By "assimilation" Cohen meant not the self-transformation of Jews into "mere imitations," again, "of the English, Scotch, Irish, Dutch, Swedes, Huguenots, or Germans" who inhabit America, but rather "being our own selves" in the process of participating "fully in all America's cultural activities." It was "neither safe nor desirable" for Jews to "isolate" themselves from their fellow citizens, especially liberals who

were their "only friends" anyhow. The liberal element in the American
tradition was what made America hospitable to the Jews, and this tradition ought to be defended not only for its own sake, but also as a tactic
of Jewish self-defense:

If we should do anything to antagonize [our liberal friends] by adopting an antiliberal philosophy, we should certainly cut ourselves off
from any possibility of having the cooperation of any part of the American public when we are in trouble. That is a real danger because our
Jewish nationalists *are* adopting an antiliberal philosophy.[34]

It was an abstract liberalism that Cohen employed to justify his participation in Jewish affairs. His concern for "Jewish survival" was always
a defense of Jews, as human beings, against genocide, persecution, and
discrimination; it was never an attempt, consciously at least, to perpetuate Jewish identity. Cohen believed it was inevitable that the Jews
would eventually cease to exist as an identifiable racial, religious, ethnic, and cultural group, simply because "no one can reasonably suppose
that the present divisions of mankind will last forever." He professed
his willingness to accept, "in the end," total assimilation.[35] His concern, then, was not with the preservation of Jewishness, but with the
preservation of that part of humanity that would, also inevitably, remain an identifiable social group called "the Jews" for many centuries.
In this long interim, he asserted, Jews ought not to be *compelled* to
shed their particularism, nor ought they to reassert it in ways that prevent them from sharing more fully in the benefits of human life. When
he endorsed the teaching of Jewish history to Jewish children, therefore, he was careful to justify it according to the Greek maxim, "know
thyself," not according to the need for preservation of Jewish traditions.[36] The line between these two justifications may be thin, and no
worthy purpose will be served by denying the possibility that Cohen,
covertly at least, shared the hope that the progeny of the Jewish people
would survive not only as humans but as Jews. Yet he used his entire
public life to announce as unmistakably as he could that he was not
simply a Jewish liberal, but a liberal.

Political debates among American intellectuals during the twentieth century, notes Christopher Lasch, have often turned on the success with which partisans have been able to depict each other as "sentimental, timid, effeminate, and 'utopian.' " This cult of "hard-boiled" political realism, most evident during the 1930s and 1940s, values "direct political involvement" over detachment, and demands that intellectuals diligently practice the art of the possible.[37] It was this ideal of "realism" that Thurman Arnold and other spokesmen for the New Deal's left flank used to distinguish their own views from conventional liberal capitalism; it was the same "toughness" that Reinhold Niebuhr, as a radical, used first to distance himself from Arnold-type liberals and then, in the following decade, to justify his own abandonment of radicalism for the centrist liberalism of the Americans for Democratic Action.[38] Whether or not Niebuhr, or Arnold, or anybody else, was "really realistic" could be debated at length, but the salient fact about the political style of Cohen was his conspicuous refusal to serve the realistic ideal; he remained always outside of the sphere within which these arguments were pursued. "It would be sad," he often remarked, "if all the priests deserted their altars and became soldiers."[39]

Cohen first offered this defense of priestly aloofness at the end of World War I, during which he had, by remaining neutral, managed both to offend friends and colleagues who devoted themselves to the war effort, and to disappoint Joseph Freeman and other young radicals who expected him to push his neutralism to the point of outright opposition to the war.[40] Even when he did become publicly committed to a cause, he tried to maintain this priestly posture, as in 1938, when he was determined that the anti-Nazism of himself and his friends not become so partisan as to blind them to the injustices the Czechs had perpetrated against the Sudeten Germans.[41] There were, to be sure, issues that seemed to him so clear-cut that a blunt pronouncement on one side or the other was a defense of "truth"; and Cohen was recognized as a critic of fascism in general well before antifascism became a theme of American liberal discourse.[42]

Cohen would assist the growth of liberal social democracy by practicing and promoting the tolerance and free inquiry that this form of government was peculiarly designed to promote. He did not deny that other forms of political action were necessary, including military defense, but he had no insight to offer into the exercise of force. He did not withhold the "liberal" appellation from those who took up arms against fascists, but there was no clearly defined place for them in his political outlook.[43] What Cohen had to contribute, both in theory and practice, was the politics of truth and tolerance that the division of labor, as he understood it, assigned to scholars. Against evil he offered education, moral suasion, and "a tenacious clinging to truth."[44] In this role, he was chiefly an exemplar of what he took to be liberal ideals and not a substantial contributor to liberalism as a political philosophy.[45] His theoretical contribution to liberalism was not made in a political context at all, but in the setting of philosophy of history.

NOTES

1. Sidney Hook, review of *RN*, in *JP* XXIX (1932), 24.

2. See pp. 167-169.

3. *FL*, 85 (originally published under the pseudonym "Philonous," *NR* XXI [1919], 19-20). Prior to its appearance in *FL*, Cohen also reprinted this piece, "A Slacker's Apology," in *Student Outlook* II (1934), 10-11, at a time when the pressure to "follow the banner of Lucifer" was strongest.

4. *DJ*, 159.

5. *DJ*, 257 (emphasis added).

6. *DJ*, 171; cf. *DJ*, 184.

7. Charles S. Liebman, "Towards a Theory of Jewish Liberalism," in Donald R. Cutler, ed., *The Religious Situation* (Boston, 1969), 1047, 1051-1052, 1055.

8. Charles B. Forcey, *Crossroads of Liberalism* (New York, 1961), x.

9. MRC, "Property and Sovereignty," *Cornell Law Quarterly Review* XIII (1927), 8-30 (*LSO*, 41-68).

10. MRC, "The Basis of Contract," *Harvard Law Review* XLVI (1933), 553-592 (*LSO*, 69-111).

11. MRC, "Constitutional and Natural Rights in 1789 and Since," *National Lawyers Guild Quarterly* I (1938), 92-103 (*FL*, 175-193). Cohen differed with his friend Felix Frankfurter over court reorganization; see their correspondence in *Portrait*, 263-267, 271-274, 277-281. Cf. also MRC, "Fallacies about the Court," *Nation* CXLI (1935), 39-40 (reprinted in Howard Zinn, ed., *New Deal Thought* [Indianapolis, 1966], 351-367).

12. Bruce Bliven to MRC, January 5, 1938, Cohen MSS.

13. *Portrait*, 176.

14. MRC, "Why I Am Not a Communist," *Modern Monthly* VIII (1934), 148-149, 163-165.

15. Sidney Hook, "Why I Am a Communist," *Modern Monthly* VIII (1934), 148-149, 163-165.

16. Paul Salter and Jack Librome, "Dewey, Russell and Cohen: Why They Are Anti-Communist," *New Masses* XII (1934), 22-23. Salter and Librome concluded that Cohen was "by far the most sophistic, the most patently reactionary" of the three liberals under attack.

17. Daniel J. Bronstein et al., *Basic Problems in Philosophy* (New York, 1947), 219-224.

18. *DJ*, 241. Cf. MRC to prospective members of the Conference on Jewish Relations, June 5, 1933, in *Portrait*, 219.

19. MRC to prospective members, 219. For a list of leading members as of 1936 see MRC to James N. Rosenberg, October 26, 1936, in *Portrait*, 223. Cf. *DJ*, 243.

20. *Portrait*, 220.

21. *DJ*, 243.

22. *DJ*, 248, 250; *Portrait*, 226.

23. *DJ*, 246-247; MRC, "As a Liberal Views It," in Marvin Lowenthal et al., *Proposed Roads for American Jewry* (New York, 1938), 56 (*RWJ*, 8-9).

24. MRC to Jay Leo Rothschild, February 1, 1939, in *Portrait*, 229. Cf. MRC, "As a Liberal Views It," 53 (*RWJ*, 7).

25. *DJ*, 238-239.

26. MRC, "As a Liberal Views It," 53-54 (*RWJ*, 7). This paper was first given as an address in 1936, before the National Council of Jewish Women.

27. MRC, "Zionism: Tribalism or Liberalism?" *NR* XVIII (1919), 182-183 (*FL*, 327, 329-330, 332). When this essay was reprinted in *FL*, it was followed by a "Postscript" disavowing "some views that have been falsely associated, in the public mind, with opposition to Zionism," especially laws against the immigration of Jews to Palestine. Cf. the recollections of Cohen's daughter of a fiery argument between Cohen and the Zionist leader David Ben-Gurion in New York in 1941 (*Portrait*, 218). Cf. also Cohen's recollections of having been branded an anti-Semite on account of his attitude toward Zionism (*DJ*, 226).

28. Horace Kallen, "Zionism: Democracy or Prussianism," *NR* XVIII (1919), 311-313.

29. *DJ*, 250.

30. *Portrait*, 236.

31. MRC to Henry Levy, May 16, 1935, in *Portrait*, 215-216. Cf. the petulant remarks of Felix Cohen in response to the observation of Horace Kallen that the events of 1933 inspired Cohen's increased interest in Jewish activities: letter to editor, *Jewish Social Studies* XIII (1951), 381-382. For Kallen's interpretation see 85-86 and 382.

32. MRC, "Cohen Forecasts Disappearance of Yiddish," *American Hebrew* CXXXV (1932), 553, 577. Cf. MRC, "Remarks," *Foreign-Born* III (1922), 168-169.

33. MRC, "As a Liberal Views It," 68-69 (*RWJ*, 15-16).

34. MRC, "As a Liberal Views It," 73, 77 (*RWJ*, 17-18, 20).

35. MRC, "As a Liberal Views It," 70 (*RWJ*, 16).

36. MRC, "As a Liberal Views It," 68, 73 (*RWJ*, 14-15, 17-18). Cf. *RWJ*, 23-29.

37. Christopher Lasch, *The New Radicalism in America: The Emergence of the Intellectual as a Social Type, 1889-1963* (New York, 1965), 289.

38. Reinhold Niebuhr, *Moral Man and Immoral Society* (New York, 1932), and Reinhold Niebuhr, *The Children of Light and the Children of Darkness* (New York, 1944).

39. *FL*, 85.

40. Joseph Freeman, *An American Testament* (New York, 1936), 94-95; *FL* 84-88.

41. Lewis Feuer remembers an evening in Cohen's home during which a group of Cohen's students and former students argued with him at length over this point (conversation with author). Cf. Feuer, "The Philosophy of Morris R. Cohen: Its Social Bearings," *Philosophy and Phenomenological Research* X (1950), 474.

42. John P. Diggins, *Mussolini and Fascism: The View from America* (Princeton, 1972), 260.

43. MRC, "Sacco and Vanzetti Compared with Dreyfus," *Sacco-Vanzetti Dawn* (n.d.), clipping in Archives of C.C.N.Y., "Cohen, Morris R., 1900"; MRC, review of Osmond K. Fraenkel, *The Sacco-Vanzetti Case*, in *Nation* CXXXIII (1941), 702-703 (*FL*, 193-198); MRC, "A Scandalous Denial of Justice: The Bertrand Russell Case," in John Dewey and Horace Kallen, eds., *The Bertrand Russell Case* (New York, 1941), 131-147 (*FL*, 198-210). Cohen testified in defense of a communist colleague, Morris U. Schappes, in the Court of General Sessions, New York City, June 25, 1941. Cf. *Portrait*, 109, 172.

44. Undated diary note, in *DJ*, 270.

45. For Cohen's closest approaches to systematic justifications of liberalism as a political philosophy see *FL*, 437-469; MRC, "What I Believe," *Nation* CXXXIII (1931), 128-131 (*FL*, 3-10); MRC, "The Intellectual Basis of Individualism," *League for Industrial Democracy Monthly* X (1932), 3-4, 11 (*FL*, 59-67). Cohen's scattered aphorisms about liberalism as a political philosophy are intelligently pulled together and discussed by Herbert G. Reid in "Morris Cohen's Case for Liberalism," *Review of Politics* XXXIII (1971), 489-511.

Is it in hopes
to find or lose
          myself
that I
fill up my table now
with Michelet and Motley?
To "know how it was"
or to forget how it is—
what else?
Split at the root, neither Gentile nor Jew,
Yankee nor Rebel, born
in the face of two ancient cults,
I'm a good reader of histories.
And you,
Morris Cohen, dear to me as a brother,
when you sit at night
tracing your way through your volumes
of Josephus, or any
of the old Judaic chronicles,
do you find yourself there, a simpler,
more eloquent Jew?
          or do you read
to shut out the tick-tock of self,
the questions and their routine answers?

Adrienne Rich

American intellectuals of the 1940s and 1950s were often uncertain about the nature of man and the pattern of his history, but they were determined at least to shun excessively optimistic, simplistic, and arrogant beliefs. The "human condition" was complex; and insofar as any general qualities could be attributed to it, they were tragedy, irony, paradox, and ambiguity. Such was the mood of tract after tract in the postwar decade, during which theologian Reinhold Niebuhr very nearly replaced the militantly secular John Dewey as the reigning national sage. Secular liberals were suddenly eager to take account of the "limitations" of man, allegedly slighted by a tradition that looked to "social intelligence" for a transformation of the terms on which life was to be lived. Now wisdom consisted in acknowledging the permanence, not the mutability, of the most salient features of human experience.

The intellectuals of the 1940s and 1950s were not the first thinkers to regard themselves as wiser than their predecessors,[1] but not every generation claims for itself the same kind of moral superiority. These prophets of humility and contrition did not, for example, view their own insights as more "progressive" than those of "reactionary" forebears, nor did they claim for themselves a more passionate commitment to the liberation of human potentialities from foolish fears and needless constraints. They did not announce a bold, clear vision to replace one encumbered by contradictions, antinomies, and obscurities. Rather, they took possession of "profundity," "realism," and "sophistication"; they rejoiced in their ability to get beyond "superficiality," "idealism," and "innocence." They warned against "the sins of pride." To be sure, all of these labels are general enough to serve a variety of polemical uses, but American attitudes toward man and history had changed sufficiently from 1920 to 1950 to produce vividly contrasting rhetoric.

The "liberal interpretation of history" was chastised in one representative critique for having too often "ignored the evil in human nature, attributing human evils to externals" instead of to internal, endemic conditions. The liberal tradition was obtuse, also, about "irrationality," which, however we may respond to it, is "primarily" responsible for how people behave. It was a mistake, further, to assume that "men always want freedom," for in fact adults, "like children, love to follow a leader. Far from loving to be free to decide, most people find the necessity of making decisions a strain and prefer to have it taken off their shoulders." Liberalism also "ignored the influence of traditions and institutions," "sinned in believing in steady, inevitable progress," and erred in "minimizing the powers of darkness." "No candid observer of man's past can find in it any guaranty of the triumph of light."

These strictures were made by Morris Cohen,[2] and not for the first time in 1947. Cohen was not the only moralist to sound "dark notes" during the preceding thirty years, but he was distinctive among leaders of "liberal social thought" in the frequency and conviction with which he did so. Well before American entry into World War I, Cohen began to scold his contemporaries for a naive belief in "progress."[3] By the early 1920s, when Dewey was still defending the "infinite perfectibility of man,"[4] Cohen had identified himself with the contrasting emphasis on the permanent limitations and iniquity of humankind: "Neither in love nor in work, neither in society nor in solitude, neither in the arts nor in the sciences will the world of actuality permit us to attain perfection," for we are powerless against the "ineradicable evil" that haunts our efforts. Such sentiments were drawn out of Cohen by Dewey in particular, whose hopes Cohen repeatedly scoffed at during the interwar years. In 1920 the *New Republic* published what was to be Cohen's paradigmatic assault on Dewey's alleged failure to confront "the incurable evils which, in an imperfect world, every child of mortal man and woman must face before reaching the crowning agonies of death." Oblivious to "the mystery of the universe," Dewey marches on, curiously confident that he and his fellows can shape the world to purposes dictated by human reason. However genuine were Dewey's services to freedom and reason,

the future may wonder at the naive and entirely uncritical way in which such a keen mind could accept . . . the myth of universal evolution, and [at] his failure to recognize that despite its supreme worth, human intelligence is frail, pathetically impotent in the face of great physical stress, or vital impulse.

The virtue Dewey and his followers most lacked, insisted Cohen, was "wisely cultivated resignation."[5]

"Man's silly pretensions to exalt himself as master of the universe"[6] were bound up with what Cohen believed to be the impossible dream of escaping from history. One cannot brush away the past and start with a clean slate, he repeated in almost every context in which he found himself. His critique of popular Baconianism stressed that inherited interpretations of the world, even if "mythical," are the inescapable and indispensable starting points for science. One cannot simply "look at the facts," he said hundreds of times; instead, one has to employ a theory, a set of categories for understanding the object of knowledge. In jurisprudence, his defense of rule and precedent was likewise grounded in the sense that judges respond to the "particulars" of a case, not in a vacuum, but in the context of a body of categories, principles, and priorities created by the history of relevant social and legal experience. He doubted that the elimination of the class system would terminate troublesome social evils, for he saw these evils as rooted in conditions transcending class that would inevitably define the character of both violent socialist revolution and the society produced by it. Although he rejected the use of history to undermine or to justify a given doctrine— this was the hated "genetic fallacy"—he felt strongly attached to history as a source of security and as an expansion of experience beyond the concreteness of the present. No single feature of *Reason and Nature* more readily distinguishes it, on mere perusal, from Dewey's *Experience and Nature* or Lewis's *Mind and the World Order* than its abundance of historical allusions; Cohen was almost "choked" by his historical erudition, as more than one of his contemporaries lamented.[7]

If too inclined to ignore the benefits and inevitabilities of history, Cohen's age seemed to him similarly prone to thrust aside certain commonsense notions about human nature in favor of such shallow enthusiasms as Freudianism, Marxism, and behaviorism. Although he frequently sneered at Freud and his followers, Cohen actually grasped very little of Freud's conception of the ultimate dynamics of human history, and he would not have understood a phrase like Auden's "made of eros and of dust." Cohen's most sustained discussion of Freud was a review of *Moses and Monotheism*, a book he read only as an unsuccessful contribution to the scholarly field of "Jewish history," based on scanty research in the ancient sources. Freud's idea "that all history begins with the father killing the sons and then the sons killing the father" was a triumph of the "mythic" over the "scientific" way of thinking.[8] Most often, Cohen dismissed Freud as a monocausal mental determinist, whose concept of "subconscious mind" had never been shown to have a real, biological counterpart. Cohen acknowledged, however, that psychoanalysis, like Christian Science, did achieve some therapeutic success. He was not really a critic "of Freud" at all, but rather a debunker of the popular Freudianism that informed such works as Jerome Frank's *Law and the Modern Mind.*[9] By laughing simplistic doctrines out of court, Cohen, in effect, kept the more complex Freudian view of man at a distance. There was simply no rapport between Cohen's own general sense of man's "passionately irrational drives"[10] and Freud's specific attempt to analyze them. Cohen was happy enough with the categories of "reason" and "passion," as handed down by the eighteenth century.

Cohen understood Marx better than Freud, but here, too, his attention was fixed on contemporary interpretations, which were marked by a single-minded "economic determinism." His admonitions were aimed only indirectly at Marx's notions of class and of the historical inevitability and function of class conflict. His direct targets were social critics like Bernard Smith, whose attempt to relate literary attitudes to economic structure Cohen characterized as a reduction of "a wide range of very complicated and highly individualized phenomena to too simple a pattern."[11] By simply affirming the authenticity of noneconomic motives in human behavior, Cohen disposed of any supposed obligation to probe more deeply the Marxist insight into the foundations of culture.

Cohen's positive ideas emerged a bit more in his dissents from behaviorist psychology and its analogues in the social sciences generally. Neither the categories of the physical sciences nor those of "stimulus and response" are able to handle the complexity of social objects, Cohen held, for human life contains an irreducibly "teleological" element, and the social sciences must therefore discuss a human act "in terms of its goals." Not only is the "purposive" as real in society as the "physical," so, too, is the "ethical," for social acts are "problems for us," requiring normative responses. The object of knowledge in social inquiry is sufficiently distinct from that in physical inquiry that the application of "scientific method" must never be taken to mean making over society in the image of "electrons in motion."[12]

By the end of the 1930s Cohen's "philosophical anthropology"—if this term can refer to opinions about the dynamics of human experience as a whole—was manifest chiefly in these critiques, and in his occasional marginal references to "polar" drives such as security and adventure, reason and passion, the contemplative and the sensual, the centrifugal and the centripetal. He sometimes alluded to a cyclical pattern in which "the whole universe, with its rhythmic seasons of growth and decay," experiences "periodic waves" of hope that inevitably "shatter themselves in turn against the sands of actuality."[13] Then he decided, late in life, to write what he called his "magnum opus,"[14] a systematic philosophy of civilization that would explore "the meaning of human history."

The appeal speculative philosophy of history had for Cohen was undoubtedly a result, partially, of the rise of fascism and anti-Semitism, and the onset of war. The pursuit of "cosmic issues" was also a way of dealing with those personal concerns of his late middle age that led to the writing of an autobiography: ambivalent about his achievements and aware that most of his life was behind him, Cohen in the late 1930s became increasingly confused about the meaning of it all. In a short dramatic sketch of 1938, which he called a "dialogue," he sought to express his vision of the "relation of personal experience to history."[15] This piece uniquely mirrors both the personal preoccupations that would soon find fuller expression in *A Dreamer's Journey* and the universal scope Cohen would aim for in *The Meaning of Human History*.

King Saul's Daughter was inspired by the life of Michal, as described in 1 and 2 Samuel. While reading and reviewing in the general area of Jewish history since 1933, Cohen had been drawn frequently back to the Old Testament. Suddenly, while studying Samuel, his imagination was "gripped" by Michal, daughter of King Saul, a marginal figure in the narrative of David's life and times. Once the inspiration took hold of him, Cohen "was forced to write it out almost in one sitting." He then spent a full month polishing it, reading sections to his wife and to his grown children during the evenings of that summer of 1938, when the family was together at Blue Mountain Lake in the Adirondacks.[16] The Bible presented Cohen with an almost infinite variety of types of experience, and his ability to identify so fully with Michal in particular is hence of interest.

Cohen's preface sets forth the salient facts about Michal. Happily married to David ("the only woman in the Biblical history of whom we are told that she loved her husband"), she is deprived of her beloved by the arbitrary wrath of her father, who then gives her to another man; Michal finally lives down her loss of David, and after many years achieves perfect love for her new husband, only to lose him when political events force her own return to David, who then quarrels with her and participates in the killing of the five sons of her second marriage.[17] Even this characterization is partially the product of Cohen's imagination: Samuel says that Michal's second husband walked after her and wept when she was taken from him, but there is no specific indication that Michal herself experienced a grief as profound as his.[18] This addition to the story reveals some of what Cohen was looking for in Michal: someone who has suffered intense pain while being battered about by events beyond her control. When evidence was lacking for truly acute pain, Cohen created it. The play was not intended as a historically accurate reconstruction of events, so the point here concerns not the mere fact that Cohen embellished the Bible—such was his whole idea—but rather the specific directions taken by his imagination. His preface also attributes to the Bible the sense that Michal was "proud and unbendingly dignified, intellectually resourceful and withal intense in her affections."[19] This characterization of Samuel's implications is not manifestly wrong, but Cohen chooses to sketch these qualities very boldly as his drama proceeds.

Michal is never an agent of fate; she is a being to whom things happen. Cohen admires her inner strength, sensitivity, and courage; inert as a recipient of fate, she wins dignity and respect through her stoic ability simply to endure, to remain alive and intact during years of tribulation. She is the ultimate expression of tenacity, which Cohen felt to be the quality most central to himself, and which he believed had come to him from another long-suffering woman, his mother.

Bessie Farfel Cohen had died but two years before Michal became the vehicle for Morris Cohen's emotions, and the identity of Michal with Bessie can scarcely be missed. Not only does Cohen attribute to Michal the same general traits he associated with his mother; he reveals the identification more explicitly at several points. For example, in speaking of her second husband, Phaltiel, Michal uses words almost identical to those Cohen proposed for the epitaph of Bessie's husband, Morris's own father: "he never said nor did anything base."[20] Elsewhere, a minor figure in the play characterizes Michal's marriage to Phaltiel in almost exactly the same terms Cohen used to describe his own parents' marriage: "the love that is developed by living together is the most enduring."[21]

If Michal was mother, on another level Michal was also Morris. The intimacy with which his own ego was identified with his mother is revealed in an entry of Cohen's diary written shortly after Bessie's death: "all the dreams of my life, my long communings with myself directly or indirectly connected with her, seem to be endowed with some of her tenacious vitality despite physical frailty."[22] Hence Cohen could get inside Michal, through the persona of his mother, and make her the spokesman for certain of his most deeply felt responses to human experience. "If your life is full of such extremes," Michal says to David, who, along with King Saul, is a symbol for the dynamic yet anarchic world of affairs, "I fear that you will soon wear out even your titanic energy." Then Michal, the passive receiver of history, whom David accuses of being "too detached," breaks into tears and confesses: "As for myself—I do not trust myself to say any more. Please leave me with my thoughts."[23]

"Not in victory is heroism," Cohen had noted to himself in his early twenties, "but in the long, continued, painful struggle."[24] For nearly forty years Cohen had "endured," employing modes of covert dogmatism and open, often brilliant, "rapierlike" criticism; now, near the end of life, the "tenacious clinging" that had found only incomplete expression in his public career as a cleaner of stables surfaced with avenging intensity in what was, for him, an aberrant genre. Cohen, who years before had mocked belles lettres with the observation, "anyone can write a poem; but now, to do a piece of *criticism*!,"[25] was finally attracted to a freer, more imaginative outlet. Here, in *King Saul's Daughter*, less private than his diary yet less public than his published work, Cohen could more amply express his affinities with those quiet, virtuous, and unhappy souls for whom dogmas were to be held dear, not exposed to constant criticism; and for whom the brooding of tenacious self-absorption, of being alone with "one's thoughts," was *not* an obstacle to be overcome in the interests of going into some activity "with all one's might and main," but rather a necessary and rational defense against a chaotic world. The sense that something long submerged was being let loose in *King Saul's Daughter* is confirmed by the extent to which Cohen luxuriates in the fatalistic supernaturalism of the Old Testament (an effect he seeks to mitigate by having Michal perfunctorily denounce superstition and fanaticism),[26] and by the abruptness with which childlike, clearly uncontrolled emotions protrude into the

play's otherwise dark and resigned mood: to depict the early stages of
Michal's relationship to David, for example, Cohen falls back on the
conventions of fairy tales.[27]

"Wisely cultivated resignation" had long been part of Cohen's advice
to his fellow humans, but the message was marginal, at best, to his
metaphysics, his philosophy of science, his jurisprudence, and even his
politics; now, in speculations on "history," this sentiment would
achieve its full expression. Yet in moving from *King Saul's Daughter*—a
"philosopher's holiday"—back into formal philosophical writing, the
tensions that had been partially released by writing the play were again
renewed. *The Meaning of Human History* was to be a systematic treatise; it was to be his Carus Lectures, and would thus find its inevitable
place on the shelf next to Dewey's *Experience and Nature* and Lovejoy's *Revolt Against Dualism.* It was exactly the sort of writing that had
always frustrated Cohen most. And pressure of a related sort soon developed, for once Cohen began to work out his ideas about history, he
was drawn back, inexorably, to pick up the loose ends of his career.
The *meaning* of human *history* became yet another assault on the old
ontological problem, the relation of the two orders: logic, value, meaning, and form on the one hand; history, time, existence, and matter on
the other. Now the struggle would be renewed in its most challenging
setting, the temporal experience of man. Here, at last, Cohen would
speak to what his critics among metaphysicians accused him of ignoring: the actual *relation* of "meaning" and "logic" to the contingencies
of life. What is man, under the ordinance of time? What logical pattern,
what meaning, is to be found in the totality of experience? These questions Cohen would confront at last; now his oblique fatalism and his
senses of teleology and tragedy would, hopefully, find their relation to
the scientific ideal.

One can only guess what *The Meaning of Human History* might have
looked like had its author been able to complete it to his own satisfaction. In 1942 the manuscript became the responsibility of Felix Cohen,

who helped his disabled father prepare it for its eventual publication in 1947. It is a fragmented and disconnected book, and it only just begins to pursue and integrate the concerns that had impelled Cohen to undertake it in the first place. The very incompleteness of the work is an apt, if sad, metaphor for Cohen's attempts, generally, to get beyond his critical style and do sustained, systematic philosophical analysis. Still, despite abrupt shifts of focus from paragraph to paragraph and chapter to chapter, *The Meaning of Human History* has an unmistakable, if implicit, unity. The book moves from a consideration of the nature of historical knowledge to an analysis of the object of knowledge itself, from the historian's task to the temporal experience of man that the historian and the philosopher of history seek to understand.

As history "oscillates between poetry . . . and the desire to know what actually happened," so, too, does all science employ our imaginative energies at one stage or another, wrote Cohen in an attempt to bring historical knowledge within the scope of scientific knowledge in general. The fact that history "deals with unique events" does not make their comprehension any less a "scientific" act, for judgments about such happenings can presumably be tested and eventually integrated into a coherent, organized system. Drawing on the conception of scientific method he had defended for thirty years, Cohen attacked two old enemies: the popular "Baconian" sense that science consists in looking upon facts without any preconceived ideas, and the "relativist" or subjectivist claim that all knowledge is created by man, rather than discovered in nature.[28] But Cohen's problem was not quite the same this time, for skepticism about "objectivity" was greater with reference to history than to other "scientific" disciplines, especially in the early 1940s after a radically relativist position had been popularized in the previous decade by Charles Beard and Carl Becker, then the two most influential theorists among historians.[29]

Hence Cohen, while quick to acknowledge the influence of the historian's values, assumptions, and principles of selection, was more concerned to deny the implication that historical knowledge is subjective.

The "categories," the "perspective" a historian brings to his work do not prevent the "objective" determination of truth.

> It may be admitted . . . that all selection involves an arbitrary cutting off and even a distortion in the picture of the past. But if the meaning of an event denotes its relations to other events connected with it, the meaning of history is not created by the historian but discovered by him. . . . What the historian makes is not the past but findings about it.[30]

There are "objective underlying patterns" in historical reality which the historian, by using his chosen categories critically and scientifically, may hope to discover. "A battle," for example, must not be seen as "merely a number of movements." Its *meaning* can be discovered only when the historian is equipped with categories which enable him to see that "each movement has significance": "a battle is part of a war, which is generally an outcome of national politics," and so forth.[31] That historians provide different accounts of closely related events need not be taken as an indictment of the objectivity of their accounts or of the reality of the meanings they claim to have found in an event. The variation in what historians say follows not from their "subjectivity," nor from the lack of real meanings in history. Rather, it follows from the fact that historians choose to ask different questions about the same events. In their answers to "given specific questions," historians are not so distant from one another. As for what questions ought to be asked, the choice is itself "part of the process of rational inquiry."[32]

Within his various "perspectives" and "categories," Cohen added, the historian "must assume causal laws according to which the phenomena of human life are connected." While historians do not seek to discover universal laws, they must employ them to understand the specific, individual, temporal events that draw their attention. A historical account may be coherent because we assume, for example,

> that men will generally seek their economic advantage, that ambitious generals will get their countries into war, that rebellions are commonly due to misgovernment, that custom will control conduct, but that

travel, discovery of new lands, or contact with other peoples tends to break down the unquestioning acceptance of custom and traditions.[33]

Cohen's list was made up of what today's philosophers of history would call "lawlike generalizations." They are not hard and fast in the same sense as is the law "water freezes at 32 degrees," but they do express relations that are frequently found to hold. The distinction between the "causal law" and the "lawlike generalization" became central to philosophical discourse about history shortly after Cohen wrote; and his lack of rigor, from today's viewpoint, ought not to conceal the fact that few American philosophers had, by 1942, written similarly cogent accounts of historical knowledge.

Philosophy of history was scarcely a discipline at all in the United States until the end of the 1940s, by which time Carl Hempel's 1942 classic, "The Function of General Laws in History," had created the now famous controversy over the nature of historical explanation.[34] "Explanation," too, was a concept Cohen did not use specifically, for in 1940 the distinctions between "understanding," "account," "explanation," "truth," and "meaning" were not significantly operative in theoretical discourse about history, especially as pursued by the working historians who were then doing most of the talking.[35]

Cohen's fate as a theorist of historical knowledge was, therefore, not unlike his destiny as a philosopher of science: soon after he made a series of relatively rigorous advances in formulating and resolving certain problems, the sophistication of the discussion increased abruptly, and his views rapidly became passé among his fellow philosophers. Among historians, however, Cohen's basic attitude toward the conflicting claims of "objectivity" and "relativism" made good sense, and he is remembered even today for having helped to moderate the more thoroughgoing relativism of Beard and Becker.[36]

The Meaning of Human History's analysis of the object of knowledge begins with a commentary on "causation." The causal relation between events is, Cohen felt, perhaps the most important sort of connection— and therefore "meaning"—to be fished out of "the living stream of history." Logic is to be found amid the flux not simply in the relation of part to whole (as the battle is part of a war, etc.), but in the relation between an event and the "reason why it should occur in the way in which it does." Defining the "cause" of an event as no more and no less than the "sum of [its] necessary and sufficient conditions," Cohen sought to establish the applicability of the concept to human affairs.[37] His approach was first to assume that it *is* applicable, on the grounds that human experience is, after all, part of "nature," and then to elucidate those features of human experience that make it more complicated than the rest of nature. In this view, the search for causal relations in history consists chiefly in avoiding "hasty generalization"—a warning that recurs in the book[38]—while taking as much as possible into account.

The reality historians study, Cohen explained, is so complex that we cannot dare to hope for causal explanations comparable in exactness to those of the physical sciences. "Physical systems," for example, "can generally be restored to previous conditions and the effects of intervening history thus be eliminated," but not so in "the organic and human realm where the effect of age and experience cannot be wiped out." Moreover, "human volition," however dependent upon physical systems, remains notoriously unreducible to the laws of physical causality. Furthermore, the forces at work in human affairs are easily confused with one another: a "religious" cause is not necessarily mutually exclusive with an "economic" one. Most important of all, historical study proves that "one-factor" interpretations will almost certainly fail: the plurality of operative forces simply demands a "multidimensional" approach.[39]

Cohen supported the claims of "multidimensionality" through an analysis of "The Geographic Factor in History," based on his eclectic reading of Pliny, Vitruvius, and scattered modern texts. He found that topography, climate, and natural resources were all "necessary but not sufficient conditions of any particular course of human development." Not surprisingly, to those steeped in Cohen, the discussion of plurality turned into another dualistic go-around between "mind" and "matter," with both the "spiritualists" and the "environmentalists" shown to be one-sided. "Every human act contains human and nonhuman elements inextricably intertwined," Cohen concluded; we must recognize "both mind and matter as polar components" of history.[40] So, too, in the following chapters, were "physiology" and "intellect" balanced, and "great men" commingled with "social forces."[41]

The principle of polarity continued to guide Cohen once he left the problem of causality to take up the ultimate dynamics and pattern of historical development. Neither the "progressive" view of history nor its opposite, the "theory of human degeneration," will stand the tests of reflection, he began, but the "intermediate" view of cyclical change "may guard us against the more violent extremes of optimism and pessimism." The radical distinctness of each civilization makes it impossible for the cyclical view to work "as a guide in the actual writing" of the history of given civilizations, but the "recurrences" we see in distinct societies and periods are nevertheless "the stuff out of which generalization in the social sciences emerges." The specific form taken by most cyclical views, he complained, was the analogy to the "individual life cycle," with its birth, growth, decay, and death. One ought to look for other repeatable episodes in history. But the metaphor Cohen preferred to "growth" was more general and, as he failed to acknowledge, less conducive to the achievement of precise scientific generalization: "the tides of the sea." This conception, said Cohen, recognizes the reality of both permanence and change:

The oscillations of history about a given norm are at least as real as the norm. High tide and low tide are as real as mean sea level. And though the tides of history are less easily charted than the tides of the sea, their charting is still the chief task of the historian.[42]

Cohen certainly did not believe that human history had so regular and predictable a pattern as the tides of the Atlantic on Long Island, but the metaphor expressed both his sense of history's vastness and his faith in cosmic order.

It was in this context that he wrote the critique of the "liberal interpretation of history" quoted earlier. The liberals had weakened their
position by their extravagant expectations, by their easy belief in the
goodness of man and in his historical progress; liberals had failed to
take into account "the idea of polarity and oscillation," and had thereby simply turned upside down the errors of the extreme conservatives,
who could see only evil and degeneration. "The dominant forces in
human nature," said Cohen, coming now to the marrow of his view of
man as a temporal and social creature, are "fear" and "freedom." These
"two poles of human life" are "the expansive forces, which involve
adventure, and the centralizing or organizing forces, which protect us
against those elements that would destroy us." Liberalism would be
stronger, Cohen implied, if it recognized the importance and positive
value of our fears, just as those "who are opposed to innovation of any
sort" have not seen that "without freedom to expand or grow life
would be impossible."[43] This advice was of course perfectly consistent
with the messages Cohen had been sending his fellow liberals throughout his career, for it was organization and caution, not expansion and
daring, that defined his scientific ideal. While he did not in this volume
invoke the metaphor of the coachman, caught between inertia and
stampede, the ambience was identical. "Oscillations in the direction of
total freedom and . . . total restraint may be inevitable," Cohen wrote
now, and the "balance" any society attains "is always precarious."[44]

Cohen was frankly uncertain about the form to be taken by the
"new" balance "between fear and freedom" that would replace traditional liberalism, but he was at least sure that disillusioned liberals
ought not to accommodate too quickly with religion. In the final chapter of *The Meaning of Human History*, he sought to mitigate the potentially messianic implications of his "tides of the sea" sense of history.
The insights of "fear" must not lead toward an abject submission to
history; such an error would betray the promise of "human intelligence" and "wipe out any real distinction between good and evil." The
old message, "whatever is, is right" emerged, for example, from the

view of Christian existentialist Nicholas Berdyaev that any demand for human justice was resistance to the will of God.[45] Cohen's "wisely cultivated resignation" thus had its limits: the temptation to trust, like Job, in the ultimate goodness of the "mysterious tides, mighty and deep" that swept along Michal, and Morris Cohen, had to be checked by the determination to make distinctions. Hence one must defend the tiny flame of inquiry in "the dark and boundless sea of being," for only through the practice of reason could one hope to align oneself with the truth and goodness that are endemic to history, and to avoid their equally endemic opposites. It was the reality of these polar qualities in human history itself—not simply in a subjective realm—that made "fear" a necessary and wise response to life, but this very fear needed to express itself through the active pursuit of the happily self-corrective "Socratic ideal of free inquiry."[46]

Hence the question of history's relation to truth and value divided into two: How does what we know of history assist us, as free and rational agents, in making the right decisions? And what is the actual historical fate of "truth" and those who seek it? To the first question Cohen's answer was, as always, that history can expand our scope of knowledge and insight but cannot determine the "right," for that would become "the genetic fallacy."[47] To the second question Cohen offered what he called "the tragic view of history." In this view, man, however committed a seeker and teller of truth, is "a crooked stick," in Kant's phrase, an imperfect being living in a distinctly "limited" environment; hence a recurrent theme of history must be "the triumph of brute power over idealistic aspirations and generous hopes." Truth and goodness are defeated again and again, but they live on as ideals which, "even though not completely attainable at any one time," guide our efforts. Defeat is never permanent, for the "spirit of truth," like the tides, makes its eternal return: "The Hellenic spirit has outlived the Roman conquest, and Napoleon could not permanently wipe out the ideal of Liberty, Equality, and Fraternity."[48] It is thus a pattern of history that "truth, even though for a time crushed to earth, rises again."[49] Mill believed that truth's great advantage over error lies in the fact that it is always there to be confronted, sooner or later, whenever men lapse from it.[50] This was essentially Cohen's view, with the important caveat that evil has powers of persistence virtually equal to those of truth.

The Meaning of Human History's postscripts to Cohen's earlier work in metaphysics, philosophy of science, and moral philosophy were not substantive enough to influence professional philosophers. Even Cohen's analysis of historical knowledge was destined to attract only limited attention.[51] The book's role in contemporary discourse was not remotely comparable to that of *Reason and Nature*, or *Law and the Social Order*, or many of Cohen's briefer efforts. Yet the volume did bring Cohen's sense of life to more complete articulation, and at a time when some of his insights were in vogue. It won a certain amount of acclaim as a sober and wise answer to the superficialities of the liberal tradition,[52] and it might even have become one of the more quoted texts of the postwar revision of liberalism had it not been so doggedly aloof from one central concern of revisionist liberals: the moral responsibilities of power.

The Meaning of Human History expressed a passive sense of "tragedy," unmistakably different from the view of Reinhold Niebuhr, for example, in which man is seen as a tragic *agent*, destined to participate in evil while achieving limited good. History, for Cohen, was something that happened *to* people, and a "tragic" event in history was the defeat, whether by inner limitations or external forces, of the right values. "Power," moreover, was for Cohen a pole to "truth," and this was indeed the term he most often used for the force that periodically crushed truth. Cohen's philosophy of history turned out to have the same parameters as his politics, although the latter was presumably a politics for intellectuals, as intellectuals. His "tragic view of history" was not similarly limited, officially, but in practice it addressed the destiny of man primarily as a seeker of and a witness to truth, and only secondarily as a being who must bear the responsibility for the exercise of power.

American liberals in the 1940s and 1950s were disposed toward a sense of tragedy less passive and less purely cerebral; they were concerned to understand the moral significance of the unprecedented aggregate of power at the disposal of man in general and Americans in particular. It was the possessors of power, not its victims, who were looking for the meaning of history; the bombers of Hiroshima, not the bombed. Such special needs could scarcely be met by someone who, only a few years before, had offered the story of Michal as representative of the "relation of personal experience to history."

NOTES

1. Some members of this particular generation were in revolt not only against their predecessors, but against views they themselves had held as young men in the "utopian" movements of the 1930s. For a straightforward expression of the view that this generation had been "twice born," and hence distinctly wise in comparison with other generations, see Daniel Bell, *The End of Ideology* (New York, 1960), 299-314.

2. *MHH*, 269-270.

3. MRC, "The New Philosopher's Stone," *NR* III (1915), 338-339 (*FL*, 404); MRC, review of Robert Michels, *Political Parties*, in *NR* VIII (1916), 303-304 (*FL*, 160-161).

4. E.g., John Dewey, *Reconstruction in Philosophy* (New York, 1920), 49, where Dewey adds the following: "Man is capable, if he but will exercise the required courage, intelligence, and effort, of shaping his own fate. Physical conditions offer no insurmountable barriers."

5. MRC, "American Philosophy: John Dewey and the Chicago School," *NR* XXII (1920), 82-86. Cf., from among the many examples, Cohen's Presidential Address of 1929, "Vision and Technique in Philosophy," *PR* XXXIX (1930), 127-152 (*FL*, 365-391), and his overview of Dewey's faults on the occasion of the latter's eightieth birthday, "Some Difficulties in Dewey's Anthropocentric Naturalism," *PR* XLIX (1940), 196-228 (*SPS*, 139-175). Cf. also the revised and expanded version of "Dewey and the Chicago School" in *AT*, 363-380.

6. MRC, "Dewey and the Chicago School," 86.

7. E.g., John Dewey to Arthur F. Bentley, July 9, 1945, in John Dewey and Arthur F. Bentley, *A Philosophic Correspondence*, ed. Sidney Ratner and Jules Altman (New Brunswick, N.J., 1964), 439.

8. MRC, review of Sigmund Freud, *Moses and Monotheism*, in *Jewish Social Studies* I (1939), 469-475 (*RWJ*, 139-146).

9. MRC, review of Emile Boutroux, *The Contingency of the Laws of Nature*, in *NR* XIII (1917), 192 (*FL*, 433); MRC, "Amor Dei Intellectualis," *Chronicon Spinozanum* III (1923), 9-10 (*FL*, 313); MRC, "The Faith of a Logician," in George P. Adams and William P. Montague, eds., *Contemporary American Philosophy* (New York, 1930), I, 238 (*SPS*, 22); MRC, review of Jerome Frank, *Law and the Modern Mind*, in *Nation* CXXXI (1931), 259-260 (*LSO*, 357-362).

10. Diary, July 4, 1938, in *DJ*, 274.

11. MRC, review of Bernard Smith, *Forces in American Criticism*, in *Journal of the History of Ideas* I (1940), 241-251 (*FL*, 213-277, esp. 277). Cf. Cohen's review of the non-Marxist, but socially and economically oriented work of Vernon L. Parrington, *Main Currents of American Thought*, in *NR* LXV (1931), 303-304 (*FL*, 249-255).

12. MRC, "The Natural Sciences and the Social Sciences," in William F. Ogburn and Alexander Goldenweiser, eds., *The Social Sciences* (New York, 1927), 437-466 (*RN*, 335-346).

13. E.g., MRC, review of Michels, 304 (*FL*, 160-161).

14. MRC, quoted by Leonora Cohen Rosenfield, in *MHH* (2nd ed.), x.

15. *KSD*, prefatory note.

16. *KSD*, prefatory note; *DJ*, 205; *Portrait*, 210-211.

17. *KSD*, prefatory note.

18. 1 Samuel 18:20, 27; 19:11-17; 25:44; and 2 Samuel 3:13-16; 6:16-23.

19. *KSD*, prefatory note.

20. *KSD*, III, viii; *DJ*, 283-284.

21. *KSD*, II, viii; *DJ*, 12: "The love that grows out of devotedly living together in common efforts proved at least in their case more enduring than the romantic love that is often only a temporary attraction."

22. Diary, November 30, 1936, in *DJ*, 283. Cf. note of 1940, in *DJ*, 262.

23. *KSD*, IV, iv, v.

24. Note of 1904, in *Portrait*, 29.

25. Cohen made this response when asked to evaluate a poem for a periodical. The anecdote was first told to me by Samuel Haber.

26. *KSD*, esp. III, iii.

27. E.g., *KSD*, I, ii, v, vi; II, ii.

28. *MHH*, 28-41, esp. 31, 37.

29. For a succinct discussion of "relativism" in the historiography of the 1930s see John Higham et al., *History* (Englewood Cliffs, N.J., 1965), 117-131.

30. *MHH*, 46, 49.

31. *MHH*, 66.

32. *MHH*, 67-68.

33. *MHH*, 37-38.

34. For Hempel's essay in the original see *JP* (1942), 35-48. Of the many discussions of this controversy, among the most cogent are Maurice Mandelbaum, "Historical Explanation: The Problem of Covering Laws," *History and Theory* I (1961), 229-242, and Rudolph Weingartner, "The Quarrel about Historical Explanation," in Ronald H. Nash, ed., *Ideas of History* (New York, 1969), II, 140-157.

35. The word "explanation" does appear several times in *MHH* (e.g., 99), but Cohen felt free to use the word "establish" as a synonym when discussing what historians were trying to do with events. The one work of distinction addressed to the problem of historical knowledge by an American philosopher during the 1930s was Maurice Mandelbaum, *The Problem of Historical Knowledge* (New York, 1938).

36. E.g., Michael Kammen's reference to Cohen in *History and Theory* XI (1972), 368. Cf. J. R. Levenson, "The Genesis of Confucian China and Its Modern Fate," in L. P. Curtis, Jr., ed., *The Historian's Workshop* (New York, 1970), 280.

37. *MHH*, 94-132, esp. 98, 100, 131.

38. E.g., *MHH*, 164.

39. *MHH*, 116-122, 225.

40. *MHH*, 133-171, esp. 137, 148, 158, 169-171.

41. *MHH*, 174-224.

42. *MHH*, 260-264.

43. *MHH*, 264-275, esp. 273-274.

44. *MHH*, 274.

45. *MHH*, 280-285. Cf. *FL*, 449-462, where Cohen tries to qualify the idea of progress in the interests of a wiser liberalism of the future.

46. *MHH*, 293.

47. *MHH*, 291.

48. *MHH*, 294-296.

49. *MHH*, 296. The phrase is from William Cullen Bryant's poem *The Battlefront*, ninth stanza, although Cohen does not put it in quotation marks.

50. Cohen's conception is sufficiently reminiscent of Mill's to warrant the quotation here of lines 503-516 of *On Liberty*: "It is a piece of idle sentimentality that truth, merely as truth, has any inherent power denied to error, of prevailing against the dungeon and the stake. Men are not more zealous for truth than they often are for error, and a sufficient application of legal or even of social penalties will generally succeed in stopping the propagation of either. The real advantage which truth has, consists in this, that when an opinion is true, it may be extinguished once, twice, or many times, but in the course of ages there will generally be found persons to rediscover it, until some one of its reappearances falls on a time when from favorable circumstances it escapes persecution until it has made such head as to withstand all subsequent attempts to suppress it."

51. See, e.g., the review by Cohen's disappointed admirer, John Herman Randall, Jr., in *Journal of the History of Ideas* X (1949), 305-312.

52. E.g., Perry Miller, review of *MHH*, in *Nation* CLXVI (1948), 553-554. Cf. the same theme in reviews of Cohen's other books during the 1940s, e.g., Heinz Eulau, "Not Guide but Lantern," *NR* CXIV (1946), 583-584, and especially the remarks of contrite ex-radicals like Granville Hicks, in *American Mercury* LXII (1946), 624-629, and Jim Cork, as quoted in *Portrait*, 144.

It was only toward sleep that every wink of the eyelids could strike a spark into the cloudy tinder of the dark, kindle out of shadowy corners of the bedroom such myriad and such vivid jets of images—of the glint on tilted beards, of the uneven shine on roller skates, of the dry light on grey stone stoops, of the tapering glitter of rails, of the oily sheen on the night-smooth rivers, of the glow on thin blonde hair, red faces, of the glow on the outstretched, open palms of legions upon legions of hands hurtling toward him. He might as well call it sleep. It was only toward sleep that ears had power to cull again and reassemble the shrill cry, the hoarse voice, the scream of fear, the bells, the thick-breathing, the roar of crowds and all sounds that lay fermenting in the vats of silence and the past. It was only toward sleep one knew himself still lying on the cobbles, felt the cobbles under him, and over him and scudding ever toward him like a black foam, the perpetual blur of shod and running feet, the broken shoes, new shoes, stubby, pointed, caked, polished, buniony, pavement-beveled, lumpish, under skirts, under trousers, shoes, over one and through one, and feel them all and feel, not pain, not terror, but strangest triumph, strangest acquiescence. One might as well call it sleep. He shut his eyes.

Henry Roth

Morris Cohen entered Mt. Sinai hospital in New York on January 27, 1942, expecting to rest there for several days to overcome a general feeling of sickness and exhaustion that had recently become acute. He turned out to be suffering from a mild cardial infarction, or "coronary." A number of prominent physicians were called in, and they agreed that Cohen's brain was being damaged by emboli. Bodily movement could prevent the clotting that threatened his life, but Cohen refused to cooperate. Time after time he was lifted out of bed but would drop to the floor and refuse to move. He appeared to have the muscular strength, but he lacked the disposition. He adamantly refused to eat, and after two months of steady decline he was sent home from the hospital, presumably to die.[1]

Once confronted with the possibility that death might be at hand, Cohen all but welcomed it. This response is not altogether surprising when seen in the context of the sentiments he had been confiding to his diaries during the preceding several years. In 1940 he mused that "blank annihilation may be preferable to a life in which the balance is on the side of torture." "When the living are deprived of suffering," he said, "they are relieved." "The thought of death," he admitted a few years earlier, "is ever present in my mind." Cohen knew that Spinoza held that "a free man thinks never of death," but he made a point of insisting that in this one instance his philosophical hero had been wrong. In the wake of his mother's death, especially, Cohen wrote cryptic notes about death:

I shall not be dead. For the dead will not be I. The dead body of what was my mother is not the Bessie who lived, suffered, and yet kept a masterful grip on life. Death is the absence of life where it once was.[2]

Cohen was intrigued with the possibility that his own body, "changed, will continue in some form." More conventionally, he took comfort from the fact that his books "perhaps will be read," and that his children would live on.[3] *King Saul's Daughter* concluded with a wistful reference to the "mysterious tides, deep and mighty," beyond the control of human beings.[4]

Even as an adolescent, Cohen's diaries recorded a preoccupation with thoughts of death,[5] and his cultural criticism during the intervening decades reminded his readers, tangentially but repeatedly, that the "crowning agonies of death" await everyone.[6] Well before the age of fifty he had taken on the posture of a "grand old man," and was inclined to stand on the prerogatives of one who had already lived long and hard.[7] He saw his life as an epic, in which he walked through "the valley of the shadow" at twenty-five (the nervous exhaustion that sent him to Watkins Glen in 1906), only to fight off illness, humiliation, and poverty thereafter.[8] "Once in a while," he explained to Ernest Nagel in 1939, "I have very distressing symptoms of death gripping me. One would suppose that having had them so often one would get accustomed to them. But that is not the case." Cohen did not describe these symptoms in detail, but he attributed them to a malfunction of his "pneumogastric nerve," which made his "heart and stomach misbehave."[9] The reality of his suffering is not to be denied, although its sources do not lie open to further view. Its importance lies in Cohen's having always carried with him the sense that his physical body was on the verge of disintegration; that he was too weak to function properly. "For the last forty years," he said to Nagel, "I have always been more or less of an invalid."[10]

In the late 1930s Cohen was markedly uncomfortable with the responsibility for control over his own affairs. Committed to the Conference on Jewish Relations and to the completion of a number of books, he fretted about his inability to concentrate on any of his tasks, on his apparently constitutional impediment to the setting of priorities:

The real evil . . . can be put in psychologic terms. . . . I am distracted not only by different objectives but also by perpetual doubts as to whether it is all worthwhile and it would not be better to ease up and live to enjoy myself in my own quiet way . . . in as much peace and comfort as the opportunities afford.[11]

But "what is life without any tasks to drive us?" he asked elsewhere.[12] He could neither surrender any of his interests nor "concentrate to

bring any of them to ripe fruition," so he was left, bewildered and bur-
dened, to muse, "most of my life seems wasted."[13]

Continually in these later years, Cohen expressed his vow to write a
half-dozen or more books, to complete not only his autobiography and
his philosophy of history, but also, at the very minimum, a systematic
work on metaphysics and another on the history of American thought.
He told friends and colleagues about these plans, and announced them
in interviews with newspapers.[14] After his nominal retirement in 1938,
he felt obliged to do the creative work that his heavy teaching duties
had kept him from pursuing more single-mindedly. His great fear, he
confessed, was that death would take him before he could finish his
task, that he would die "with all the accumulated reflections on life"
still within him, unexpressed.[15] Yet, simultaneously, he was not so
sure he had anything to say: he wondered whether the effort was
"worthwhile," whether his arid message deserved to be carried further,
whether he had anything to offer beyond a "distillation of old common
sense passing through a skeptical sieve." Unfortunately, many of the
"accumulated reflections" he feared would die with him were rather
disappointing when he wrote them out: he so often began with a "brilliant idea," only to discover that it was but "a poor little common-
place."[16]

It was in these years, too, that Cohen became the most "obsessed
with the idea" that his mind was "drying up." "Many things properly
planned and started, fail because at the last moment the energy is not
there to carry it through properly."[17] He suspected that the difficulty
was partially psychological, so he set out to free himself from "anxiety
neuroses" by "concentrating more" on his work.[18] Yet the solitary
enterprise of writing was more difficult than lecturing or leading discussions; aiming now to think systematically, rather than on an hoc basis
for a class, a book review, or a short critical essay, Cohen was increasingly preoccupied with the sense that his "mental life" was mostly "dry
desert sand." The latter had "oases" and "fresh faucets," which could
be opened sometimes by "contradiction" but more reliably by the stim-

ulation of appreciation: he wanted to be sure that "the flow is worth something."[19] The evidence may be lacking for the conclusion that Cohen was looking for a way out, that he was eager for an excuse *not* to follow through on his promises to produce a magnum opus and its supporting volumes, but there is no question that his ambivalence was profound.

Not until Cohen's brain had been badly damaged did he begin to respond to treatment. Even then he resisted, and he was induced to eat and to move his body only after a new physician began to handle him differently. Dr. Mack Lipkin, a personal friend of the Ryshpan family, had only recently completed his internship when he agreed, at Mary's behest, to take over the care of her husband after the latter's release from the hospital. By then the patient was virtually a "vegetable," who had gone without a proper meal for several months. Lipkin began as other doctors had, trying to get Cohen to stand up, or at least to move his limbs about. When this failed, Lipkin settled for less: he managed to persuade Cohen to allow his head to be propped up for five minutes a day, and after that, ten; each step was taken with Cohen's permission and greeted with enthusiastic congratulations and encouragement on the part of Lipkin and the practical nurse carrying out his instructions. The procedure was unusual for 1942, when the practice of "rehabilitation medicine" had not yet become a professional routine. As a result of this gradual escalation of demands and the carefully controlled expression of appreciation, Cohen was walking on the street in several weeks. But his brain had been so damaged by the stroke that even Lipkin's attention was unable to restore to normal levels his patient's ability to speak, read, and write; Cohen's mind went "in and out" for the next five years, till his death, and manifested "marked mental tension defects" even when he was at his strongest.[20]

Lipkin's approach might have worked on another patient, but its success with Cohen is almost eerie when viewed in the context of Cohen's own remarks about his "vital fluids" and the conditions under which they could be induced to "flow." Years before, Thomas Davidson had gotten hold of Cohen when his "soul was parched" and had caused his "living waters" to flow forth; now Lipkin, in very different circumstances, reestablished Cohen's will to live. In the intervening years Cohen had worn himself out in "measured straining in opposite directions," in devoted service to his version of the scientific ideal; he had kept his craft out of treacherous currents, and now, were it not for Lipkin, he would have drifted quickly and quietly into the sea. After months of decline, and injury to his brain, he was no longer in a position to send out the message of King Lear, as he had done, in effect, when the doctors first tried to arouse him:

You do me wrong to take me out o' the grave.
Thou art a soul in bliss; but I am bound
Upon a wheel of fire, that mine own tears
Do scald like molten lead.

By the time Morris Cohen died, much of American intellectual discourse took place on ground he had helped to chart. If he did not, himself, settle the issue of what were the metaphysical, methodological, and moral implications of the scientific endeavor, he at least helped to ensure that the next generation would be more reflective than his about the ways in which modern culture was "scientific." The lacunae he found in the thought of his contemporaries were among the most obvious starting points for the intellectual labors of the following generation. If Cohen did not create a metaphysical alternative to temporalism and nominalism, he brought to the surface of debate a number of reservations about these tendencies. If he did not produce a philosophy of science, he helped to create a discipline devoted to it, and one that took for granted the critique of popular empiricism over which he had labored for so long. If he did not, as a philosopher of law, positively advance the work of that field, he identified what were to be remembered as the most crucial vulnerabilities in the work of his contemporaries. If he did not solve, theoretically, the problem of scholarly objectivity's relation to political advocacy, he helped through sheer force of asser-

tion to keep alive the hope that "progressive" political values could be
defended though the use of disinterested intellect. If he did not formulate a detailed philosophy of historical knowledge, he outlined the position that Hempel and Popper, and others, were to make the starting
point for at least thirty years of technical discourse. If he did not
achieve an interpretation of man's historical destiny satisfactory to the
needs of a world power, he expressed both a vision of humanity's limitations and a stance of "resignation" that were central to the post-
World War II discourse of most American intellectuals.

In context after context, the general axioms Cohen had tried to reinforce were, indeed, institutionalized, but understood now in relation
to the specific demands of increasingly sophisticated disciplines, or in
relation to other conditions peculiar to the changing times. Cohen's
actual formulations were less and less quotable, for the usable principles
they contained were indissolubly bound up with arguments Cohen had
made against what now seemed to be straw men. Why read Cohen on
philosophy of science when one could read Nagel? Why read Cohen on
historical knowledge when one could read Hempel? Why read Cohen on
the failures of liberalism, even, when one could read Morton White or
Lionel Trilling?

In 1949 White and Trilling published what were soon to be recognized as definitive assessments of the tradition to which American intellectuals saw themselves as heirs. White's *Social Thought in America*
surveyed "progressive" academic thinking from the 1880s to about
1930. It spoke loudly and firmly for its author's generation when it
articulated a series of caveats against the thinking of Dewey, Holmes,
Thorstein Veblen, Charles Beard, and James Harvey Robinson. These
were the great leaders of the "revolt against formalism"; they were
"suspicious of approaches which are excessively formal; they all protest
their anxiety to come to grips with reality, their attachment to the
moving and the vital in social life." For all the values of liberalization
these tendencies brought with them, Dewey and his colleagues lost their
sense of balance: "the revolt was speedily followed by a reign of terror

in which precision and logic and analytic methods became suspect."
This "fear of rigidity" made the liberals too scornful of "principles";
hence they were never very good at defining just what they meant by
"liberalism," "scientific method," or just about anything else. Something called "science" was central to their social vision, but their greatest theorist, Dewey, authored "no impressive reflections on science,"
and the other four "never said anything about the logic of scientific
procedure which has not been either elementary or obscure." Moreover,
neither Dewey nor any of the others managed to articulate goals for
social action. In their concern with *how* to reorganize society, the liberals lost sight of the need to say *what* it was one wanted to do. Randolph Bourne was essentially correct in his famous charge that instrumentalism had means but no ends; Bourne "saw that we cannot be engi-
neers without knowing what to build."[21]

White was amused by Robinson, the "latter-day Bacon" who
amounted to little more than a "cheerleader" for "the liberation of
human intelligence," a movement he could not even define clearly.
Robinson's and Dewey's highly optimistic "forward glance to the brav-
est of all possible worlds" seemed quaint to White, and their "patroniz-
ing attitude toward the Greeks" a little irritating. Robinson's *Making of
the Modern Mind* was too often "devoted to damning the past," and
Dewey's attempt to refute Plato and Aristotle, not by logic, but by
showing their views to be rationalizations of social and economic interest, was about as effective as "the application of a crowbar to the skulls
of the classical philosophers."[22]

Trilling, in *The Liberal Imagination*, was especially put off by the
studied practicality he found in American liberalism, by the anti-intellectualism that seemed always to lurk just beneath the surface. Liberals,
he complained, believed "that there exists an opposition between reality and mind and that one must enlist oneself in the party of reality."
Taking as his chief text the work of Vernon Louis Parrington, the
grandest name in liberal literary criticism, Trilling mocked the view that
an interest on the part of a novelist in the "odors of the shop" should

be praised for being more completely "real" than, and hence morally superior to, Henry James's concern with the "idea of intellectual honor." America's "liberal, progressive culture," ambivalent about affairs of the mind and heart, tolerated the "vulgar materialism" of such novelists as Theodore Dreiser, with their "huge negation," their simple cry of "Bunk!" Liberals felt that Dreiser's art, while perhaps not "intellectually adequate," was to be praised anyhow: it was "certainly very *strong*, certainly very *real*."[23]

Cohen had found almost exactly these same deficiencies, not only in the progressive tradition in general, but specifically in Parrington, Robinson, and Dewey.[24] The point is not that Cohen had "anticipated" White and Trilling, but that in the pre-World War II community of discourse they analyzed, a sensibility common to their own had in fact been forcefully articulated, and by one of the most prominent participants in that discourse. If this fact serves to qualify some of the impressions left by White and Trilling about their predecessors, it serves simultaneously to support those impressions: Cohen was not, after all, in the majority. His rapport with his age was intimate, but this intimacy was not based on simple agreement.

It was certainly not because of Cohen, alone, that the generation of the 1940s and 1950s developed a critical perspective on many of Cohen's contemporaries, but he undoubtedly helped to create the skeptical conditions under which such criticism could thrive. Cohen's role was to formulate, popularize, and reinforce certain suspicions about ideas more or less "accepted" in his day; when the intellectual traditions of his era were subsequently updated and revised, the weaknesses he had helped to identify were exactly those the new generation was most eager to consign to the realm of the "history of liberal social thought." Although White's book did not mention Cohen,[25] its critiques of historicism, instrumentalism, and temporalism fulfilled Cohen's purposes masterfully, and they achieved for White the influence Cohen had always sought.

The works of Trilling and White were contributed to the discourse of an intelligentsia that did not exist when Cohen began his career in 1910. To be sure there was, early in the century, plenty of intellectual discourse, and there were on hand a number of critics—liberals, nonbelievers, and persons of various ethnic stocks—but there was no distinctly secular, ethnically diverse, liberal intelligentsia devoted to cosmopolitan ideals. What had happened in the intervening years was more than the assimilation of many persons of Cohen's ethnic background into the American academic and literary world; that world had, in fact, been changed by this process. If the children of the Yiddish ghetto were often eager to escape provincialism and to seize the opportunities of a larger world, so, too, were many "Mayflower descendants" looking for ways to transcend what they perceived as the provincialism of their own upbringings.[26] The two antiprovincialisms reinforced each other and promoted, in concert, a cosmopolitan ideal that became one of the root values in the community of discourse into which young intellectuals of the 1940s—whatever their ethnic origins—were absorbed.

The career of Morris Cohen was one of the chief agencies by which this single, avowedly cosmopolitan sphere of intellectual discourse came into existence. If young Jews looked to him for an example of how to practice the life of the mind freed of the limitations of Jewish particularism, so did the likes of Harry Overstreet, Randolph Bourne, and Perry Miller look to him for an intellectual style that refreshingly supplemented the native traditions to which they were heir. Cohen was thus used by both "sides"; his life was a field on which the inheritors of two cultures met to talk and look each other over. Once this process had been essentially completed, once a single sphere of discourse had been firmly established, Cohen had outlived one of his principal functions. His writings would never again—except for the historian—be endowed with the special social significance they carried in the 1910s, 1920s, and 1930s. Henceforth, a book or essay by Morris Cohen would be no more and no less than a treatise on whatever was its announced subject, be it "Meaning and Implication" or "The Philosophy of Spinoza."

From the perspective of the history of the newly consolidated intelligentsia, then, Cohen was an almost ancient figure by the time of his death in 1947. Even if many of his basic ideas were accepted, he was, as a social being, anything but a contemporary. It made sense to let him slide into history along with the intellectual errors he had exposed and the cultural particularism against which he had revolted. Affectionate as they were toward Cohen's memory, intellectuals of the 1940s and 1950s, including many who had studied under Cohen, were as eager to distance themselves from certain of his characteristics as they were to disown those excesses of the past that he had helped them to discover. They were troubled by his lack of originality and by his relentlessly negative mode of criticism.[27] Cohen's overtly antiseptic style was an embarrassment to a generation for whom "compulsive anality" was a trait to be either laughed at or transcended through psychoanalytic awareness and broadened experiences. This generation was also ready to disown the pretentiousness of the "Jewish boy who made it," and who could then restrain himself neither from boasting of his friendships with Holmes, Frankfurter, and Einstein, nor from posturing as a much greater thinker than he was, nor from taking seriously as a mature philosopher the platitudes that ought, perhaps, to have remained within the confines of undergraduate discourse.

The tendency to associate these failings with Cohen was ironically reinforced by the filial piety of Felix Cohen, whose devotion led him to publish fragments of works his father could not bring himself to complete. At first the reviewers made a brave effort, but when *Preface to Logic* (1944), *Faith of a Liberal* (1946), and *The Meaning of Human History* (1947) were followed quickly by the Holmes-Cohen correspondence (1948), then by *A Dreamer's Journey* (1949) and *Studies in Philosophy and Science* (1949), enthusiasm began to wane. Soon came *Reason and Law* (1950), *Reflections of a Wondering Jew* (1950), *King Saul's Daughter* (1952), and *American Thought* (1954). These volumes included some of Cohen's strongest work, but in aggregate they served chiefly to bring to light again Cohen's least impressive, most dated work, and to append unpublished manuscripts that tended, especially in the cases of *The Meaning of Human History* and *King Saul's Daughter*, to focus attention on exactly those disabilities that most readers found sad and unattractive. Forced by the sheer magnitude of Felix's program of publication to say more about Morris Cohen than they might have wished, even Cohen's admirers began referring to him less and less. Cohen's neglect by his immediate successors may have been unfortunate in some respects. Conceivably, closer attention to Cohen might have rendered American intellectuals of the 1940s, 1950s, and 1960s more sensitive to the limitations of logical positivism, or more determined to explore and articulate publicly the general philosophical implications of the specialized work their generation pursued so successfully in so many disciplines. Yet the impression persists that Cohen's successors, by looking beyond him, expressed their own growth. It was partially because they had learned so much from him that they found themselves able to transcend him. Like so many influential teachers, Morris Cohen was consumed by the history he had helped to create.

NOTES

1. Mack Lipkin, M.D., conversation with author, New York City, June 2, 1971.

2. Diary, July 18, 1937, in *DJ*, 261, and undated notes of 1940, in *DJ*, 262.

3. Undated note of 1940, in *DJ*, 262.

4. *KSD*, 93. Cf. MRC to Felix Frankfurter, January 2, 1939, in *Portrait*, 285.

5. Diary, January 20, 1897, in *Portrait*, 9.

6. E.g., MRC, "American Philosophy: Dewey and the Chicago School," *NR* XXII (1920), 82 (*AT*, 366).

7. E.g., MRC, "Address," in *Tribute*, 72, 75.

8. Diary, August 25, 1937, in *DJ*, 268.

9. MRC to Ernest Nagel, August 18, 1939, in *Portrait*, 407. Cohen may have been referring to his fainting spells, which were frequent in the 1930s (Lewis Feuer, conversation with author).

10. MRC to Ernest Nagel, August 18, 1939, in *Portrait*, 407.

11. Note of 1939, in *DJ*, 274-275.

12. Note of 1939, in *DJ*, 280.

13. Note of 1939, in *DJ*, 275.

14. *New York World-Telegram*, December 21, 1937; MRC to Ernest Nagel, July 11, 1939, in *Portrait*, 405-406.

15. Diary, July 4, 1938, in *DJ*, 274; Diary, May 29, 1940, in *DJ*, 262.

16. Undated note, in *DJ*, 271; note of 1939, in *DJ*, 274-275; Diary, June 26, 1940, in *DJ*, 277.

17. Diary, June 16, 1934, in *DJ*, 273; Diary, February 14, 1935, in *DJ*, 262.

18. Diary, June 30, 1940, in *DJ*, 277.

19. Diary, August 19, 1936, in *DJ*, 271; Diary, November 30, 1936, in *DJ*, 271; note of 1938, in *DJ*, 271-272; note of 1939, in *DJ*, 272.

20. Mack Lipkin, conversation with author.

21. Morton White, *Social Thought in America: The Revolt Against Formalism* (New York, 1949), 6, 239, 241, 244-245.

22. White, *Social Thought*, 190, 194-195.

23. Lionel Trilling, *The Liberal Imagination* (New York, 1949), 8, 11, 18.

24. E.g., MRC, review of Parrington, *The Beginnings of Critical Realism in America*, in *NR* LXV (1931), 303; MRC, "Dewey and the Chicago School," 82-86 (*AT*, 363-380); [MRC,] "Liberalism and Irrationalism," *NR* XXX (1922), 333-334 (*FL*, 67-71).

25. White does refer in a footnote to the tendency of "philosophers like Dewey and Morris R. Cohen" to interpret Holmes in ways partial to their own philosophical ideas (*Social Thought*, 282-283).

26. For a general overview of this process see David A. Hollinger, "Ethnic Diversity, Cosmopolitanism, and the Emergence of the American Liberal Intelligentsia," *American Quarterly* XXVII (1975), 133-151.

27. E.g., John Herman Randall, Jr., review of *MHH*, in *Journal of the History of Ideas* X (1949), 305-312, esp. 305; Lewis S. Feuer, "The Philosophy of Morris R. Cohen: Its Social Bearings," *Philosophy and Phenomenological Research* X (1950), 471-485, esp. 480-482. Some of Cohen's admirers did continue to speak of him in an exclusively hagiographic idiom; see, for example, Milton R. Konvitz, "Morris R. Cohen," *Antioch Review* VII (1947), 487-501, and Irwin Edman, "Morris Raphael Cohen—A Tribute," *City College Alumnus* XLII (1947), 5, 18.